D

+ B

Rights, Killing, and Suffering

Rights, Killing, and Suffering

Moral Vegetarianism and Applied Ethics

R. G. FREY

Basil Blackwell

First published 1983
Basil Blackwell Publisher Limited
108 Cowley Road, Oxford OX4 1JF, England

British Library Cataloguing in Publication Data
Frey, Raymond
    Rights, killing, and suffering.
    1. Vegetarianism
    I. Title
    613.2'62'01 TX392

    ISBN 0-631-12684-8

Typesetting by Cambrian Typesetters, Aldershot, Hants
Printed in Great Britain by Billing & Sons Ltd, Worcester

Contents

Preface   ix

Acknowledgements   xii

Part I

1 Ethics, Argument, and Practice   3
     Argument as the Basis of Practice
     Critical Thinking
2 Moral and Non-Moral Vegetarianism   6
     Non-Moral Grounds
     The Argument from Health
     Moral Grounds
     Coercion on Behalf of Vegetarianism
3 Two Types of Moral Vegetarianism   17
     The Redistribution Argument
     The Increased Shortage Argument
     The Waste Argument
     The Argument from Effect on Character
     The Argument from Violence
     The Argument from Pain and Suffering
     Focus upon Animal Welfare

Part II

4 The Three Arguments from Animal Welfare   27
     Failure of the Arguments
5 Two Conceptions of the Status of Vegetarianism   30
     Partial and Absolute Exclusions
     Conditional and Unconditional Conceptions
     Counter-Arguments and Competing Tactics

6 Positive and Negative Moral Vegetarianism 36
  Ascendency of the Argument from Pain and Suffering
  Change in the Requirement for Success
  Effectiveness and the Choice of Tactics

Part III

7 The Appeal to Moral Rights 43
  Dispensing with Rights
8 Rights, their Grounds, and the Problem of Argument 46
  Rights and the Moral Concepts
  Wrongs, Rights, and Protection
  Principles and Superfluity of Rights
  Conflicts of Rights
  Prima Facie Rights, Strict Intuitionism, and Utility
  The Correlative Thesis
  Repudiating Rights and Eliminating Clashes
  Basic Moral Rights
  Dispensing with the Diversions Rights Create
  Acquired and Unacquired Rights
9 Rights, their Nature, and the Problem of Strength 67
  Rights as Trumps
  Rights as Mirrors of Absolute Wrongs
  Absolute and *Prima Facie* Rights
  An Act-Utilitarian Account of Strength
  Loosening Some Preconceptions about Rights
  Rights and the Duty to Compensate
10 Rights, Consequentialism, and Act-Utilitarianism 83
  Mill and Bentham: Accommodation and Hostility towards
    Moral Rights
  Consequentialism and the Place of Rights in
    Act-Utilitarianism
  Consequentialism and Rights Compartmentalized
  Hare's Two-Level Account of Moral Thinking
  The Two-Level Complication as the Model for
    Compartmentalization
  Consequentialism and Practice

Part IV

11 The Appeal to the Wrongness of Killing 99
  At the Mercy of Competing/Conflicting Theories
12 The Value of Life 103
  Life Principles
  Kinship and Reverence for Life
  The Value of Animal and Human Life
  Diminution in Value

The Value of Life, Vivisection, and the Appeal to
Benefit
13 Killing and the Doctrine of Double Effect   118
Conditions for Employment
Direct and Oblique Intention
Responsibility
Attempts to Render Control Responsibility Superfluous
Bringing Aid and Avoiding Injury
The Order of Causation between Effects
14 Value in Nature: On the Alleged Possibility of an   141
Environmental Ethic
Moral Standing and Inherent Value
Conflicts in Values
Feelings and Attitudes
Mistakes about Inherent Value
A Leopoldian Picture of Inherent Value
Artifacts and Nature
From Value Theory to Ethics

Part V

15 Killing, Replaceability, and the Amelioration Argument   159
Killing, Side-Effects, and Preferences
Diminution in Pleasure and Replaceability
Self-Consciousness and Food Animals
Population Policy
Miserable Lives
Failure to Bar Replacement
Replaceability and Animal Generations
16 Pain, Amelioration, and a Choice of Tactics   174
Bases of the Argument from Pain and Suffering
The Argument's Appeal
The Argument and the Concerned Individual
Suffering: Miserable Life and Single Experience Views
The Concerned Individual's Tactic as a Response to
the Argument
Attempts to Prejudice the Choice between Tactics
17 Alleged Reasons for the Choice of Vegetarianism   190
The Claim of Symbolic Gesture
The Claim of Political-Economic Power
Utilitarianism and Vegetarianism: Some Reflections
on Practicalities
The Claim of Progressive Collapse
The Claim of Practicality/Effectiveness
The Claim of Knowledge
The Appeal to Thresholds
The Concession

18 Sincerity and Consistency   218
        An Overview
        The Charge of Insincerity or Hypocrisy
        The Charge of Inconsistency
        Approval and Action
        The Demands of Consistency
        Two Views of Strictness in Demands
        The Good Man
19 Needless Suffering   243
        The Factual Side to the Charge
        The Moral Side to the Charge

Preface

This book is an essay in practical or applied ethics. Though essentially it takes the form of an enquiry into the ethics of eating meat, most of the central issues it raises have an interest and importance which transcend any narrow concern with animals and vegetarianism.

It suggests that the three main arguments from animal welfare, by which modern proponents of vegetarianism seek to demonstrate the wrongness of eating meat, do not succeed, with the result that we have no reason to think, at least from the point of view of animal welfare, that eating meat is wrong. Because these three arguments focus upon the violation of moral rights, killing, and the infliction of pain and suffering, however, it should be apparent that they raise numerous issues which, quite apart from their prominence in discussions of our treatment of animals, figure widely in discussions of our treatment of human beings. For this reason, though concerned with animals, my narrative is very far from confined to them, and at times they are left entirely in the background. I have not hesitated, in other words, to comment upon important matters linked to the themes of rights, killing, and suffering, whether or not animals are in question.

This is a philosophical book, but I have tried hard to make its arguments and language completely accessible to non-philosophers, students, and the educated public. It can be regarded as a critical introduction to (some themes in) modern moral vegetarianism. I must, however, issue certain warnings in this respect. First, the book is in no sense a history or survey, whether of relevant positions or of past and present literature; it is a sustained, argumentative whole, a committed treatise. Second, it makes no pretence to be an exhaustive summary of the rights and wrongs of one view after another; it confronts the arguments from rights, killing, and suffering and develops its own line of argument with respect to them. Third, it is not a book without a point of view; it takes a stand on the issues it confronts and attempts to mould that stand into a coherent, consistent whole.

A word about the book's origin. Several years ago, Peter Singer and I tentatively agreed to do a joint book on vegetarianism, roughly on the model of the volume by J.J.C. Smart and Bernard Williams, *Utilitarianism, For and Against*. Soon, however, the project was put aside. As we went into exactly what it would require of us. Peter's heavy existing commitments not only gave him second thoughts about taking on more but also made it quite clear that we would come nowhere near the completion date we had earlier envisaged, whereas I judged that a delay of the sort he would require would prove disruptive to my own commitments. In fact, these commitments soon got the better of me, and Peter's reluctance to to forward in the end saved me the ignominy of having repeatedly to stall him.

Though the project with Peter was set aside, my plan to write a book on moral vegetarianism, which I had promised in the final footnote to *Interests and Rights*, and on Peter's contribution to that cause was not.This is that book, much expanded from what it would have been, of course, had the earlier project gone forward and more wide ranging than the format of that project would have allowed. It develops the case I should have presented for Peter to reply to, and it can in its way, I suppose, be regarded as a response to *Animal Liberation, Practical Ethics*, and other of his writings on animals and vegetarianism. Though it refers to my *Interests and Rights*, it neither duplicates nor presupposes acquaintance with that work, though someone familiar with it will know how I might respond to certain theoretical questions, e.g., about moral rights or interests or self-consciousness that the text here might elicit in some readers.

Of the three arguments for moral vegetarianism noted above, I think the argument from pain and suffering is the strongest; so, too, does Peter. But not everyone does; and were I to have concerned myself principally with the work of someone who relied for the most part upon, say, the argument from moral rights, then the book would have had a different look, with the examination of still further suggestions about the nature and ground of rights, about the theoretical structure in which rights are to figure, about the strength of rights, and so on, included.

I have had the good fortune to be able to read virtually all of the book in the form of papers to discussion groups, university audiences, and popular as well as learned societies, particularly in the United States, and I owe a debt of thanks to all the many people who bothered to come along and argue with me. Some of these occasions, such as the conferences on The Moral Foundations of Public Policy, organized by Harlan B. Miller and William H. Williams, and held in Blacksburg, Virginia, were particularly fruitful, and I am grateful for having been asked to participate.

I have discussed the issues of this book with and have been helped by far too many people to list here, so I hope a general acknowledgement of thanks will not be thought lacking in generosity. I do want especially to thank, however, those people who, though not knowing me, called upon or wrote to me in order to register their opposition to, or (less frequently) their support for, views of mine in *Interests and Rights*, and other writings, and who were prevailed upon to continue the argument over some of my present concerns.

People whose work or comments have assisted me include Lawrence Becker, Stephen Clark, James Griffin, Bart Gruzalski, P. M. S. Hacker, R. M. Hare, John Mackie, H. J. McCloskey, Michael Martin, James Rachels, Tom Regan, Peter Singer, Carl Wellman, Peter Wenz, and Henry West. But there are many others, and I am grateful to them all. As for debts of a general kind in philosophy, numerous friends in Oxford have claims upon me; those of R. M. Hare, my former teacher, and P. M. S. Hacker are particularly deep.

Finally, I must thank Bobbie Matthews for her intelligent reading of my text, her skilful typing, and her kindness in putting up with a constantly changing schedule of work.

I dedicate this work to my father, to whom by any standard I owe an enormous amount.

R. G. F
Oxford

Acknowledgements

Some of the material presented here has appeared in reviews and articles by me, and I wish to thank the editors and publishers of the *Canadian Journal of Philosophy* ('Some aspects to the doctrine of double effect', 1975), *Mind* (review of P. Singer's *Practical Ethics*, 1982), *Environmental Ethics* (review of M. W. Fox's *Returning to Eden: Animal Rights and Human Obligations*, 1983), and the *Journal of Medical Ethics* ('Vivisection, medicine, and morals', 1983), as well as the Humana Press of New Jersey ('On why we would do better to jettison moral rights', in *Ethics and Animals*, H. B. Miller, W. H. Williams (eds), 1983), for permitting me to draw upon some of this material again. I have not hesitated to alter it.

Part I

Part One

1

Ethics, Argument, and Practice

*All that is necessary for the forces of evil to win is for enough
good men to do nothing.*
Edmund Burke

Burke's cry states a truth that can never be recalled too often: we as good men must act to combat the forces of evil. But exactly how are we to act? On which side of the serious moral, social, and political issues before us today are we to come down? Determining this is the problem, our problem, one instance of which we confront over the issue of vegetarianism and our treatment of animals in raising and killing them for food. Must we as good men give up eating meat, as some would urge? Or may we justifiably carry on with our present diet? All of us may agree that good men should combat evil; but we only know which way to move on this issue when we have determined for ourselves whether meat-eating is wrong.

Argument as the Basis of Practice

A presumption of those who urge the boycott of meat on moral grounds is that, if they can obtain our agreement that eating meat is wrong, we shall change our diet accordingly. They presume, that is, that we take morality seriously and so are concerned to behave according to our moral beliefs. For it is not merely a change in our views about meat-eating but also a change in our diet or eating practices which they seek.

The overwhelming majority of us not only eat meat but also very much enjoy it; if our present diet is to be changed, therefore, the case for changing it is going to have to be powerful enough to overcome our great love of meat dishes. This does not entail that the case in question will be a moral one; but unless we are in some way compelled to become vegetarians, it is difficult to think of a more powerful case than a moral one to effect the desired change, given that this case must breast the current of our enormous liking for meat. Obviously, the power of such a case, as I have said, depends upon our taking morality seriously, since only if we do so can moral claims hope to overcome our love of meat.

Importantly, the aim of those who urge the boycott of meat on moral grounds, of, that is, moral vegetarians, is not necessarily to rid us of our liking of meat (though doubtless they hope this will come in time) but to have us abstain from meat, even if we persist in liking it.

I do not consider this to be an unrealistic or excessively optimistic aim. After all, most of us do try to live up to our moral convictions and, in this sense, take morality seriously; and even when we fail and fall victims to backsliding, we usually or at least very often resolve to do better. The feeling of guilt can be a powerful factor in boosting this resolve: once we believe it wrong to eat meat, and once we can be brought as a result to feel guilty about continued meat-eating, we are increasingly likely to try to rid ourselves of this feeling by greater efforts at living up to our convictions.

It is not lack of realism or excessive optimism, then, which is the problem; it is rather the necessity of showing that eating meat is wrong. If this were our conviction, most of us would try to live up to it; but it is decidedly not the conviction of the overwhelming majority of us, who see nothing wrong in eating meat and, consequently, no need to change a diet we very much enjoy. Plainly, we lack the very conviction on which the moral vegetarian hopes to rely to bring about the desired change in our diet. In order to succeed in his aim, therefore, the moral vegetarian must supplant our present view of the morality of eating meat with his own, and this requires at a minimum that he show both that and why it is wrong to eat meat. Hence, the arguments from moral rights, killing, and pain and suffering. (Later, after the distinction between positive and negative moral vegetarianism has been introduced, this requirement will be seen to lapse, when the argument from pain and suffering is regarded in a certain light.)

The examination of arguments for moral vegetarianism is an important task. This fact can be overlooked, especially by non-philosophers, who may be passionately in favour of action or who may have grown sceptical — all too often, I fear, with reason — that those given to argument will ever cease arguing and act. To these people, Burke's cry is, at one and the same time, a reminder of one of the pitfalls of prolonged academic speculation and a call to arms. Arguments do matter, however, and for a reason of vital concern to many vegetarians. For though there are doubtless people who would be vegetarians no matter what, there are nevertheless a great many others who are vegetarians *only because* they embrace the argument from moral rights or from killing or from pain and suffering. To these people, an increasing percentage of vegetarians, I suspect, it is absolutely imperative that the argument which has turned them into moral vegetarians succeed; conversely, to the extent that that argument is compromised or rendered doubtful, then to that extent they must rethink their positions. The argument is the basis of their eating practices, so that, if it is compromised or rendered doubtful, they *per se* have no reason to abstain from meat.

Critical Thinking

The assessment of arguments is an important part of thinking critically about moral issues, and it is an exercise characteristic of moral philosophers. For most people wrestling with moral problems, if and when they turn to philosophers, they turn to them, not for wisdom (at least, in the grand sense), not for ultimate and lasting insight into the nature of the universe and of man, but for help. They seek assistance in their own critical thinking on the problems, and this assistance in the end comes, not through the opinions which philosophers accept or reject, but through careful consideration and analysis of their arguments for accepting or rejecting them. In the deepest sense, their opinions themselves do not help with the problems: if we are trying to think through a particular moral problem, then we gain very little by having some wise man of Cambridge or some wizened gentleman at the top of the Himalayas simply whisper his answer to us. It is not showing a person an unravelled knot but showing him how to unravel it that matters to him in the deepest sense.

In the end, no one can do our moral thinking for us. We can seek assistance with the problems, but ultimately we have to think them through and to reach conclusions about what to do for ourselves. Nor can we escape responsibility for our actions by surrendering our moral decisions to some alleged, moral authority. The decision to surrender our moral decisions to another is ours, and for this and for what we do as a result of it we are answerable.

2

Moral and Non-Moral Vegetarianism

If vegetarianism is the boycott of meat, then moral vegetarianism is the boycott of meat on the ground that it is wrong to eat meat. Two things should be apparent at once.

First, not eating meat is by no means the same thing as vegetarianism. Vegetarianism consists in boycotting or abstaining from meat and represents a conscious choice or deliberate policy with respect to one's diet, which is something quite different from, say, increasingly forgoing meat because it is too costly. In speaking of a conscious choice or deliberate policy, I do not mean necessarily that there is an explicit all-or-nothing decision and that becoming a vegetarian cannot be a gradual process, only that, once one has settled upon vegetarianism, one consciously or deliberately boycotts meat, even when it is relatively inexpensive.

Second, forced vegetarianism does not represent a choice or policy in respect of one's diet and so does not amount to moral vegetarianism. A person being treated for ulcers, who avoids meat as part of his treatment, is compelled by concern for his recovery to abstain from meat, just as someone who happens to live in an area where little fresh meat is available is compelled by scarcity to forgo meat. More controversially, perhaps, young children of moral vegetarians are not themselves moral vegetarians: they do not eat meat (they are not fed it), but they are not moral vegetarians, since they have not chosen or decided anything with respect to their diet. In time, of course, they may become moral vegetarians. (It is sometimes suggested that the moral vegetarian does wrong in restricting his children's diet in the way he does. This seems to me a mistake. If parents are obliged to look after the moral upbringing of their children, then they must try to educate them morally as best they can, and no small part of this education is starting children off on the right track. To the moral vegetarian, abstaining from meat is on the right track; by his own lights, he is doing the best he can for his children.)

On three matters connected with this view of moral vegetarianism, I shall have nothing to say; they are not problems for someone of my views, but for moral vegetarians.

First, I know several people who would not eat meat in their own homes but who, when invited into someone else's home, would do so, rather than cause their hosts social embarrassment. Much of the problem could be avoided, of course, merely by revealing, when accepting a dinner invitation, that one is a vegetarian. Nevertheless, to go ahead and eat meat on social occasions rather than cause embarrassment is, I suspect, a serious temptation to many vegetarians, which, if indulged, other vegetarians may condemn as a form of hypocrisy. Condemnation can appear somewhat harsh on such wayward vegetarians, who might instead be seen as in a situation of conflicting values, which they resolve in favour of not causing embarrassment. But they *could* have resolved the conflict differently; I confess to a sneaking admiration for a Dr Johnson-like dismissal ('Away with it, Madam; I'll have none of that disgusting carcass').

Second, moral vegetarians may or may not be vegans and so abstain from animal products, such as cheese and eggs, as well as meat. In some sense of the phrase, vegans are more strict than moral vegetarians, and it has been thought by some that a fully consistent moral vegetarian should embrace veganism. Whatever the truth of the matter, I am concerned in these pages with (the more minimal view of) moral vegetarianism.

Third, throughout this book, I use the term 'meat' to refer not only to (for example) beef, pork, and veal, but also to poultry. I leave aside fish and other sea creatures, since moral vegetarians often argue among themselves about the morality of eating these. Among my own moral vegetarian friends, about half eat (for example) shrimps, but I do not know whether such a high percentage is the case generally.

Non-Moral Grounds

It should be obvious that there are numerous reasons why one may boycott meat which have nothing fundamentally to do with the view that eating meat is wrong. It may be useful for purposes of contrast to set out a few of these.

Some people may not like the taste of meat. Normally, this occurs with respect to only some meat, such as liver, but it is possible to imagine it occurring with respect to all, including the cooked meats which figure prominently in sandwiches, snacks, pizzas, etc. How likely this is is, for our purposes here, irrelevant.

Others may abstain from meat on aesthetic grounds. A contribution to the *Sunday Times* expressed such a view very clearly: 'To me, the idea of eating a chopped-up animal is repulsive. A butcher's shop is horrific and obscene, quite apart from smelling of death. If I pass a butcher's window, I look away instinctively, so horrified am I at the sight of bloody carcasses.'[1]

Some people may abstain from meat on the ground that it is not natural for man to consume it. In this regard, they may, as most books on vegetarianism now seem to do,[2] point to the facts, for instance, that we lack the speed, claws, and teeth of the true carnivore and instead, like the vegetarian animals, are equipped to pick, grind, and masticate our food. They may point to differences in our digestive systems and their various processes. They may point to the facts that, compared with carnivores, we lack the instincts and the keen sense of smell displayed in their hunting behaviour. On the whole, however, whether as the result of a change in metaphysics and in a teleological conception of the universe and man or whatever, arguments about what is and is not natural for man would appear to exert far less of an appeal today than in the past, as readers familiar with some of the arguments over contraception and human sexuality will know.

Some people may abstain from meat out of religious conviction. Abstinence here may or may not be periodic. When I was growing up, rather strict Catholics did not eat meat on Fridays. Today, during Lent, many Protestants abstain from meat, particularly during the period from Good Friday through Easter Sunday. The Muslim holy month of Ramadan is a time of fasting, and solid food of any sort is avoided before sunset. During Bairam, a period of meditation and prayer that concludes Ramadan, it is not uncommon for Muslims to forego solid food altogether. Followers of Jainism, on the other hand, abstain all the year from meat.[3] The same is true of many Hindus: it is not so much moral as religious conviction which motivates their complete abstinence, though it is doubtless true that their moral precepts may in the end come to be moulded around and so reflect their religious convictions. But it is perfectly possible that someone should have religious but not moral objections to eating meat or certain cuts of meat, such that, were he to give up his religion, his particular objections to eating meat would appear. A Jewish friend of mine in Oxford, when still an adherent to orthodoxy, objected to eating certain cuts of meat; over a period of time, however, he proceeded to lapse from orthodoxy and, indeed, from religious conviction altogether, with the result that his objection to these cuts of meat was removed, as was his objection to eating the flesh of animals that had not been slaughtered in the approved (orthodox) manner.[4]

Just as numerous people cannot bring themselves to eat snails or fried ants, so some may find emotionally that they cannot bring themselves to eat meat. Perhaps it is the whole idea of chewing and swallowing flesh which inhibits them; in any event, after a time, they avoid flesh foods. This and the aesthetic ground for abstinence may come to the same thing, but they need not, I think; for one may well be able to deploy the aesthetic objection even if one is not especially squeamish. But squeamishness cannot be overlooked: if each of us had to slaughter, skin, and gut the animals we ate, would the number of meat-eaters increase or diminish? (The fact that this number would almost certainly diminish, however, must not obscure the equally important fact that a good many people *do* slaughter and prepare the animals they eat. Before coming to England, I lived and went to university in several farming areas of Virginia, where just such activities were commonplace and not infrequently involved women and children. In West Virginia, where my grandparents lived, women not too many years ago had, in order to prepare the customary fried chicken for Sunday lunch, to go out back, take up a chicken, wring its neck or chop off its head, and then pluck and gut it. In fact, in the United States at large, until only a relatively few decades ago, it was mostly only city-dwellers who were at a distance from the animals they ate.)

Some people may abstain from meat on the ground that rearing animals for food is simply wasteful of resources. They need not give this view moral overtones (though they may, as we shall see later); rather, they may hold it as the result of a cost/benefit analysis of animal farming. It may be argued, for instance, that it is grossly inefficient to continue to rear more and more animals to deplete still further our grain supplies, since the grain consumed can feed more people than the flesh of the animals nurtured on it. Some such view as this emerges from Frances Moore Lappè's well-known book *Diet For A Small Planet*,[5] though she does not restrict her efficiency argument there merely to the example of grain.

We live in the age of the mini-bikini, the age of tight pants, hot pants, no pants; and it is not difficult to imagine people who are figure-conscious adopting a meat-free diet, in the hope of acquiring and retaining an alluring appearance. Several years ago, I read a newspaper article which said that, among women under 65 in the United States, the amount of money spent on enhancing their appearance − e.g., on cosmetics, hair styles, dietetic aids, figure salons, cosmetic surgery, particularly fashionable clothes, underclothes, and footwear, etc. − exceeded the Gross National Product of a great many nations. When the 'slim look' came in, diets became very fashionable (fortunes have been made on many fronts as a result), and one of the first things eliminated or radically reduced in the weight-watcher's diet is meat. The meat industry, of course, has long tried to fight this picture of meat as very fattening, and it has been successful to some extent. At least, a number of planned diets can be found today which feature various (non-fried) meats, in some portion or other.

Finally, we must not overlook some 'unusual' reasons for abstaining from meat. For example, I have heard it said − in the guise of a piece of psychology − that members of the opposite sex are attracted by people who are 'different' in some degree. I do not know what the evidence for this claim is, but possibly the personal advertisements at the back of the *New York Review of Books* count. In any event, should vegetarianism become more prevalent, the vegetarian's 'unusualness' must, I suppose, diminish. Again, an acquaintance of mine in San Francisco swears that a vegetarian diet increases sexual potency; according to him, vegetarianism, ginseng tea (which he maintains is an aphrodisiac), and a well-thumbed copy of the *Kama Sutra* are essentials for a better sex life. Then there is the matter of movement in society: in some cosmopolitan circles in the United States, vegetarianism, Eastern religions, the occult, science fiction, black holes, yoga, mysticism generally, horror films, health food lunches, and books on the late Marilyn Monroe are very much the fashion, and one cannot very well move in, as opposed to around, these circles without participating in their practices.

I have said that moral vegetarians are concerned to effect a change not merely in our moral views about meat-eating but also in our eating practices. The above, non-moral grounds for vegetarianism, however, do not seem likely to bring about a wholesale change in our diet. For, it is unlikely that most of us are suddenly going (a) to cease liking the taste of meat, (b) to protest on aesthetic grounds to eating it, (c) to find it unnatural to eat it, (d) to convert to religions which proscribe some or all of it, (e) to become squeamish about eating it, (f) to find, emotionally, that we cannot bring ourselves to eat it, (g) to become so enamoured of cost/benefit analysis as to give it up, and (h) to become so chic and fashion-conscious or so obsessed with our sexual potency and allure or so utterly cosmopolitan as to give it up altogether.

The Argument from Health

Some people may boycott meat on grounds of health. There are several possibilities here. On the one hand, one may point to the benefits conferred by a diet based upon vegetables, grain, and roughage generally; on the other, one may point to the harms that await the voracious meat-eater. The latter has become one of the main arguments in the vegetarian armoury,[6] and it doubtless has produced converts.

The harms alluded to are generally of three sorts. First, a diet high in calories, cholesterol, and saturated fats, of which meat is typically a part, is widely thought not to be good for one, and warnings not infrequently appear, especially for men with heart problems, of the probable links between such a diet and ill-health. Second, animal feed is increasingly laced with drugs of all sorts (mainly to prevent and combat disease and to spur growth), and residues of these drugs in the flesh we consume, if ingested in quantity, are increasingly thought to pose health problems. Third, there is also the worry, as a recent television documentary in Britain brought out very vividly[7] and as the Office of Technology Assessment in the United States warned in its report of 25 June 1979,[8] that the liberal use of antibiotics in animal feed may, in time, build immunity in animals and, through them, in us, to these drugs, some of which may play a role in the treatment of human diseases.

Not even considerations of health strike me as sufficient to bring about the complete demise of meat-eating, and for a number of reasons.

Though over-consumption of animal flesh may be bad for one, and vegetarians are doubtless correct to stress this, moderate consumption does not appear in the same light. A person who watches what he eats and exercises regularly is unlikely to have a shorter life because three or four times a week he has a modest portion of meat at his evening meal, particularly if he is careful to avoid or cut down on greasy foods. The health warnings of vegetarians, in other words, may lead meat-eaters to moderation, not to abstinence. And this is important; for it means that, coupled with the fact that he is unlikely to be swept away by the other non-moral grounds for vegetarianism, the moderate meat-eater may well fall beyond the reach of non-moral vegetarians.

Indifference to health is, up to a point, commonplace. Cigarette packages have carried health warnings for some years, and certain types of cigarette advertising have been proscribed; but tens of millions of people in the United States and Britain still smoke, and the industry continues to thrive.[9] Just how well it thrives can be seen from a single statistic: in the United States alone, 28.8 billion taxed packages of cigarettes were sold in 1979, an off-year for the US tobacco industry.[10] Newspapers and magazines have long been filled with stories about the effects of a high intake of cholesterol, but such stories appear to have had only minimal effect upon the national diets of the United States and Britain. The market for eggs, milk, and cheese, for instance, has not collapsed, with the revelation that these foods are high in cholesterol. (Prices, of course, affect sales. It has long been thought, for example, that a switch from battery cages to free range methods of egg production would result in a dramatic increase in the price of eggs.[11] In Britain, the staff of the Ministry of Agriculture, Fisheries, and Food told a Commons Select Committee on Agriculture in 1980 that this was indeed the case, that the switch envisaged would mean an 80 per cent increase in the price of eggs.)[12] Soft drinks which contain saccharin, a much-publicized, suspected carcinogen, continue to retain, if not increase, their share of the market. Indeed, so successful have diet drinks proved in the United States that virtually every soft-drink manufacturer has one on the market. (This upsurge in diet drinks has coincided with a health craze among some people, as the result of which fortunes have been made by the authors of this or that diet or exercise routine, by the authors of books on jogging and on how to diagnose your illnesses in your own home, by the manufacturers and retailers of running and sporting attire, by owners of health food shops, and so on. It is not only soft-drink manufacturers who have been quick to cash in on this craze. I should perhaps note that this health fad exists among meat-eaters as well as vegetarians; it would be quite wrong to think that the upsurge in jogging, the sales of yoghurt, and the presence of salad bars in American restaurants is to be traced solely or even primarily to vegetarians.) The sale of, for instance, bacon and hot dogs in the United

States has not plummeted, though they contain sodium nitrite, which the media there have widely purveyed as another suspected carcinogen. And for all the attention recently given to residues of chemicals and antibiotics in the animal flesh we consume, meat-consumption remains firm; indeed, a great many countries, and not merely those of the Soviet bloc, seek increased consumption. Just how firm consumption remains is revealed by two statistics. In December, 1979, it was projected that the average consumer in the United States would eat 214.4 pounds of meat during 1980, a figure more than sufficient to keep the meat industry afloat.[13] In Britain, in the second half of 1980, Mintel, a marketing intelligence organization, published a survey which showed that, despite a sharply worsening economy, meat sales in Britain rose in the first half of 1980.[14]

Some people, of course, will not be even the least bit indifferent and will change their meat-based diet for health reasons; and, as I remarked earlier, the health argument does produce converts to vegetarianism. The problem, however, is that the number of people who give up meat for health reasons is simply dwarfed by the vast number of meat-eaters coming into (as well as remaining in) the market. The truth is, I suspect, that unless a government ban for reasons of health is imposed on all meat, or unless the link between disease and even moderate or minimal consumption of meat is established beyond a doubt, the health argument is not going to bring about the demise of meat-eating.

Even if a link between disease and even moderate or minimal consumption of meat were established, one must not simply assume that meat-eating would disappear as a result. The evidence for a link between smoking and disease is now substantial, but smoking is still widespread. A friend of mine who smokes moderately usually replies to those who urge him to quit that he so enjoys a good smoke at several points during the day (health warnings have produced moderation, not abstinence) that he is quite prepared to bear the cost to his health, should there be any for a moderate smoker. So, one must not overlook a further kind of response to the health argument: a moderate meat-eater, who is very fond of meat so many evenings a week, may not be in the least indifferent to his health; he may be quite prepared to take his chances and to bear the costs as a result.

We still tend to regard health as essentially a personal or private affair (and so to tolerate indifference with regard to it). A man may be imprudent if he smokes heavily, but we still tend not to regard him as immoral. Because some people do not care to be engulfed with tobacco smoke, smoking in confined, public areas, such as railway carriages, aeroplanes, and waiting rooms, is increasingly restricted; but, if a man were to smoke in private, the likes and dislikes of other people are generally held not to the point. Recently, some evidence has emerged in Japan about the harmful effects of tobacco smoke on non-smokers (specifically, on the wives of smokers, who are exposed to the noxious fumes for prolonged periods);[15] but if a man smoked in private, where non-smokers, including his wife, were unaffected, we on the whole still tend to think other people are not licensed to interfere with him.

Any vegetarian who is content to rest his case upon a similar observation of prudence in the case of meat-eating seems likely to meet with much the same sort of response. Even if it could be shown that meat-eating was imprudent, we are not thereby licensed to interfere with any individual meat-eater, unless we assume a degree of paternalism wholly at odds with the usual emphasis we place upon autonomy. And as for what the meat-eater himself makes of the claim of his imprudence, he may well reply *'chacun à son gout'*. It is hard to see the claim of prudence in this context bringing about the demise of meat-eating, especially if the meat-eating is moderate.

Confirmed meat-eaters who have long enjoyed robust health will be more difficult to convince, for example, that chemical residues in meat are undermining their health. Not even the claim that some residues can be retained in our systems and so can build up over time to dangerous levels may persuade the moderate meat-eater to abstain; for he may reason that (a) the amount of meat he consumes is not very great, (b) the danger level is so high that it will take years to reach, and, most especially, (c) he, like everyone else, varies the meats he consumes and so does not consume in a determined way the ones against which, at a particular time, he is warned.

Besides, the presence of possibly toxic residues in meat will almost certainly lead the meat-eater to the tactics presently adopted, namely, to seek a ban on those drugs which are harmful to us,[16] to seek a reduction in the amount of this or that drug used, to foster the development of new drugs to combat disease and to spur growth which are not toxic to humans, and to abstain temporarily from that kind of meat against which, at the time, we have been warned. If more drugs of the appropriate sorts are developed which are not toxic to humans, the problem will be solved, and the meat and drug industries are presently engaged in such projects. (I have seen in print the claim that fully 80 per cent of the new drugs coming onto the market are intended for use in animals.)

There are three observations it might be useful to append to the above points, which reinforce them and the direction in which they point.

The whole question of quantity bedevils discussion in this area of harm to health. Take the case of suspected carcinogens: present evidence in many instances seems to suggest that the substance must be ingested in quantities that are enormous, far exceeding anything a moderate person is likely to consume; as a result, the public often casts a dubious eye upon claims that this or that is a carcinogen. The battle over saccharin is a case in point, where, at least in some tests, the quantity of saccharin fed experimental animals, and in concentrated form over prolonged periods, vastly exceeded anything a human is likely to ingest. Even then, at that dosage in that form over that period, only a small minority of the animals developed cancers. The fact that some did eventually enabled the US Food and Drug Administration to compel soft-drink manufacturers to place a health warning on the containers of their sugar-free drinks; British authorities, however, unconvinced by the evidence, did not so compel the same firms in Britain.[17] The Canadian authorities have tested, and as a result allowed on to the market, aspartame, a sweeter sugar-substitute, with no after-taste, to replace saccharin; but the US Food and Drug Administration has, as of mid-1981, refused to license its use without more testing.

Queries are increasingly raised about extrapolations from laboratory animals under test conditions, which often means prolonged exposure at high dosage to concentrated forms of some substance, to ordinary human beings under ordinary conditions. These queries focus, not on whether test animals are sufficiently 'like us' (if they were thought not to be, the value of the tests would be compromised from the outset), but on the usually wide gulf between test conditions and the conditions in which ordinary human beings live and work and come into contact with the substance in question.

So many claims and counter-claims have recently been made in the area of health and diet, with medical evidence arrayed on all sides, that the public not infrequently does not know what to believe. The situation seems at times to be in danger of turning into what one expects in court-rooms these days, where the prosecution and defence each has its psychiatrists in the wings, to be brought on, from time to time, to contradict each other.

Even 'commonly received' claims come under fire. Thus, in the United States, the Food and Nutrition Board of the National Academy of Sciences issued a report in 1980 entitled *Toward Healthful Diets*, in which the Board found itself at odds with previous claims about cholesterol and health and refused to make any recommendation (such as radically reducing one's intake) in respect of cholesterol. Its general advice was not to worry about eating foods containing saturated fats[18] and cholesterol. Needless to say, this report caused a furore and has itself since come under fire. Again, the *International Herald Tribune* carried a report on 2 January 1981, about evidence to suggest that overweight people live longer than thin people. And so matters proceed. Confronted by a series of claims and counter-claims, with often widely discrepant suggestions about what to do, laymen will be tempted, I suspect, to carry on as before and to await further developments in the evidence.

In fine, not even the health argument appears likely as yet to eliminate meat-eating or to reach the moderate meat-eater, who is increasingly aware, if he was not already, that eating meat to excess, indeed, eating to excess, may not be prudent.

Moral Grounds

How, then, is the vegetarian to come to grips with the moderate meat-eater and to eliminate meat-eating?

Short of actually compelling people not to eat meat, moral vegetarianism is probably the best means of persuasion, for reasons set out in chapter 1. Here, I shall only observe that a moral case for changing our diet seems more certain than any of the above non-moral cases both to overcome our intense liking for meat and to reach even the moderate meat-eater. What is to make us abstain in spite of our love of meat, what is to make even the moderate meat-eater abstain from his modest portions is the conviction that eating meat is wrong. If all of us thought this, then, given that we were morally serious, meat-eating would disappear.

If the moral vegetarian can make his case, the health argument becomes superfluous. For if it is morally wrong to eat meat, then the case for abstaining from it is made, without having to mention or appeal to some illness one may possibly contract through eating it. In fact, to the moral vegetarian, if his position can be successfully established, I think the health argument may well appear as something of a red herring, as diverting attention away from the real reasons for becoming a vegetarian, which are not prudential but moral.

Coercion on Behalf of Vegetarianism

For moral vegetarians, the very essence of whose position is choosing to abstain from meat for moral reasons, coercion of others seems precluded as a possible policy option. Yet, I think it not unlikely that moral vegetarians may well in the end have to envisage something of the sort, though for a reason which is perhaps not immediately obvious.

It is exceedingly unlikely that anyone reading this book in the 1980s will see a vegetarian United States in his lifetime. Change, if it comes at all, is going to come very slowly. Quite naturally, the temptation will arise to try to speed it up, and one way of trying to do this is to force other people to behave as one wants them to. This much is obvious; but it is not the reason for coercion that I want to isolate.

As the years pass, what the moral vegetarian has to be sure of, quite apart from making fresh converts, is that he retains what converts he has already made; for if his gains are cancelled out by his losses, he has achieved nothing. But victory is far into the future; he cannot hold out its immediate prospect as a means of holding his supporters. True, he and they may be convinced that they are morally in the right; but the United States continues in its meat-eating ways, with no sign of change in the offing. So what does the moral vegetarian do?

Possibly the moral fervour of his allies will last their lifetimes; but possibly it will not. Anyone who has become a vegetarian in the past 30 years has witnessed the beginning and the absolutely phenomenal growth of the fast food industry, with its staggering sales of meat products (I return to this later); and he must see the prospect of success in his efforts at changing our diet, if not having actually receded, at least not having improved. The moral vegetarian is as far from his goal as ever. In these circumstances, coercing others can draw the prospect of success nearer, which in turn can help to hold his allies to their task.

Notes

1 David Ealey, 'Neglected vegetarian', *Sunday Times*, 10 Feb. 1980.
2 See, for example, Barbara Parham, *What's Wrong With Eating Meat?* (Denver, Colorado, Amanda Marga Publications, 1979), pp. 3–11; Vic Sussman, *The Vegetarian Alternative* (Emmaus, Pennsylvania, Rodale Press, 1978) pp. 131–46; Jon Wynne-Tyson, *Food For A Future* (Sussex, Centaur Press, 1979), pp. 27–44; Dudley Giehl, *Vegetarianism: A Way of Life* (New York, Harper and Row, 1979), pp. 23–42.
3 For a discussion of the beliefs of this relatively unknown sect (unknown, that is, in the West), see Padmanabh S. Jaini, *The Jain Path of Purification* (London, University of California Press, 1979). For a thumb-nail sketch, see Janet Barkas, *The Vegetable Passion* (London, Routledge & Kegan Paul, 1975), pp. 21–4.
4 In Britain, controversy periodically breaks out on whether the orthodox Jewish method of slaughtering animals for food — the animals are not rendered unconscious, before a knife is, in a single action, taken to the jugular vein and windpipe — is painful.
5 Frances Moore Lappè, *Diet For A Small Planet*, New York, Ballantine Books, rev. edn, 1975.
6 See, for example, Barbara Parham, *What's Wrong With Eating Meat?*, pp. 14–34; Vic Sussman, *The Vegetarian Alternative*, pp. 53–75; Jon Wynne-Tyson, *Food For A Future*, pp. 52–72; Dudley Giehl, *Vegetarianism*, pp. 26–52.
7 For a discussion of the content of this programme, see Robin Stringer, 'Intensive farming images upsetting', *Daily Telegraph*, 10 May 1979.
8 For a discussion of this report, see Victor Cohn, 'Antibiotics in animal feeds are seen as an increasing risk to human health', *International Herald Tribune*, 26 June 1979.
9 See, for example, Bill Sing, 'US tobacco earnings show strong rise', *International Herald Tribune*, 30 July 1980. In recent years, there have been dramatic increases in the number of smokers among women and girls in the United States and Britain and among the populace at large in Third World countries.
10 See *US News and World Report*, 24 Sept. 1979, p. 63.
11 See, for example, Frances Turner, John Stark, 'Which comes first — chickens or eggs?', *Guardian*, 24 Oct. 1979.
12 See Hugh Clayton, ' "Real eggs" fail price test', *The Times*, 8 Nov. 1980.
13 See Sue Shellenberger, 'Pork gains on beef as meat choice in US', *International Herald Tribune*, 24 Dec. 1979.
14 See *The Times*, 11 Aug. 1980.
15 See L. K. Altman, 'Wives of smokers face lung cancer risk', *International Herald Tribune*, 17 Jan. 1981.
16 I do not mean to imply that a ban may not have to be sought in the face of opposition from the meat industry. Such has been the case with the synthetic estrogen diethylstilbestrol, a drug widely used in the past for fattening cattle. It has now been banned by the US Food and Drug Administration for causing cancer in humans, but not without considerable opposition from meat industry groups; see 'Seven-year dispute over drugs ends with FDA ban', *New York Times*, 1 July 1979.
17 More recent studies in the United States are, I believe, divided on the issue, some giving saccharin a relatively clean bill of health, others not. I suspect it will eventually be banned there, if another artificial sweetener, e.g., aspartame, is ready to take its place and thereby to reduce the economic losses involved in its elimination.
18 For an especially interesting discussion of some evidence pointing in the opposite direction, see Colin Tudge, 'Polyunsaturates are good for you after all', *New Scientist*, 2 Oct. 1980, pp. 20–1.

3

Two Types of Moral Vegetarianism

We can distinguish broadly between two types of moral vegetarianism, depending upon whether it is human or animal welfare which is the central moral ground upon which we are to abstain from meat. I do not mean to imply that a concern with human welfare may not in the end result in an increase in animal welfare, only that it is human welfare in numerous cases upon which moral vegetarianism is made fundamentally to turn. Some examples should make this distinction clear.

The Redistribution Argument

It is a fact that numerous people are presently starving throughout the world. It is also a fact that we have already in our possession at least in part a means by which to do something about this. By forgoing meat in our diet, we could save the enormous quantities of grain used in feeding and fattening livestock, which could then be redistributed to the starving poor. Even if not every such person could be fed or fed to anything like an adequate degree, at least a good many of them could, and this is what counts. It is wrong not to try to save these people and wrong, therefore, to persist in diverting grain into feed for animals, whose numbers we are constantly increasing merely in order to satisfy our desire for meat.

This argument makes out the moral ground of vegetarianism to be the enhancement of general human welfare through the feeding of the starving poor. The argument from (animal) pain and suffering, on the other hand, makes out the moral ground of vegetarianism to be the enhancement of general animal welfare. A person who is a moral vegetarian on the basis of this latter argument may, if his and others' boycott of meat leads to a reduction in the number of animals bred, think it right to redistribute to the poor of the world the grain saved in feed for animals; but he is not committed to this. It is animal suffering, not human welfare, upon which his case for vegetarianism turns, and it is merely a happy consequence of that case that there is grain to be redistributed to poor human beings.

The Increased Shortage Argument

There are numerous versions of this argument, but perhaps the most prevalent is that developed around a present or future world food crisis. Not merely are we unable to feed everyone in the world today, whether through scarcity of food or problems in its distribution, but we are also reproducing ourselves and depleting our resources at such a rate as to ensure that we shall not be able to feed an ever-increasing number of people in future. Advances on a number of fronts have failed to prevent dramatic increases in the starving poor, particularly in those countries and in those segments of their societies which are already in serious difficulty. In short, as the number of mouths to feed rapidly begins to outstrip the increase in food production, it is wrong to use grain and other precious resources in producing meat, especially since relatively few poor countries may be able to afford much of the meat so produced.

Several additional factors affect this argument. First, there has been a decrease in world production of rice, wheat, and coarse grains,[1] and it is projected that world food consumption will exceed world food production during the 1980s. In other words, present shortages are expected to persist. Second, other, food-related resources that are in finite supply will become the object of intense competition,[2] and quite apart from the fact that wars and other violence are likely to attend this competition, poor countries on the whole are in no position to engage in, let alone win, it. This is especially true where the resource requires modern technology in its extraction and/or development or where it requires market outlets which are in the hands of multinational corporations or where the country which possesses the resource cannot control market forces sufficiently to prevent prices form collapsing (as has happened, for example, to Cuba and Jamaica over sugar and Zambia over copper). Third, many Third World countries are themselves anxious to obtain intensive farming technology. The West is sometimes castigated for exporting this technology[3] because, in order to feed the animals being farmed, poor countries will be forced to divert grain from human to animal mouths or to find more hard currency with which to import grain for animal feed. On the other hand, if these possibilities are pointed out to Third World countries, and if, nevertheless, even given time and education, they persist in wanting new, animal-farming technology, then what are we to do? We could refuse to supply it; but it is hard to believe that, if we do refuse, this will not be seen as another instance of economic imperialism. Of course, we could treat such countries paternalistically and refuse to supply the technology on the ground that we are better judges of what is in their interests, but this approach is hardly likely to recommend itself to many people today. So what are we to do, if the possible hazards are pointed out, but Third World countries continue to desire increased meat supplies? (Very few underdeveloped countries are vegetarian (by principle), and a reading of the major financial papers will reveal the breakdown of their agricultural expenditure. Given a burgeoning population, these expenditures will be directed towards the greatest farm productivity affordable; it is no accident, in other words, that population and population growth are major spurs to the acquisition of factory farming technology.) Fourth, if developing countries import massive quantities of grain in order to feed intensively farmed animals, then the price of meat, in the absence of subsidies, may be forced up there, to a point where it outstrips the cost of non-intensively produced meat.[4] This is a serious possibility, which must be taken into account by Third World countries in deliberating about the import of factory farming technology. Of course, so long as these countries remain meat-eating, they are likely to want to increase meat production, which is what intensive farming is all about.

As with other versions of the shortage argument, this one essentially appeals to what happens or is held likely to happen to human beings unless we embrace vegetarianism. And though on all versions of the shortage argument it is true that the number of animals bred may diminish, since there will doubtless not be enough grain, etc., to sustain a vast animal population, and true, therefore, that total animal suffering may diminish, it is not a reduction in animal but in human suffering with which the argument is centrally concerned.

The Waste Argument

I indicated in the last chapter that the argument from waste might be held to have moral overtones.[5] It is obvious how this may occur: it will be argued that it is wasteful and, therefore, wrong to use grain and other foodstuffs on animal feed and on increasing the size of the food animal population when people are going hungry. Not uncommonly, the charge of waste is levied against commercial farming on other counts as well; for instance, it is alleged that modern factory farms utilize great quantities of land, water, and energy,[6] all of which could be put to a less wasteful use, especially so far as factory farms in developing countries are concerned.

(Could it be wrong to waste resources *without* bringing in the effect upon human beings? The problem would be to understand what makes it wrong. There is little doubt that we are presently squandering water; but it is difficult to see how this could be morally wrong, unless *some* reference to its effect upon present and/or future human beings were made. For to look at the situation from the point of view of the water is impossible, since, in the absence of some reasonably persuasive argument to the contrary, water, grain, trees, etc., unlike humans, do not have a point of view from which they can be wronged.[7] Though animal welfare is here encompassed by the waste argument, at least to the extent of encompassing those creatures to whom we are prepared to attribute a point of view on the world,[8] it remains human welfare or alleviating human suffering in connection with which the waste of resources is usually condemned.)

The Argument from Effect on Character

Some people have come to believe and fear that, in the suffering and killing which occurs in commercial farming, we demean ourselves, coarsen our sensitivities, dull our feelings of sympathy with our fellow creatures, and so begin the descent down the slippery slope of torture and death, to a point where it becomes easier for us to contemplate and carry out the torture and killing of human beings.

This very popular type of argument likewise appeals to human welfare. It is not the killing and suffering of animals but the effect all this killing and suffering has upon those who inflict and those who tolerate it which this argument makes the moral basis of vegetarianism. Conversely, to someone who objects simply to the killing or suffering of animals, it is the actual taking of life or the actual suffering inflicted which is the moral basis of his vegetarianism. To this individual, even if the killing and suffering of animals in no way demeans or coarsens us or dulls our feelings of sympathy, it by no means follows that we ought not to refrain from killing animals or from making them suffer.

The Argument from Violence

This argument tries to connect meat-eating with (heightened) aggression in human beings, with the fighting, mugging, and other violence prevalent in Western societies. (Presumably, violence in Eastern societies with a high percentage of vegetarians is to be explained differently.)

No doubt we all to some extent share Wordsworth's lament:

> To her fair works did Nature link
> The human soul that through me ran;
> And much it grieved my heart to think
> What man has made of man.

But is meat-eating the explanation of our ills, or, more narrowly, the explanation of the mindless violence that has engulfed our cities and blighted the lives of so many who inhabit them? Must we give up meat, if our streets, parks and subways are again to be safe? The problem is to establish the relevant connection; otherwise, I suspect, meat-eating would not occur to one as part of the explanation of inner-city decay.

Sometimes, the argument from violence is held in an almost cosmic form. The following passage by Isaac Bashevis Singer illustrates the point perfectly:

> I personally believe that so long as human beings will go on shedding the blood of animals, there will never be any peace. There is only one little step from killing animals to creating gas chambers *à la* Hitler and concentration camps *à la* Stalin — all such deeds are done in the name of 'social justice'.[9]

If vegetarianism were the price of peace on earth, if abstinence from meat would rid the world of Hitlers and Stalins once and for all, who would hold back? But how many of us think these things? And is not the reason we do not simply that we cannot see the connection that would render Bashevis Singer's claims plausible? (Even so, it might be said, I cannot show him wrong, cannot show that there is no connection between killing and eating animals and Auschwitz or the Gulags. But this reply mislocates where the burden of proof falls with such claims.)

More generally, I am extremely sceptical of 'slippery slope' arguments. This is not the place to rehearse all the reasons why, but it is typical of such arguments that little evidence is adduced for supposing that one must slip on to the slope in the first place. Someone who says 'kill animals and you will find it easier to kill humans' would appear to be relying upon some thesis of psychology or human nature as support. Even if we leave aside questions about the nature and status of such a thesis, it surely cannot be assumed that it operates on each and every occasion without regard to anything else. Consider, then, the matter of the value of life: there is no reason to think, because one tolerates animals being killed for food, that one will be irresistibly led to erect gas chambers or will find it easier to erect concentration camps or will be more likely than a vegetarian to do either of these things; for the different values typically assigned animal and human life enable one to demarcate rather more markedly than Bashevis Singer allows the morality of killing animals from that of killing humans. (I return to this issue in chapter 12.) Such demarcation provides, given exactly the same assumption the vegetarian is working with, namely, that we take morality seriously, at least plausible grounds for maintaining that we shall not slip on to the slope that is supposed to extend from killing animals to killing humans.

All five of the above arguments are human-based arguments for moral vegetarianism. By way of contrast, I have been focusing upon the argument from (animal) pain and suffering, and some further discussion of it may help to make the contrast more plain.

The Argument from Pain and Suffering

This argument, championed by Peter Singer in *Animal Liberation*[10] and *Practical Ethics*,[11] by Stephen Clark in *The Moral Status of Animals*,[12] and by many others, moves either directly or indirectly to moral vegetarianism from the pain and suffering which animals undergo in being bred, raised, and slaughtered for food. (Perhaps the most common way the argument moves from pain and suffering to moral vegetarianism indirectly is via the notion of interests. This requires that animals have interests, and one aim of my *Interests and Rights* was to deny that they do, at least in a sense that enables the argument to work.)

The argument from pain and suffering, of course, has a past; its use by Singer and others is but the most recent among several. The significance it has come to have, especially under the stimulus of *Animal Liberation*, stems from its application to intensive methods of food production, to factory or commercial farming. What Singer, amongst others, has done is to give the argument new and important life, by describing how some aspects of intensive farming involve animal suffering and then using the argument to combat these farming practices.

I do not believe it betrays undue sensitivity to find certain practices employed on factory farms profoundly disturbing. To put no finer point on the matter, there are practices afoot on them, pre-eminently in the cases of laying hens and veal calves,[13] of which we cannot be proud. Even if such practices are necessary to sustain the level of profits by which farmers, their families, the meat industry as a whole, and, through it, a very great many others prosper, we still do well not to be proud of having to resort to them. Some might suggest that the great pleasure human beings receive from consuming veal more than outweighs the suffering (no grain, no straw-bedding, no exercise, perpetual confinement in tiny slatted stalls, little muscle-growth, induced iron-deficiency and anemia, almost no daylight, tethered to prevent seeking iron and exercise)[14] which these calves undergo in reaching the table. Even so, treatment such as this is not the sort of thing in which, morally, we take pride; and if it is something required in order to sustain a level or style of life to which we have become accustomed, we still do well to be distrubed that this is so.

As information about the treatment of, for example, veal calves has been more widely disseminated, more people have come to see this treatment as wrong. But this is by no means the end or even the essence of the matter for Singer; for it is central to his position − in fact, it seems the main feature of his position − that moral vegetarianism is *the means by which each of us* can move directly to eliminate the pains of food animals. Once we come to see our treatment of veal calves as wrong, vegetarianism is seen by Singer as the means by which each of us can do something about this treatment. This emerges very clearly from the central argument of *Animal Liberation*.[15]

Animals can suffer, and since they can suffer, they have interests. In view of this fact, the moral principle of the equal consideration of interests applies to them, and this means that we are not morally justified in setting aside, ignoring, or otherwise devaluing their interests.[16] This, however, is precisely what some factory farming practices, with their accompaniment of animal suffering, appear to involve, and the immorality which this represents is, if anything, accentuated by the fact that we do not need meat in order to survive and to lead healthy lives.

We can, on the other hand, do something about this situation: by boycotting meat, we can draw down market forces upon the head of the factory farmer and so reduce or eliminate the suffering of food animals. When demand slackens, prices fall; when prices fall, profits diminish; and when profits diminish, the factory farmer has less capital to re-invest in food stock. (The same is true for farmers who employ traditional methods of farming.) By becoming a vegetarian, then, each of us hits directly and immediately at factory farming; for in giving up meat, we reduce the number of food animals bred and raised for market and thereby total animal suffering. Accordingly, a genuine concern for the interests of animals and so with a diminution in their suffering requires that we cease rearing animals for food and cease eating them.

The picture one carries away from Singer's book, then, is that becoming a moral vegetarian is the means by which each of us can reduce animal suffering and so help in the effort to right a wrong. Once we have identified certain farming practices as wrong, we can use vegetarianism as the tool, as the direct and immediate means for eliminating or mitigating those practices. What is more, this means is relatively painless on us, given that there are wholesome and nutritious alternatives to meat readily available.

This picture is enormously appealing and has contributed in no small measure, I think, to the impact of Singer's book. Later, in considering some aspects of the argument from pain and suffering, I shall challenge this picture of the effects of one's becoming a moral vegetarian; indeed, Singer himself, partly in response to my arguments, which he saw in earlier draft, has returned to it in his recent paper 'Utilitarianism and vegetarianism'[17] and has tried partially to redraw it, and I shall have something to say as well about these more recent remarks. Here, however, I am concerned only to make plain the contrast between this animal-based argument from pain and suffering and human-based arguments for moral vegetarianism.

Focus upon Animal Welfare

Doubtless to many, it will appear strange that I should focus upon arguments from the enhancement of animal welfare to the exclusion of those cases for vegetarianism based upon the enhancement of human welfare. After all, it is almost certainly true, in the United States in particular, that Frances Moore Lappè's *Diet For A Small Planet*, which has now sold millions of copies, has proved vastly more effective in producing converts to vegetarianism than the works, say, of Singer and Clark (and a great many others) combined. Why, then, follow the course I do?

I hope the answer is clear: cases for vegetarianism based upon human welfare have nothing essentially to do with the plight of those animals who have become, under modern conditions, a part of the human food chain, and it is this matter of what we now do to certain animals in converting them into food which has recently given the question of vegetarianism a new focus. If people have always starved, veal calves have not always suffered in the way they presently do, on our behalf. I am not suggesting, of course, that a concern for animal welfare is a new reason for becoming a vegetarian; but the rapid growth of intensive farming and the wholesale application of technology to food production have, in the eyes of many, given the whole question of vegetarianism a new importance and, it must be said, a sense of moral urgency.

Notes

1 See Melvyn Westlake, 'Food: the deepening crisis', *The Times*, 8 Jan. 1981.
2 See Michael Tanzer, *The Race for Resources* (London, Heinemann, 1980).
3 See Geoffrey Brown, 'Animal welfare group attacks "factory farms" ', *Daily Telegraph*, 12 Nov. 1979.
4 For an example of such a computation, see John Madeley, 'Battery hens may cause grain shortage', *Observer*, 12 Oct. 1980.
5 See James Rachels, 'Vegetarianism and "the other weight problem" ', in W. Aiken, H. LaFollette, (eds), *World Hunger and Moral Obligation* (New Jersey, Prentice-Hall, 1977), pp. 180–93.
6 See Dudley Giehl, *Vegetarianism*, pp. 102–15.
7 See ch. 14. I have also touched upon this issue at a number of places in my book *Interests and Rights: The Case Against Animals* (Oxford, Clarendon Press, 1980); see especially ch. 4 and pp. 164 ff.
8 How limited or extensive the list of such creatures is I shall leave to readers to determine. One point only I stress: if you attribute a point of view on the world to other creatures to the extent that you can imaginatively represent them as 'like us' in certain minimal respects, such as having experiences or the capacity to feel pain or the ability to respond to changes in the environment, then unless you can rebut the view that some of sentient and all of non-sentient nature is not 'like us' in many of these respects they gain no foothold by these means in the camp of who or what can be wronged. See ch. 14.
9 From Isaac Bashevis Singer's Foreword to Dudley Giehl's *Vegetarianism*, pp. viii–ix.
10 Peter Singer, *Animal Liberation*, London, Jonathan Cape, 1976.
11 Peter Singer, *Practical Ethics*, Cambridge, Cambridge University Press, 1980.
12 Stephen Clark, *The Moral Status of Animals*, Oxford, Clarendon Press, 1977.
13 Later, I shall mention some recent innovations — and improvements — in the treatment of these animals.
14 Slaughter normally occurs anywhere from 12 to 15 weeks of this treatment.
15 I have discussed a number of aspects of this argument, with which I am not concerned in this work, in ch. 9 of *Interests and Rights*.
16 As Singer makes plain in chs 2 and 3 of *Practical Ethics*, the principle of the equal consideration of interests encapsulates for him the basic minimum of the analysis of the concept of equality.
17 Peter Singer, 'Utilitarianism and vegetarianism', *Philosophy and Public Affairs*, vol. 9, 1980, pp. 325–37.

Part II

4

The Three Arguments from Animal Welfare

By moral vegetarianism, then, I have in mind those cases for vegetarianism which locate the moral basis for boycotting meat in our treatment of animals in rearing and converting them into food.

Modern proponents of vegetarianism on this basis have relied principally upon three arguments to show that eating meat is wrong.

The argument from moral rights. This is the view that our present treatment of animals in converting them into food violates their moral right to life and/or freedom from unnecessary suffering. It is wrong to eat meat, then, because animals' moral rights have been violated in the course of their reaching our tables.

The argument from killing. This is the view that it is wrong to kill animals or to kill them for food, except, if at all, under conditions which few of us can pretend to be in.[1] It is wrong to eat meat because animals have undergone the irretrievable wrong of being killed, in the course of becoming food for human consumption.

The argument from pain and suffering. This is the view, to repeat, that it is wrong to eat meat, because factory-farmed (and perhaps even some traditionally-farmed) animals have suffered a good deal and, thus, been wrongly treated, in the course of being turned into food.

Two things should be apparent at once from these arguments, so far as non-moral bases to vegetarianism are concerned. First, they indicate why moral vegetarians will be wary of the argument from health. Given any one of the above bases to their moral vegetarianism, they simply will not concede that what one eats is one's own affair in quite the way that smoking and using saccharin are usually thought to be; for they will insist that the obvious moral dimension to their objection to meat-eating quite explicitly separates it from these things.[2] Second, as for the other, non-moral bases to vegetarianism, moral vegetarians will insist that all of them seriously understate the case against eating meat. This case is far stronger, they will maintain, than *any* non-moral ground for vegetarianism can possibly encompass.

One can also understand how some moral vegetarians may be led to violence. If a person does not like the taste of meat or is preoccupied with his appearance and fashion, he does not thereby acquire a licence for insisting that others share his taste or preoccupation. But if vegetarianism has one of the above moral bases, then a vegetarian may well think that he has a reason not merely for condemning a flesh diet but also for actively taking steps to discourage others in its continuance. After all, he may maintain, if moral issues are worth troubling about, they are worth doing something about.

Failure of the Arguments

I hope that it will already be fairly clear to readers that these three arguments do not in fact *establish* that it is wrong to eat meat.

All three arguments seek to demonstrate the wrongness of eating meat by showing that something else altogether is wrong. For instance, the argument from moral rights makes the wrongness of eating meat contingent upon the wrongness of violating an animal's alleged moral right to life and/or freedom from unnecessary suffering, and only if this can be shown to be wrong can meat-eating be wrong. But how will showing that it is wrong to violate an animal's rights show that it is wrong to eat meat? Obviously, any argument which tries to move from the wrongness of A to the wrongness of B depends upon establishing the wrongness of A; but it also depends upon whether the wrongness of A logically entails the wrongness of B. Only if it does can showing the former show or demonstrate the latter. In the argument from moral rights or the other two arguments, however, there is no such entailment: even if violating an animal's moral rights can be shown to be wrong, and even if every single one of an animal's alleged moral rights has been violated, it does not in the least follow that eating meat is wrong, any more than it follows, if we allow that it is wrong to be cruel to animals, that it is, therefore, wrong to eat them. So, meat-eating has not been shown to be wrong.

In the absence of entailments, the transitivity of wrongness from A to B is not quite as open and shut as the arguments from moral rights, killing, and pain and suffering would have it. Suppose my neighbour shoots and kills a turkey: even if it was wrong of him to kill it, is it wrong of me to eat it? It is not obvious how the argument from killing (or the other arguments) can show that it is, when the person who does the eating is different from the person who does the killing, which is the case, of course, with the meat we buy in the supermarket. After all, where killing or violating rights or inflicting suffering is concerned, it is normally the person who does these things who is morally suspect. And even if we allow that most abattoirs would not exist if most people did not eat meat, it does not follow that the wrongness of the slaughterer's act of killing, if it is wrong, somehow mystically transfers to the consumer's act of eating. It is true that animals are killed in order to be eaten; but it is killing, not eating, which carries the moral force in the argument from killing and which is being condemned.

Much the same is true of cannibalism: it is killing the person in order to eat him, not eating him once he is dead, that is typically the focus of legal and moral condemnation; and if the people who do the eating are different from the people who do the killing, it by no means follows that the wrongness of the latter's act somehow transfers to the former's. (In the well-known case of *Regina v. Dudley and Stephens*,[3] two shipwrecked and starving men killed and ate a cabin boy who was adrift at sea with them. It appears to have been the finding in this case that the saving of one's own life, even in extreme circumstances, is no defence to murder. In other words, if the two men had waited for the cabin boy to expire naturally,[4] there would have been no case for them to answer.)

Finally, even if we were to suppose that wrongness *is* transitive in the three arguments, we obtain a result not quite to the liking of their proponents. For do not the arguments themselves implicitly concede the wrong of eating meat to be far less serious than the wrong of violating rights or killing or inflicting suffering? For example, the focus of the argument from pain and suffering is upon inflicting pain and suffering on animals, not upon benefiting as a result; so even if we were to concede for the sake of argument that it is wrong to benefit from painful practices, an issue to which I return later, *this* argument appears to make that wrong a far less substantial one than the wrong of actually engaging in those practices. The same is true of the other arguments; thus, in the turkey example, if I am wrong to eat the turkey, nevertheless, on the argument from killing, the wrongness of my act is as nothing to the wrongness of your act of killing it.

Notes

1   I have in mind conditions of necessity, where the killing and eating of animals is necessary for our survival.
2   As I indicated in ch. 2, if such things were to have an effect upon people in addition to users, then moral arguments might possibly arise in connection with their use. I emphasize use, in order to distinguish this issue from another, in which morality can enter the picture differently; thus, if a person smokes, contracts cancer, requires hospitalization, and cannot defray the entire costs involved, then the rest of us as taxpayers will have to do so. It might be argued that it is morally wrong to make us use resources on what might be regarded as avoidable illnesses, when there are so many people with unavoidable illnesses.
3   1884: 14 QBD, 273.
4   They did not so wait, of course, because they not unreasonably believed themselves in imminent danger of starving to death.

5

Two Conceptions of the Status of Vegetarianism

There is a curious feature of the arguments from moral rights, killing, and pain and suffering that I am sure many readers have noticed. It consists in the fact that, even if we were to regard the arguments as completely successful, they would by no means bar or eliminate all meat-eating. In this can be found the basis for distinguishing two very different conceptions of the status of vegetarianism.

Partial and Absolute Exclusions

When I first arrived at Oxford from Virginia, I became friendly with a mathematician from Calcutta. He was a vegetarian and abstained from all meat. Meals in college were very unpleasant for him, since they invariably featured meat dishes, and what vegetables there were were unappetizing, always the same, and — the great English gastronomic failure — overcooked. He regarded eating meat as an abomination; there were no circumstances — apart, perhaps from direst necessity, and even this was uncertain — in which he would allow it to be right. Eating meat was simply excluded from consideration, and there was an end to it.

The arguments from moral rights, killing, and pain and suffering do not have the same absolutely dismissive effect. The reason is that the objections which they severally pose are not actually to eating animals but to the treatment animals receive in the course of being converted into food. The result is obvious: to animals which have not undergone the treatment in question, the arguments do not apply. Thus, since the argument from moral rights makes the wrongness of violating animals' moral rights crucial, it places no objection in the way of eating meat from animals whose rights have not been violated. Someone who is a vegetarian solely on the basis of this argument, then, has no reason *per se* to abstain from such meat, any more than someone who is a vegetarian on the basis of the argument from pain and suffering has any reason *per se* to abstain from eating the flesh of animals who have not been cruelly treated in being turned into food. This does not mean, of course, that these individuals will eat the meat in question, only that they must have one more shot in their lockers, if they are going to abstain on principle from this meat as well.

To my Indian friend, this situation would appear very strange indeed. For here are purported vegetarians who, *prima facie*, have no reason not to eat this meat. *He* does not eat meat at all; eating meat is quite excluded from consideration, whether the animal has had its rights violated or been killed or been made to suffer, or whether it has simply fallen from the heavens at one's feet or miraculously appeared in one's cooking pot. To him, it would be exceedingly peculiar to think that his vegetarianism required him to look carefully into the question of whether this chicken has had its rights violated, or had dropped dead from heart seizure, or had not suffered at some point in the past, as if one as opposed to some other answer would make it right for him to eat meat. The plain fact is that, so far as *his* vegetarianism is concerned, such questions are beside the point. Conversely, to the proponents of the three arguments, these questions are very much to the point, and their vegetarianism is conditioned by the responses given in their respective cases.

To this Indian, then, proponents of the three arguments appear more exercised by rights, killing, and suffering than by eating animals. What the arguments make out to be morally wrong is not actually eating animals but violating their alleged moral rights or killing them or making them suffer. Do none of these things, and the wrongness of eating meat vanishes. Here, then, are vegetarians of whom vegetarianism is only demanded if animals are treated one way rather than another. (In the case of the argument from pain and suffering, this result gives rise to a view which *prima facie* seems very strange. For there seems something odd indeed about a view which says in effect that when animals are (treated in such a way as to be) miserable they may not be eaten but when they are (treated in such a way as to be) happy and content they may be eaten. One's natural inclination would be to say the opposite, that when animals are contented, their lives are a benefit to them and that then, if ever, vegetarianism is demanded of us. I shall return to this point later, in connection with claims about the replaceability of animals.)

Conditional and Unconditional Conceptions

If we think of the position of this Indian mathematician as unconditional vegetarianism and that of the proponents of the three arguments as conditional vegetarianism, then how might we characterize the essential difference between these two conceptions of vegetarianism?

In his paper 'Utilitarianism and vegetarianism', Peter Singer objects to

Cora Diamond's claim[1] that his position yields the curious result that it is perfectly permissible to eat animals which are accident victims:

> Why is this curious? It is only curious on the assumption that vegetarians must think it *always* wrong to eat meat. No doubt some vegetarians are moral absolutists, just as there are absolute pacifists, absolute anti-abortionists and absolute truth-tellers who would never tell a lie. I reject all these forms of moral absolutism.[2]

Doubtless Singer would regard unconditional vegetarians as absolutists, and doubtless there is a significant difference between my Indian friend and Singer on this score. But the suggestion of the above passage — that some people think it always wrong to eat meat, whereas others, including Singer, think it only sometimes wrong — is not quite explicit as to the full difference between them.

If we think in terms of a distinction between unconditional and conditional vegetarianism, then the point I was making earlier can be put this way: when conditions of food animal treatment are one way rather than another, conditional vegetarianism ceases to have a ground, the result of which is, in the circumstances, to remove from conditional vegetarians their reason for abstaining from meat. When conditions are one way rather than another, vegetarianism is pointless; for the whole point of conditional vegetarianism is to improve the conditions in which animals are bred, raised, and slaughtered for food, and if conditions are already of the appropriate sort, then there is no point in adopting vegetarianism as the tactic by which to make them of that sort. Here, it seems to me, is encapsulated the essence of conditional vegetarianism: it is a tactic by means of which one hopes to improve the treatment of food animals. This is especially clear in the case of Singer, who, as we saw in chapter 3, regards vegetarianism based upon the argument from pain and suffering as the means by which to combat the pains of factory-farmed animals.

At the core of conditional vegetarianism, then, is a conception of vegetarianism as a tactic for combating the treatment or pains of food animals. But tactics are appropriate to circumstances, and a change in circumstances can, as we have seen, render one's tactics pointless. In the case of a conditional vegetarian, to persist in abstaining from meat, even when circumstances are of the desired sort, becomes a needless gesture.

Accordingly, to say merely that what separates my Indian friend from Singer is a form of absolutism, to say merely that conditional vegetarianism is limited (or applies only in respect of some animals) whereas unconditional vegetarianism is unlimited, leaves out any mention of the tactical conception of vegetarianism, which essentially defines the conditional position. This omission is of the utmost importance; for no one even remotely in sympathy with the views of my Indian friend could accept such a conception of vegetarianism. To this Indian, vegetarianism is something quite different: it represents a decision about how he will live in the world, a decision tantamount in part to the adoption of a way of life, for a world which contains a multiplicity of creatures and things, each as much a part of the whole as he is. It represents an attempt to live in harmony with the creatures and things he finds around him and to encroach on them as little as they on the whole encroach on him. It represents an effort to see himself as part of the world, and not a world — and law — unto himself. So far as I can see, nothing could be further from a tactical conception of vegetarianism than this conception of how we shall live in a world where we are but part of the whole, of which conception vegetarianism is a constituent.

(Someone armed with such a conception of vegetarianism is very likely to find Singer's emphasis upon pain rather puzzling. For though my Indian friend is not indifferent to the pains of animals, it is not by virtue of the fact that they can feel pain that he thinks they warrant and obtain his respect. If asked whether it was because animals can feel pain that he tries to live in harmony with them, as one part of nature with another, he would, I think, view both the question and the questioner with deep puzzlement, not least because many portions of the whole of which he sees himself as a part *cannot* feel pain. In time, I believe he would come to think that only someone with a particular theory would seize upon pain in this way and elevate it or its avoidance to supreme importance in ethics.)[3]

I myself am as much opposed to moral absolutisms as is Singer and, I suspect, for many of the same reasons. I have used the example of this Indian mathematician simply in order to bring out the tactical conception of vegetarianism, which lies at the heart of conditional vegetarianism, especially that of Singer.

Counter-Argument and Competing Tactics

Apart from the fact that, as we have seen, some vegetarians reject the tactical conception of vegetarianism, this conception is exposed to counter-arguments of a specific type. If we stick with Singer as our example, then these counter-arguments stem directly from the literature on utilitarianism.

The specific type of counter-argument is this: if vegetarianism is a tactic for combating the pains of food animals, then this tactic ceases to have any point whatever, if we develop ways of breeding, raising, and slaughtering animals painlessly. In this eventuality, we could eat all the meat we liked, and Singer would have no ground for complaint.

It will be claimed, however, that there is no meat available from animals which have not, in particular, been reared by painful methods. To this, there are three responses.

First, it is factually false; there are millions upon millions of animals presently being farmed but not factory-farmed. It is both tempting to argue and not obviously wrong to suggest that because traditional farming methods are held, even by vegetarians, to be vastly less painful than intensive ones, the argument from pain and suffering does not provide a reason for abstaining from the flesh of traditionally-farmed animals. (As we shall see, in connection with his views on killing, Singer himself appears prepared to accept this point about traditional farming.)

Second, not all intensively farmed animals suffer to anything like the degree of veal calves, or have the same methods of production used upon them. To give but a single example, in the United States, dairy cows are commercially farmed, and when their days as milk-producers come to an end, they are sent to slaughter. However, their lives are by no means as miserable as those of veal calves.

Third, if we focus solely upon factory-farmed animals, then we can see clearly to what the tactical conception of vegetarianism finally exposes Singer. For just as not eating meat is a tactic for dealing with the pains of food animals, so, too, is the package involving, among other things, maintaining and expanding traditional farming techniques, progressivly eliminating painful practices in intensive farming, and funding research into and developing pain-killing drugs. As tactics, both are on all fours; one is not *per se* more morally correct than the other. Moreover, the latter tactic has two further attractions: first, it enables us not only to deal with animal pain but also to retain our present, meat-based diet intact, and second, it enables us to meet the claim that the heavy demand for meat today can only be satisfied by intensive methods of production.

In this way, vegetarianism, Singer's tactic, is confronted with competition. That is, we are confronted with different tactics for combating the pains of food animals, and the central issue between them becomes simply the degree of effectiveness in achieving this end. The determination of which of two tactics is more effective in lessening animal pain is not a piece of theory but a matter of fact. If technological developments succeed in the encompassing way the one tactic envisages, then it may well be, on grounds of effectiveness, the preferred one, as new and better pain-killers, administered painlessly, reach more and more animals. This very real possibility cannot be eliminated *a priori* through any theoretical considerations. This is especially true for utilitarians such as Singer, for whom it must always remain a contingent affair whether the implementation of one policy has consequences which, in comparison with those of the implementation of another, make it the preferred or right policy. Effectiveness, then, is everything, and vegetarianism must confront and defeat (or at least not be defeated by) one after another competitor on this score; it by no means is *obviously* the most effective tactic for reducing the pains of food animals, so that all potential competitors can be ignored *ab initio*. (Later, I shall argue that the view that vegetarianism is the most effective step one can take to reduce and eliminate food animal suffering is false.)

To my Indian friend, of course, all this squabbling over effectiveness is beside the point; for whether it is Singer or his opponent who has the more effective means for coming to grips with animal pain, eating meat remains an abomination, and that is that.

Notes

1 Cora Diamond, 'Eating meat and eating people', *Philosophy*, vol. 53, 1978, pp. 465–79.
2 Singer, 'Utilitarianism and vegetarianism', pp. 327–8; italics in original.
3 It is not accidental that many of those concerned to develop an environmental ethic, especially if they have been influenced by the work of Aldo Leopold, are hostile to the use of pain to confer moral standing. See ch. 14. See also Frey, *Interests and Rights*, ch. 4.

6

Positive and Negative Moral Vegetarianism

The arguments from moral rights, killing, and pain and suffering neither establish that eating meat is wrong nor establish, even if successful, that eating all meat is wrong. We can broadly distinguish, however, between positive and negative moral vegetarianism. Positive moral vegetarianism consists in showing that eating meat is wrong; negative moral vegetarianism consists in bringing a case against (and, by means of it, perhaps doing something about) some of the practices employed on factory farms. Even if the arguments from moral rights, killing, and pain and suffering do not establish the former, they may well be thought to be important in accomplishing the latter.

(Positive and negative moral vegetarianism are not entirely unrelated, of course, since the case against factory farming, should it lead to a significant reduction in the number of food animals, would thereby result in a decline in meat-eating, which in part is what positive moral vegetarianism hopes to achieve. As we shall see, however, and this is the reason I have introduced the distinction, one can be a negative without being a positive moral vegetarian.)

Ascendency of the Argument from Pain and Suffering

Viewed in this light, as part of the case against factory farming, the three arguments may be thought to gain renewed life. In fact, only the argument from pain and suffering does so, and in a way which reveals why it is, in my opinion, the most forceful and important of the three arguments.

Moral rights

What is wrong with some intensive methods of farming? What is objectionable about the treatment meted out to veal calves? Why are some people up in arms about this treatment? The answers to all these questions turn upon the suffering which the animals undergo. To say that what is wrong with painful farming practices is that they violate moral rights merely introduces an extra and unnecessary item into the picture. Why make such a detour? Why insert some item between the painful practices and their wrongness? (In the case of some philosophers, of course, it is because they have a theory of rights to sell the public.) What is wrong with painful farming practices is that they are painful. Similarly, it would be utterly perverse to point to a man writhing in agony as the result of being tortured by scalding and to claim that what was wrong there was that the man's moral rights were being violated, as if, were I able to convince you that there were no moral rights or that that man did not possess any or did not possess the requisite ones, there would be nothing wrong in continuing to scald him. Moral rights are excess baggage here; for there is nothing required to mediate between the (extraordinarily) painful character of the act and its wrongness.

Killing

In the case of the argument from killing, there are two similar problems. First, to maintain that what is wrong with painful farming practices is that the animals are eventually killed, is to overlook the painful character of those practices. In this light, the argument has nothing specifically to say to factory farming and to (for example) the suffering of veal calves. Moreover, it should be borne in mind that there is no inconsistency in condemning the killing of animals but not their harsh treatment. (In some Eastern societies, this is arguably the norm.) In this eventuality, the treatment of animals could reach hideous levels without provoking condemnation; yet, already, some aspects of the present treatment of some factory-farmed animals have given rise to concern. Second, to maintain that what is wrong with painful farming practices is that the animals are eventually killed makes the wrongness of those practices dependent upon somewhat esoteric (and difficult) questions about the value of animal life and allied issues. In this case, were I able to convince you that animal life had no, or only very slight, value and certainly nothing approaching the value of human life, then the wrongness of these farming practices would disappear, though their painful character endured.

Pain and suffering

This argument is directly concerned with the pains of animals and so with their treatment on factory farms. Indeed, if we recall the picture that

Singer draws around it, namely, of the boycott of meat as the tactic, as the direct and immediate means for coming to grips with and lessening the effect of painful farming practices, then the argument can appear to be *mainly concerned* not with positive but negative moral vegetarianism, not with demonstrating that it is wrong to eat meat but with showing that and how factory farming must be curtailed or stopped.

In my view, then, only the argument from pain and suffering is centrally concerned with what worries people about some aspects of factory farming. The great merit and attraction of the argument lies in what it does not require to be the case in order to succeed, in the fact, that is, that *it can dispense with talk about moral rights and the value of life.* Let there be no moral rights and let animal life have no or only slight value: animals can still feel the effects of painful farming practices, and the case for negative moral vegetarianism gets underway. Significantly, too, however extensive the list of things people fail to agree upon about animals, and recent discussion of the moral status of animals show the list to be a long one, they virtually all condemn cruel suffering.

Change in the Requirement for Success

In chapter 1, I remarked that the moral vegetarian, in order to succeed in bringing about the dramatic change in our eating practices that he desires, had to supplant our present view of the morality of eating meat with his own. With the failure of the three arguments to establish positive moral vegetarianism, and with the rebirth of the argument from pain and suffering as the main hope for negative moral vegetarianism, however, there is an important change in the requirement for success of moral — now, negative moral — vegetarianism.

On the one hand, seen positively, the argument from pain and suffering does not compel us to change our view of the morality of eating meat; for even if some, most, or all practices employed on factory farms could, because of their painful character, be shown to be wrong, it still would not follow that it was wrong to eat meat. True, if many factory farms went out of business, there would be many fewer animals to eat; but it would not follow that it was wrong to eat what animals there were or, following an earlier suggestion, that it was wrong to eat traditionally-farmed animals. On the other hand, seen negatively, as an attempt to combat the iniquities of factory farming, the argument seems to fare differently, just because, in the hands, e.g., of Singer, the boycott of meat is portrayed as spelling disaster for factory farming. Thus, it is wrong to inflict undeserved suffering upon animals; certain intensive methods of farming do just this; the boycott of meat is the tactic, the direct and immediate means by which to get rid of these methods; and the elimination of these methods means the virtual end of factory farming and intensively produced meat and so the pains of food animals.

Now on this negative view of the argument, one important change with chapter 1 should be obvious. I can care about animal suffering and give up and boycott meat without in the least having to think eating meat is wrong; I just want to do something and something effective to lessen animal pain. So one's view of the morality of meat-eating need not change even if one accepts the argument: one can be a negative without being a positive moral vegetarian. In this way, it is not at all difficult to imagine someone who accepts the argument (a) boycotting meat from animals who have suffered greatly on factory farms but not meat from other factory-farmed animals, or (b) boycotting meat until the particular methods which are objectionable are cleaned up, or (c) boycotting meat except traditionally-farmed meat.

Even if one accepts the argument, then, one's view of the morality of meat-eating need not change; and what this means is that a wholesale change in our eating habits will not come through or by means of the kind of moral conversion on our parts envisaged in chapter 1. Nevertheless, one is now not eating meat, and this, it might be held, essentially gives Singer and like-minded vegetarians what they are after, namely, a change in our eating practices. In this way, negative moral vegetarianism can succeed in producing a change in our diet, even if our view of the morality of meat-eating remains unchanged. The change sought can come through or by means of our concern to take the most effective action we can to lessen animal suffering.

Effectiveness and the Choice of Tactics

Seen in the above light, the aim of the argument from pain and suffering is to mitigate, reduce, or eliminate animal suffering by directly and immediately coming to grips with those practices which cause this suffering. Success for the argument turns upon actually coming to grips with those practices: it is no longer a matter of proving or establishing that meat-eating is wrong, and in that way moving to produce a change in our diet, but purely a matter of effectiveness in dealing with animal suffering. The result, however, is that the case for changing our diet now becomes, as it were, a hostage to fortune on this issue. The more we can mitigate and reduce animal suffering in factory farming, the less extensive the application of the argument from pain and suffering. More generally, if it can be shown that boycotting meat is not the most effective step one can take to lessen animal suffering or that there is an equally efficacious course of action which allows us to remain meat-eaters, then the case for changing our eating habits will, on the argument's basis, have vanished. In which case, of course, we shall be left not only with our present eating habits more or less intact, but also with our present view of the ethics of eating meat and our present liking for meat.

I do not think most readers will find anything very surprising in the above. Plenty of people who are not vegetárians are concerned about animal suffering and concerned as well to do something about it, and this number includes a good many members of animal welfare organizations, such as the RSPCA in Britain. True, more radical members of this and of other animal welfare groups castigate the non-vegetarian members among them; but it would be false to think, especially in Britain, that the meat-eating public has no concern for the welfare of food animals. It has; the question is how to give voice to that concern. Giving up meat is one but not the only way, and the question naturally arises of why choose it as opposed to some other way. That is where the issue of effectiveness comes in.

Part III

7

The Appeal to Moral Rights

Claims to moral rights abound. In the United States in particular (moral rights are not nearly as fashionable in Britain), there is a tendency today to clothe virtually all moral and social issues in the language of rights, in order to be able to demand one's due. Thus, issues about the treatment of children have given way to children's rights, about the demands of (some) women to women's rights, about the despoilation of forests to the rights of trees or of the environment generally, about abortion to the rights of the foetus and the rights of the mother, and about the farming and treatment of animals to animal rights.

Declarations of human rights have come into their own, and an increasing number of things — from emigration to a minimum income, housing, a job, old age insurance, and medical assistance — are now simply ceded us as of right. Some groups derive further sustenance from such declarations: some homosexuals, for example, now maintain that certain (proposed) pieces of legislation infringe their human right to freedom of sexual expression. What we should do about the poor of the Third World is increasingly transformed into an issue of the poor having a moral right to subsistence (in its various facets) against us and our incomes and food supplies. Political liberals in the United States have swept up human rights into their ideologies, and governments around the world are taken to task on their treatment of their citizens.

So far as I can see, our alleged moral rights have proliferated to such an extent that they now run to every corner of our lives, and only someone completely out of touch with American social and politcal reality today would find surprising a friend's claim that we have a moral right to a society free of nuclear power plants and free of the terrible noises of modern contraptions, or Alan Gewirth's claim that we have a moral right not to have cancer inflicted upon us.[1]

Moral rights have become the fashionable terms of contemporary moral debate, and one interest group after another has moved to formulate its position in terms of them. The reason is obvious: to fail to cast its wants in terms of rights and so to fail to place itself in a position to demand its due is to disadvantage itself in this debate *vis-à-vis* other groups which show no such reluctance. And what group is prepared to do that?

I am not in sympathy with this reliance upon moral rights in order to discuss and prosecute moral issues, and I have tried to explain why, in general terms, in *Interests and Rights*.[2] This remains my position, and I try in the material on rights that follows in part to deepen it. I also try, however, to speak to the clash between (act-) utilitarianism and rights-theory, which is so prominent a part of applied ethics today, and which recurs from one substantive issue to another.

Dispensing with Rights

The great merit of the argument from pain and suffering, as we saw in the last chapter, lies in what it does not require to be the case in order to succeed, in the fact, that is, that it can dispense with talk about moral rights and the value of life. It is true that the argument *is* sometimes found today encumbered with moral rights. Ironically, such encumbrance has almost certainly been facilitated through widespread misunderstanding of the parallel Singer draws in *Animal Liberation* between discrimination upon the basis of species and sexual and racial discrimination, two areas in which moral rights are prominently claimed today on a massive scale. It was not Singer's aim to conduct the argument from pain and suffering in terms of moral rights, and he does not in fact do so; but, even if he had, it would have been a needless − and muddling − gesture on his part. For, as we have seen, rights are simply excess baggage to this argument; they are not required in order to condemn painful farming practices, are not required to mediate between such practices and their wrongness, as if what makes such practices wrong is not their painful character but their violation of some alleged right or other.

I believe that the argument from moral rights is rather unlikely to prove substantially effective in the cause of negative moral vegetarianism. The reason is simply that (claims to and about) moral rights themselves get in the way. On the one hand, they make it appear that issues such as our treatment of food animals cannot be discussed or discussed properly unless animals are ceded rights, and this is quite false. Numerous, concerned laymen have argued for years over the morality of our treatment of animals, without the intervention of moral rights; utilitarians have been in the forefront of animal reform, but, almost invariably, outside the trappings of moral rights; and Britain has long been a leader in reform legislation without its legislators and, through them, its populace having had first to cede animals moral rights in order then to be in a position to favour reform. In each case, people have thought they could condemn harsh treatment without having first to postulate moral rights in animals in order to do so. On the other hand, if one's ground for objecting to painful farming practices lies in their violation of animals' putative moral rights, then the wrongness of such practices is at the mercy of the demonstration both that there are some moral rights and that animals can possess them. Neither point is easy to establish, and both raise many difficult questions of philosophy, a number of which I explored in *Interests and Rights*. There, very broadly, I argued not only that, if there are any moral rights, animals do not possess them, but also that we are not in a position to affirm that there are any such rights. Either conclusion suffices to scuttle the argument from moral rights.

In arguing in *Interests and Rights* that we are more than justified in doubting whether there are any moral rights, I wanted, among other things, to move readers at least some way towards the views that rights do not have a fundamental role to play in ethics − in my view, they are superfluous in the face of a fully developed theory of right and wrong, which is all we need to decide how we shall act − and that, at least at the present juncture in the development of rights-theory, the value of rights-talk in ethics, apart, perhaps, from helping to put one's opponents on the defensive, is negligible. I want in the next three chapters to say something further in support of these views.

Notes

1 Alan Gewirth, 'Human rights and the prevention of cancer', *American Philosophical Quarterly*, vol. 17, 1980.
2 Frey, *Interests and Rights*, especially ch. I and the Postscript.

8

Rights, their Grounds, and the Problem of Argument

I do not believe we gain anything in clarity, precision, and understanding by trying to discuss moral issues in terms of rights, and this applies as much to the important issue of the rightness and justification of our treatment of animals as to any other. Indeed, I think obfuscation is nearly always the result of the invocation of moral rights. What inevitably ensues is that we turn away from the immediate and important problems of whether, say, our present treatment of animals is right and can be justified and away from the necessary task of thrashing out principles of rightness and justification of treatment. Instead, we come to focus upon the much less immediate, important, and easily resolvable because wholly speculative questions of whether there really is this or that moral right which some people, but not others, allege that there is, and of what the criteria are, and of how we are to decide what the criteria are, for the possession of this or that right. Speculative questions invite speculative answers, and a vast industry has arisen as a result, both as to the nature and/or type of moral rights we and others are alleged to possess, and as to the grounds in virtue of which we and others are alleged to possess them. So far as I can see, there is no internal limit to this exercise, except that of human ingenuity in being able to conjure up still different conceptions of moral rights and still further arguments in support of this or that criterion of right-possession.

There are a number of reasons why talk of rights does not shed light on important ethical questions, but I shall here concentrate upon a single one, namely, the obvious difficulty we all experience whenever we try to argue with each other about moral rights. This difficulty has (at least) three sources.

Rights and the Moral Concepts

It is not obvious how we are to move back and forth between talk of rights and talk in terms of the moral concepts of right, wrong, and ought. Several views of the matter exist,[1] but none, so far as I know, commands widespread assent. The result is clear: if we cannot link up the moral concepts and rights, then it is difficult to see not only how we could ever argue about moral rights, but also quite how we would analyse the concept of a moral right.

Consider an example: Cathy loves fried eggs for breakfast, and her husband, Heathcliff, knows this; but though Heathcliff makes scrambled eggs, poached eggs, boiled eggs, and omelettes, he never makes fried eggs for breakfast. Heathcliff and Cathy are married, there are duties on both sides, and marriage is, we say, a matter of mutual accommodation; yet, though he knows Cathy's desires and preferences perfectly, Heathcliff never makes fried eggs for breakfast.

Now I can imagine a third party saying that it is wrong of Heathcliff not to make fried eggs occasionally or that he ought to or even that, given that he is married, knows Cathy's desires, and finds making fried eggs no more trouble than making any other sort of eggs, he has a duty to make fried eggs occasionally; but does anyone really think we can move from saying these things to the view that Cathy has a moral right to fried eggs for breakfast? And if you think we *can* make this move, then how are you going to prevent the complete trivialization of the notion of a moral right, since there appears no end to the possible development of similar examples? Of course, you might say that Cathy's right to fried eggs is not a moral but an institutional right, a right arising within the confines of marriage; but many, if not most, people regard this and many other social institutions in a moral light and so regard the institutional rights which arise within them as moral rights as well.[2] I shall not labour the point; but from the fact that you think it wrong of Heathcliff not to make fried eggs occasionally for breakfast, nothing obviously follows about Cathy's having a moral right to fried eggs.

Even if we cannot move in this direction, however, can we not move in the other, from talk of rights to talk of what is wrong? That is, if we assume or concede that Cathy has a moral right to fried eggs for breakfast, can we not conclude that, *ceteris paribus*, it is wrong of Heathcliff not to make fried eggs occasionally? But this way of approaching the matter brings out its own shortcoming; for what if you are not allowed the assumption or concession that Cathy has such a right? Then, you will have to show how you reach this right, on the basis of what is right and wrong or ought to be done in respect of Cathy's breakfast, and the previous argument applies. Likewise, if you assume that squirrels have a moral right to chestnuts on the ground, then doubtless you will conclude that it is wrong of me to deprive them of these nuts; but if you are not granted your assumption of such a right, how are you going to reach it merely from your view that it is wrong for me to roast chestnuts in such quantities as to deprive squirrels of this food source? For unless by fiat you simply turn whatever you judge to be wrong into a right on the part of some creature not to have that thing done, you are constantly going to run up against the fact that it does not follow from its being judged wrong, e.g., to deprive squirrels of chestnuts on the ground that they have a moral right to these nuts. In short, to tie moral rights and the concepts of right, wrong, and ought together, requires more than the merely one-way transaction which the present line of argument envisages.[3]

One might try to argue from 'Cathy wants fried eggs for breakfast' to 'It is wrong of Healthcliff, *ceteris paribus*, to frustrate this want' to 'Cathy has a moral right not to have her wants, including this one, frustrated' or to 'Cathy has a moral right to have her wants, including this one, satisfied'. The problem is how we are supposed to get from the fact that it is wrong, *ceteris paribus*, to frustrate Cathy's wants to the conclusion that Cathy has a *moral right* to the satisfaction of her wants and so of her want for fried eggs. I can see no entailment or analytic connection here, and anything less would seem compatible with acknowledging the wrong but denying the right. One can, of course, manufacture such a connection, for example, by laying down as a conceptual truth or otherwise stipulating that merely having wants entitles one to their satisfaction. In this case, the frustration of one's wants by others will be the violation of one's entitlements or rights, which in turn, it will be maintained, is, *ceteris paribus*, wrong. A good deal of work requires to be done on the grounds of this stipulation, however, before it can be accepted. Among other things, this view looks far less a conceptual truth and much more a substantive moral judgment, one which reflects some view, for instance, about the rightness of our interference in the lives of others, as they seek to pursue and satisfy their wants.

Wrongs, Rights, and Protection

The problem of how we get from wrongs to rights is, in any event, an unnecessary one. For, as we saw in the last chapter, in connection with some painful farming practices, what makes wrong acts wrong is not that they violate some alleged moral right or other. What is wrong with torturing and killing someone is not the violation of some right of his, but the sheer agony and suffering he undergoes, the snuffing out of his hopes, desires, and wishes, and so on. What is wrong with depriving someone of a decent wage is not that it infringes some alleged right of his to this or that income but that it ruins his life and the lives of those who depend upon him. What is wrong with depriving someone of his liberty is that it thwarts his hopes and plans, circumscribes his future and what he can make of it, and so impoverishes his life. In short, there is no need to postulate moral rights as intermediaries between pain and agony, or thwarted hopes, desires, and plans, or ruined lives and the wrongness of what was done.

Even in a world without moral rights, even in the kind of world I sketched in *Interests and Rights*, however, acts can still be right and wrong and principles of rightness and justification of treatment can still be presented and argued. In *Animal Liberation* and *Practical Ethics*, not only does Singer not prosecute his case in terms of moral rights but also he does not appeal to such rights in order to reach substantive moral conclusions about our treatment of animals. He thinks that animals can feel pain, and on that basis alone, that they have interests to be weighed by us in deciding upon our treatment of them; and he plainly thinks he has a case for morally condemning some intensive farming practices for ignoring or undervaluing those interests, without in any way grounding his condemnation of these practices upon their violation of putative rights.

Nevertheless, it is fashionable today to say of moral rights that they are the last refuge of the weak and defenceless, the implication being that, in a world, probably utilitarian in character, in which there are no moral rights, the weak and defenceless will go to the wall. Three central worries are, I think, encapsulated by this refuge plea, namely, that without moral rights animals (a) will be entirely at our self-serving, self-interested mercy, (b) will, as we pursue our own advantage, cease to be regarded by us as objects of moral concern, and (c) will, perhaps, as a result of (b), cease to be regarded by us as creatures whose treatment should be of moment to us or at least of sufficient moment to make us pause in the pursuit of our own advantage. Importantly, however, the weak and defenceless do not go to the wall in Singer's work, though Singer studiously avoids appeal to moral rights; and Singer *is* an (act-) utilitarian. Indeed, far from taking advantage of animals in the above ways, he staunchly defends them, but without recourse to rights. The same is true of Stephen Clark's *The Moral Status of Animals*. Although Clark himself is no utilitarian, as he makes plain in his book's opening pages, his positive theses can all be raised and discussed outside the trappings of moral rights, and his plea for regarding animals as objects of moral concern owes nothing to some antecedent case for moral rights and for their possession by animals. Likewise, even in the kind of (utilitarian) world sketched in *Interests and Rights*, there is no suggestion that animals are or should be at our mercy, or that we should not concern ourselves with them morally, or that their treatment by us is not something with which we have morally to occupy ourselves. In fine, it is simply not true that, in the absence of moral rights, the weak and defenceless are at the mercy of our advantage and, therefore, that their protection *requires* moral rights.

Principles and the Superfluity of Rights

A second source of difficulty in arguing about rights, which I discussed in *Interests and Rights*,[4] is that what passes for such argument is in fact nearly always argument about the acceptance of the moral principle(s) which is said to be the ground of the alleged right in question. Thus, when someone maintains that women have a moral right to an abortion on demand, and when we dispute this claim, what we in the end find ourselves arguing about is the acceptability (and interpretation) of the moral principle which is alleged to confer this right upon women. The acceptability of this principle is crucial, since one only accepts that women have such a right if one accepts the principle which confers this right upon them.

In this context, however, three facts about arguments over the acceptability of moral principles are especially germane.

(1) We do not agree on moral principles, as anyone will know who has, for example, followed contemporary discussions on sexual morality, abortion, euthanasia, infanticide, suicide, capital punishment, etc. One may not, therefore, merely presume common agreement on this or that principle.

(2) We do not agree on the criteria of acceptability in moral principles. Are these criteria formal or material? Do they involve reference to 'ordinary moral convictions' and the views of the 'plain man' (or, perhaps, to some special subset of these convictions and views)? Or does such a reference simply amount to letting our intuitions in ethics have a wholly unwarranted decisiveness in the matter? Must our principles 'fit' our pre-theoretical intuitions? If so, why? Are the criteria of acceptability in principles bound up with the mutual accommodation of principles and judgments, that is, with the achievement of a condition of reflective equilibrium between our considered moral judgements and some set of principles which brings order, system, and harmony to those of our judgments which we do not wish to discard in the light of (the application of) those principles? Or is this type of criterion merely a sophisticted intuitionistic one, and so objectionable on grounds similar to those urged against W. D. Ross? Is there any restriction on the content of moral principles? Or is the acceptability of such principles a purely formal affair, with nothing whatever to do with content? In short, in order to ground a moral right, you may not presume either the acceptability of some moral principles, or, when you turn your attention to this principle and begin to consider whether it *is* acceptable, agreed criteria of acceptability in principles.

(3) We can, as we have seen, argue about the acceptability of moral principles even if no moral rights are alleged to be grounded upon them and even if there are no moral rights whatever. Thus, we can argue about the acceptability of a moral principle enjoining respect for life, whether or not we think foetuses or animals have a moral right to life; and we *have to argue* about its acceptability, if you maintain that foetuses and animals have a right to life on the basis of it.

In the light of these facts, I think an argument can be produced which shows that moral rights are superfluous. If we cannot reach agreement on the criteria of acceptability in moral principles, and if we cannot, therefore, reach agreement on our moral principles, then we are not going to agree on whether there is this or that right, conferred by this or that principle. If, however, we do reach agreement on the criteria of acceptability in moral principles, and if we do then reach agreement in moral principles, then there is no longer any need to posit the existence of a right. For if we take morality seriously and so try to live up to our principles, we shall behave in the way the right's proponent wants us to, without his having to postulate the right's existence. In other words, if moral rights are put forward on the basis of unagreed moral principles, we will not agree on whether there are such rights, whereas if they are put forward on the basis of agreed moral principles, they appear unnecessary, since our principles will now lead us to behave in the way the rights' proponents want us to behave.

Notice the effect this argument has on the earlier rights-as-refuge claim. If rights are put forward on the basis of unagreed moral principles, with the result that we do not agree as to whether there are such rights, then they will not serve to protect the weak and defenceless; whereas, if they are advanced on the basis of agreed moral principles, then they appear unnecessary to the protection of the weak and defenceless, since our principles will already be leading us to behave in what the rights' proponents see as the desired way.

It could be argued that postulating moral rights on the basis of agreed moral principles serves the function of an insurance policy, in the event that people do not take morality seriously or fail to live up to their principles or succumb to temptation. Perhaps this is so; but it is important to realize that this line of defence can no longer sustain a view of moral rights as the central concern, the very heart and soul of a theory of morality. They become mere appendages, and often not even that, to agreed moral principles.

Conflicts of Rights

A third source of difficulty in arguing about moral rights is the problem of conflicts and their resolution. Advocates of rights do well to be sensitive to this problem, and very few of them indeed do not concede that it poses serious difficulties for them. Certainly, it is clear that inability to resolve conflicts is a severe hindrance to arguing about rights.

It is to a discussion of conflicts and of several features in respect of them that I now want to turn. First, however, it is necessary to be clear as to why such a discussion, which might appear tangential to the case of animals, is in fact germane.

Advocates of moral rights invariably hold that there are a good many such rights, and in cases where animals are ascribed some moral right or other, some conflicting moral right of human beings can normally be ascribed as well.[5] (I shall overlook possible conflicts of rights between animals.) Thus, if squirrels are held to have a moral right to the chestnuts in my backyard, it is also the case that I am held to have a moral (and legal) right to the use and enjoyment of my property. If chickens are held to have a moral right to life, it is also the case that they are the property of chicken-farmers, who are held to have not only a moral (and legal) right to the use of their property but also the additional moral right to earn a livelihood and to support their families. (The same is true elsewhere, as when, for example, foetuses are ceded a right to life and women a right to control over their own bodies, or when the starving poor are ceded a right to sustenance and middle-class farmers and ordinary people a right to their resources and property.) It seems obvious that, if we are ever going to make anything of arguing moral questions such as our treatment of animals in terms of rights, we simply have to have some way of resolving these conflicts.

Prima facie Rights, Strict Intuitionism, and Utility

Traditionally, even allegedly fundamental rights have been held to be *prima facie* just because of the possibility of conflicts, which arise as the result of a theorist recognizing more than one such right. Thus, the picture we carry away from the discussion of rights by ethical intuitionists earlier this century is this: there are a number of *prima facie* rights, and these not infrequently come into conflict with each other; we resolve this conflict by means of moral intuition, by intuiting which is the more stringent and compelling *prima facie* right either on this occasion or *tout court*.

Now moral intuition, whether as an explanatory device or as a piece of moral epistemology, will not do, for reasons which countless writers have made too familiar to detain us here. So how are we to resolve conflicts?

Whatever we do appears to involve the abandonment of strict intuitionism. What we require in order to resolve conflicts are ways of measuring the relative stringencies of rights; but either these measures rest upon moral intuition, in which case they are as tainted as the earlier position, or they admit of non-intuitistic justification, in which case strict intuitionism has been abandoned. Notice that an appeal to some hierarchy of rights in terms of relative stringencies gets nowhere, since we can only compile such a hierarchy in the first place if we are in possession of the very measures we are seeking. Nor am I aware of ever having seen an ordered and argued hierarchical list of these non-intuitionistic-based measures in the writings of advocates of rights.

In sum, strict intuitionism is objectionable, a hierarchy of rights cannot be or at least has not been fashioned, and non-intuitionistic measures of stringency are not immediately or even apparently in the offing.

In this situation, how can one exclude *a priori* the possibility of a principle of utility serving among the measures of stringency? After all, it is not obviously wrong or silly to suggest that we determine relative stringency between two conflicting *prima facie* rights by appeal to the consequences of honouring (and/or infringing) each of them, which, when generalized, amounts to saying that what it would be right to do is to comply with that *prima facie* right the consequences of which compliance are productive of best consequences. In this eventuality, however, the very core of one's rights-based moral theory, almost certainly adopted in the first place as an antidote to (act-) utilitarianism, is infected with a utilitarian principle. Accordingly, if one's rights-based theory is to avoid this fate, one must provide measures of stringency which preclude the admission of a principle of utility among them but which in no way rely upon a strict intuitionism, an assumed hierarchy of relative stringencies, or merely presumed, non-intuitionistic measures of stringency in order to do so.

The Correlative Thesis

These are not, however, the only boundaries to our problem. In the earlier intuitionists, some of the *prima facie* rights claimed were themselves embedded in intuition. This was because duties and rights were seen as correlative, and many alleged *prima facie* duties, such as those of benefi-cence, self-improvement, and non-maleficence, did not themselves stem from any voluntary undertaking on our part. In other words, the *prima facie* right had its ground in the correlative *prima facie* duty, and some *prima facie* duties had their ground, not in the quasi-contractual arrangements which ensue as the result of voluntary acts on our part, such as making a promise or entering a marriage, but in intuition. It is within social, con-tractual arrangements of these sorts that the correlative thesis of rights and duties finds a home; outside such arrangements, this thesis is, I believe, of doubtful truth. But whether it is true or false is of no consequence here; if the thesis is true, then our attention turns from alleged *prima facie* rights to alleged *prima facie* duties and to the fact that many such alleged duties, including, a number of allegedly important ones, such as duties to respect life and prevent avoidable suffering, do not have their ground in any voluntary undertakings on our part but, in the earlier intuitionists, in moral intuition; if, however, the correlative thesis is false, then some of these alleged *prima facie* rights must themselves be directly intuited. Whichever it is, my point is this: to the extent that *prima facie* rights are either directly or indirectly embedded in moral intuition, to that extent *prima facie* rights are repudiated.

Plainly, therefore, there is an additional boundary to our problem of how to argue about rights in the face of conflicts. In order to resolve conflicts among *prima facie* rights, one must provide measures of stringency which preclude a principle of utility but which do not rely upon a strict intuitionism, an assumed hierarchy of relative stringencies, or merely presumed, non-intuitionistic measures of stringency in order to do so; but in order to prevent our resolving the conflict by repudiating one or more of the conflicting rights, one must sustain these rights — must, that is, sustain the claim that there really are these rights — without recourse to moral intuition.

Repudiating Rights and Eliminating Clashes

It is at least in part this fear of the repudiation of rights, I think, that has made three obvious ways of eliminating clashes of rights unattractive to *prima facie* theorists.

First, one might maintain (or stipulate) that such clashes are only apparent, not genuine, because one side to the clash is not a right but, say, a demand. Almost no theorist of *prima facie* rights has adopted this view as a general thesis. It would, if held to extend across the spectrum of alleged *prima facie* rights, defeat the whole purpose for which theorists introduced such rights in the first place, which was to cede us a variety of rights in a variety of respects. That is, if I have been ceded a *prima facie* right to life in the first place, I do not suddenly have that right reduced merely to a demand, simply because it may conflict with some other *prima facie* right. It may not be honoured in this situation, it may not be of sufficient stringency, but that is a far cry from saying I have lost the right or had it reduced to a demand, simply because it is in conflict with other *prima facie* rights.

Second, one might maintain (or stipulate) that such clashes are only apparent, not genuine, because both sides to the clash are not rights but, say, demands to something or against someone. On this view, we have not the picture of final rights issuing from compromises among conflicting *prima facie* rights, but rather the picture of rights, regarded as legitimatized demands, issuing from compromises among demands. Now, however, the purpose of *prima facie* rights — to cede us a variety of rights in a variety of respects — has been lost altogether; what has been ceded is merely a variety of demands, and it turns out that *prima facie* theorists have been wrong to call rights — and to use in their anti-(act-)utilitarian campaigns — what are not really rights at all. Moreover, to speak of demands here plays into the hands of the (act-) utilitarian; for if what are in conflict are not rights but demands, then there is even less reason to think appeals to utility excluded *a priori* as means of resolving the conflicts and so of legitimatizing demands.

Third, the desire not to lose sight of the purpose behind *prima facie* rights — to cede us a variety of rights in a variety of respects — makes another obvious way of eliminating clashes of rights unattractive to *prima facie* theorists. This is to cede us but a single right and to maintain either that it is the only right there is or that it is the most fundamental right, from which all others are consistently derived. *Prima facie* theorists have embraced neither alternative: the former conflicts straightforwardly with their desire to cede us a variety of rights, whereas the latter conflicts with their view of the equal status of the rights so ceded us. One right is not somehow more a right than another; indeed, part of the explanation of the inability of *prima facie* theorists to fashion a hierarchy of rights stems from their reluctance to alter the equal status of *prima facie* rights. We have in their eyes a variety of *prima facie* rights, and it is because these rights are on all fours that the problem of conflicts looms so large for them from the outset.

Moreover, there is another problem with the present option, which an example may help to illustrate. Ronald Dworkin, in *Taking Rights Seriously*,[6] argues that other individual moral rights are derived from the absolutely fundamental moral right to equal concern and respect. It seems exceedingly implausible to suppose, however, as H. L. A. Hart has pointed out,[7] that the full panoply of individual moral rights which contemporary rights-theorists and others purvey can be traced either to some single fundamental right in general or to the right to equal concern and respect in particular; and this is true of quite straightforward claims to moral rights which have legal overtones. A man in the United States who asserts a moral right on behalf of his child to sing Christmas carols in school (court decisions there have upheld a bar on singing carols in the public schools) is neither overtly nor in some subtle way arguing that his child is being shown a degree of concern and respect drastically at odds with that being shown to his neighbour's children; indeed, unless these terms are construed exceedingly broadly, he is not arguing about concern and respect at all. Rather, he is arguing, as he sees it, about the legitimate extent of a court's power to interfere with his child's freedom, in circumstances where he and a good many others cannot make out the clear and present danger necessary in order to justify such a limitation of freedom. Likewise, when the National Rifle Association in the United States asserts on behalf of its members a moral (and legal) right to bear arms, its claim is neither directly nor indirectly grounded in some demand for concern and respect, equal or otherwise, but in some demand to show the clear and present danger necessary in order to impose limits on its members' freedom. Of course, it is using a claim to a right in order perhaps to elicit a measure of concern and respect for its members' views, but that is not the same thing as saying that its claim is about concern and respect.

Basic Moral Rights

The boundaries set out in the preceding sections markedly circumscribe possible answers to our problem of how to argue about rights in the face of conflicts, and the boundary of sustaining the rights, in order to avoid their repudiation, is especially pressing, to philosophers who wish to maintain that there are basic moral rights. In order to illustrate these points, I want very briefly to compare and contrast the answers which three well-known advocates of rights provide to these problems. In none of their cases is arguing about rights an easy matter; in fact, it is difficult to see how argument can really take place at all.

Basic moral rights as self-evident

H. J. McCloskey, in his article 'Moral rights and animals',[8] subscribes to the view that there are moral rights, and then goes on to consider whether animals can possess them. He approaches the case of animals through a discussion of moral rights generally and of possible criteria for their possession. He distinguishes between accorded moral rights, such as a right to the use of one's property, and basic intrinsic moral rights, such as a right to autonomy and integrity; and it seems reasonable to suppose that he thinks basic moral rights more important, and their violation more serious, than less basic ones. The capacity for moral self-direction and self-determination is, according to McCloskey, the characteristic in virtue of which a creature possesses these basic rights. It follows, therefore, that animals (and, for that matter, humans) are only going to be conceded basic moral rights to the extent that they possess or can be construed as in some wise sharing in this capacity, and it is highly doubtful whether very many, if any, of them do.[9]

But this is about who can possess basic moral rights; what about conflicts among these rights and the argument by which McCloskey sustains the claim that there really are such rights, in order to prevent our repudiating one or more of them and so resolving conflicts that way?

McCloskey allows that there can be conflicts even between basic intrinsic moral rights, and he maintains that these are to be resolved 'by weighing up the conflicting rights in terms of their various stringencies'.[10] On the question of how we determine the stringencies of these rights, McCloskey says:

> It is impossible to set out priority rules for resolving such conflicts. They are to be resolved only by reference to the relative stringencies of the rights involved; and this is to be determined by reference to the ground of the right, and the basis on which the individuals concerned come to possess the rights. In many cases, the conflicts seem rationally to be irresoluble.[11]

I find this line of defence rather puzzling, and on three counts. First, if many conflicts of moral rights cannot rationally be resolved, how is light supposed to be shed upon the moral issues being discussed in these terms? For instance, should it turn out that conflicts between the rights of animals and human beings cannot in many cases be rationally resolved, what reason have we to think that we are really more likely to obtain a clearer view of the moral issues involved in our treatment of animals by discussing them in this way? Second, this impression of lack of progress, or even retreat in clarity and understanding, is strengthened, I should have thought, by the fact that this impasse over rights is reached, not after long bouts of tortuous argument on the issues, but, if moral issues are discussed and prosecuted in terms of basic moral rights, at the very outset. Third, suppose, however, we were to agree with McCloskey, for the sake of argument, that 'many cases' of conflicts were rationally irresoluble, and that it were, as he thinks, an overly harsh demand of a rights-theory to insist that all conflicts of rights be either resolved or resoluble: what, then, are we *actually to do* in these − now taking McCloskey at his word − many cases? If they cannot be rationally resolved, then I as a moral being seem compelled either to suffer a kind of moral equivalent of a nervous breakdown − where conflicts cannot be rationally resolved I just do not know what to do in such situations − or to act irrationally or non-rationally. Neither is an appealing alternative to moral beings.

My perplexity here is deepened, moreover, when, following McCloskey's directions, I look to the ground and basis of these basic moral rights to ascertain their stringency. On this matter McCloskey is direct:

> A persistent claim more common in the eighteenth century than today, has been that certain rights are self-evidently so. It is an appeal which I suggest is appropriate in respect of certain basic rights, if 'self-evident' is understood correctly, as by W. D. Ross in the context of his discussion of our knowledge of the principles of prima facie obligation. Rights such as rights to life as persons, to moral autonomy and integrity, to respect as persons, appear to be rights which are self-evident, and in respect of which, argument other than that directed at clarification of what is involved in acknowledging the moral right is neither necessary nor possible.[12]

If, however, conflicts between basic moral rights are to be resolved by appeals to stringency, if stringency is to be determined by the ground of these rights, and if their ground is held to be self-evidence, then how am I any further along towards resolving conflicts than before? For self-evidence either provides me with no measures of stringency at all or it provides me with measures, argument in support of which is, in McCloskey's words, 'neither necessary nor possible'. And without argument, how are we going to resolve, having come this far, those disputes which will arise between us, not only as to whether this or that is self-evident, but also as to which of two equally self-evident basic moral rights is the more stringent? Appeal to the basis of such rights, to be found in our capacity for moral self-direction and self-determination, does not assist us, since both of the conflicting, equally self-evident, basic rights can have this same basis.

My point about McCloskey, then, is not that some of us are not prepared to hold some selection of alleged rights, including a right to life, to be self-evident and to require no argument whatever in order to substantiate and sustain them; it is rather that, if self-evidence is the ground of a right to life or to anything whatever, if this ground is the arbiter of the right's stringency, and if other basic rights have this same ground, then we are effectively deprived of any means of arguing about whether there is such a right, about its stringency, and about conflicts between it and other basic rights. To affirm that there are such basic rights, but to leave us no room for arguing about them in the above ways, does not strike me as the most profitable way of discussing moral issues, or as a methodology likely to facilitate understanding and resolution of these issues, or as the best way of setting about trying to work out principles for the direction or re-direction of our behaviour towards other people or other creatures. Nor does the prospect of our often breaking down or acting irrationally/non-rationally augur well for (our treatment of) these people or creatures.

Fundamental moral rights as recommended

J. L. Mackie is another advocate of rights. His influential article 'Can there be a right-based moral theory?' attempts to sketch the bare bones of just such a theory.[13] Essentially, the view which emerges there is of a multiplicity of less fundamental moral rights, derived from one or a small number of fundamental moral rights. Three points are noteworthy about this distinction. First, the class of fundamental rights appears at first to be confined to the right to choose how one will live,[14] but it later appears to be expanded to include rights to life, liberty, and the pursuit of happiness.[15] Second, only persons possess these fundamental rights, though any and all persons possess them equally. One implication of this view, as Mackie realizes, is that, since animals are not obviously persons, they in turn are not obviously the subject of these fundamental rights. Third, the distinction between less fundamental and fundamental moral rights is not that between *prima facie* and absolute rights; in Mackie's view, which on the whole is in the mould cast by traditional *prima facie* theorists, because even fundamental moral rights can clash, they, too, are only *prima facie* rights.

How, then, does Mackie approach our problem of how to argue about rights in the face of conflicts? He maintains that people's final rights result from compromises between their initial conflicting rights, including their conflicting fundamental rights, and these compromises, he says, 'will have to be worked out in practice, but will be morally defensible only in so far as they reflect the equality of the *prima facie* rights.'[16] But how are these compromises to be effected in practice? Mackie suggests a model:

... we might think in terms of a model in which each person is represented by a point-center of force, and the forces (representing *prima facie* rights) obey an inverse square law, so that a right decreases in weight with the remoteness of the matter on which it bears from the person whose right it is.[17]

I think the difficulties with this model are just those which Mackie himself brings out, namely, that cases will arise in which equally vital rights clash, in which the parties do not know how vital some right is to them, in which the parties involved will sometimes be mistaken, at other times deceived on how vital some right is to them, etc. Indeed, I think this model may well underestimate the degree of conflicts; for the rights each of the parties in conflict insists is vital to them almost certainly represents an interest of theirs which they at least take to be vital to them. Clashes of this sort are common; the courts are full of them. So, if one's theory is to avoid this fate, one must have a so-far unspecified means of telling even among numerous and frequent *sincere* avowals of what one takes to be a vital interest that one is mistaken or deceived, or whatever.

In fact, though Mackie does say that it is not a reasonable requirement to demand of a theory such as his that it resolve all conflicts,[18] he nevertheless acknowledges that resolving conflicts is a serious problem for him, which implies, he says, that it will not be easy 'to determine, in concrete cases, what the implications of our theory will be'.[19] But how, then, are we better off arguing moral issues in these terms? On the one hand, it is not clear how we are to argue clashes in fundamental moral rights; on the other, if such rights represent important interests of people, it seems absolutely imperative that we have some idea of how to go about adjudicating these clashes, at least if we seek an harmonious society. Being told merely that we will have to thrash out these clashes in practice, without some decision-procedure, is not very helpful about how we are to set about this task. And what confidence have we from the outset that such clashes can be thrashed out in practice? So far as I can see, nothing in Mackie's paper provides this confidence, nor is it clear that there is anything he could point to which would.

Nevertheless, conflicts or not, it is Mackie's view that we as persons have fundamental moral rights, such as a right to choose how we shall live. How, then, does he sustain the claim that there are these rights? What is the ground he ascribes them? He says this: 'The fundamental right is put forward as universal. On the other hand I am not claiming that it is objectively valid, or that its validity can be found out by reason: I am merely adopting it and recommending it for general adoption as a moral principle.'[20] Why, however, should we accept or follow Mackie's recommendation? Judging from his paper, it is because he thinks doing so can best capture our moral intuitions (which do not, of course, have to rest upon moral intuition, as a thesis in moral epistemology). Thus, Mackie berates all forms of utilitarianism, because 'they not merely allow but positively require, in certain circumstances, that the well-being of one individual should be sacrificed, without limits, for the well-being of others.'[21] It is this anti-utilitarian intuition or judgement which recurs throughout Mackie's essay and which provides the backdrop against which his recommendation of moral rights, rights which do not allow the vital interests of one person to be sacrificed for the well-being of others, must be seen. Put simply, the basis of Mackie's recommendation of fundamental moral rights is this and doubtless other anti-utilitarian intuitions or judgements of his, and one has no reason to accept or follow his recommendation unless one happens to share these intuitions.

In the main, I find my own intuitions run in the direction of utilitarianism; to take only the example of sacrificing interests, I should have no difficulty in supporting compulsory conscription in time of war and so the sacrifice of this or that individual's interests on behalf of the well-being of an aggregate of others. But my point here is not just that people's intuitions do not agree; it is also, and much more importantly, that, unless they agree, we shall not agree that there are any (or any fundamental) moral rights. For unless our intuitions run in the direction of Mackie's, we have no reason, to use Mackie's term,[22] to 'posit' the existence of such rights. Thus, the case for positing moral rights or some scheme of fundamental moral rights must inevitably take the form of pointing to one's moral intuitions. Why, however, give our moral intuitions this degree of weight? Mackie does not explain why in his essay; and though he may think that our moral intuitions are what moral theories must account for, enough has recently been written on this issue in methodology to indicate that it is a minefield of controversy.

In short, one is only going to think there are moral rights (or reasons for positing moral rights) if one's intuitions run this way as opposed to that; if they run differently, then there are no such rights (or reasons for positing them). To a great extent, this places the moral rights we are alleged to have at the mercy of our intuitions; and though one can nurse along and perhaps even cultivate one's anti-utilitarian intuitions, so, too, can one nurse along and cultivate contrary intuitions, with obvious results. Oddly enough, then, on Mackie's view, argument about moral rights and their impact on and implications for us in concrete situations can only take place between people with similar intuitions; to people with different intuitions, the case for posting such rights in the first place is not made. Surely, however, this gets things in reverse? Those readers whose intuition it is that abortion or euthanasia or suicide or meat-eating is wrong do not want to argue with someone possessed of similar intuitions; you want to argue with me, with someone who does not share your intuitions. If Mackie is correct, however, you will not be able to do so. Or, more correctly, you will not be able to do so on the basis of rights, since our intuitions are such that we are not going to agree on the postulation of (fundamental) moral rights in the first place. (Obviously, with this the case, the question of whether animals can be the subject of such rights never arises between us.)

Thus, however you decide to argue these moral issues with me, *if* you decide to argue them with me, it will be outside the context of Mackie's rights-based theory of morality.

The right to equal concern and respect as fundamental and axiomatic

In *Taking Rights Seriously*, Ronald Dworkin opposes what he sees as the prevalent theory of law, which is the legal positivism that derives from the work of John Austin and Jeremy Bentham. One significant aspect to Dworkin's discontent with positivism is his disenchantment with utilitarianism (or what he calls 'economic' utilitarianism), which he describes in his Introduction as the normative underpinning of positivism. In large measure, his attack on utilitarianism is not so much direct,[23] by rehearsing all its many alleged difficulties in all its forms, as indirect, by showing that a theory of rights which emerges from giving consideration and weight to people's individual rights yields results antithetical to utilitarianism.

Very broadly, Dworkin's view is that persons have individual, political or moral rights which they hold against encroachment from other people and from the community on their vital concerns. Unless these political or moral rights are taken seriously, that is, are recognized, accepted, and vigorously observed by other individuals and especially by the community, in the form of its political leaders, legislators, and magistrates, we shall fail fully to recognize, accept, and observe people's absolutely fundamental right to equal concern and respect. These individual rights and, in particular, this absolutely fundamental right are not brought into being by community decision, social practice, or public legislation; they survive contrary decisions, practices, legislation, and adjudication; and, in fact, they prescribe the bounds beyond which both individuals and the community may not go in the pursuit of their aggregate goals. As in the case of Mackie, then, the underlying motif is that these individual rights and this absolutely fundamental right may not be infringed in the name of (increasing) the collective well-being of an aggregate of others; if anything, they stand as bulwarks impeding the pursuit of this ideal and, in order to protect an individual's vital interests in the face of the preponderant preferences of other people for some sacrifice of those interests, trump claims on its behalf.

Unlike the cases of McCloskey and Mackie, rights in this strong sense Dworkin is using are not *prima facie* rights. Or if this is too bold, then certainly we can say that he does not think our fundamental right to equal concern and respect to be merely a *prima facie* right. As with the cases of McCloskey and Mackie, however, because it is questionable whether animals are persons, it is questionable whether they possess the array of individual political/moral rights, or the fundamental right to equal concern and respect upon which Dworkin focuses.

How then does Dworkin sustain the claim that there is this absolutely fundamental right to equal concern and respect? He suggests: '. . . our intuitions about justice presuppose not only that people have rights but that one right among these is fundamental and even axiomatic. This most fundamental of rights is a distinct conception of the right to equality, which I call the right to equal concern and respect.'[24] Later, he maintains that his book 'suggests one favored form of argument for political rights, which is the derivation of particular rights from the abstract right to concern and respect taken to be fundamental and axiomatic.'[25] Thus, in Dworkin's case as well, we have an instance of positing a fundamental right and then attempting to derive other, dependent rights.

Though the right to equal concern and respect is not a *prima facie* right, it is not entirely clear whether conflicts with respect to this right are possible. Mackie says of this right that 'one person's possession or enjoyment of it does not conflict with another's',[26] but some examples can certainly be described in such a way as to make this appear possible. For instance, I can well imagine that those who campaign for a right to life on behalf of foetuses may hold in situations in which either the mother or foetus may be saved, but not both, that the mother's right to concern and respect clashes with the foetus's right in this regard; and this clash in fundamental rights we have no means, ostensibly, at least, of ever resolving.

But the important point to notice about Dworkin's view is that which links it to Mackie's. Why develop and then adopt this theory of rights? It is not that one finds oneself with a theory and then discovers that it yields anti-utilitarian results; rather, as with Mackie, and McCloskey as well, one finds oneself with anti-utilitarian intuitions and so one tries to develop a theoretical framework into which these intuitions can fit and in which they are taken seriously. As Neil MacCormick has stressed,[27] Dworkin's adoption of John Rawls' intuitionistic method of reflective equilibrium between intuitive judgements and principles, a methodology in morals slated by Hare[28] and attacked by others, is the bedrock upon which Dworkin's constructive model of morality rests, and Dworkin's intuitive judgements, particularly as regards the sacrifice of one person's interests for the well-being of an aggregate of others, are for the most part anti-utilitarian. Hence, the positing of an axiomatic and absolutely fundamental moral right to equal concern and respect. Ultimately, therefore, the existence of this right depends upon the way our intuitions run, and what I should say on this score in respect of Dworkin, I have already said in respect of Mackie.

Dispensing with the Diversions Rights Create

Quite apart from the fact that, in the cases of McCloskey, Mackie, and Dworkin, it is very doubtful at best whether animals have (basic or fundamental) moral rights, not much headway has been made with the problem of arguing rights in the face of conflicts; and in the case of one of the boundaries to this problem, serious difficulties arise. For in order to get basic or fundamental moral rights into existence and to sustain them, so that their observance can, for example, serve to impede the utilitarian pursuit of the collective good at some individual's expense, McCloskey appeals to self-evidence, Mackie makes a recommendation based upon his moral intuitions, and Dworkin appears to stipulate in accordance with his intuitive judgements (about what it would and would not be right to do to individuals on behalf of the well-being of a number of others). It is not easy to see how argument is possible about moral rights put into existence and then sustained on these bases; indeed, as we have seen, all three writers, for one reason or another, do not think argument even to be appropriate. Certainly, it is not easy to see how we could argue with any degree of finality about moral rights either on an intuitionism grounded in self-evidence, if we differ over whether something is self-evident and so whether argument is needed in order to substantiate it, or, in the cases of Mackie and Dworkin, on an intuitionism grounded in moral intuitions or intuitive judgements, if these vary among us, as they assuredly do. And if our moral intuitions do vary, and we cannot agree as a result on the positing of this or that right, then how are we supposed to gain a clearer understanding of the moral issues involved by going ahead and discussing them in terms of rights? Surely the only result of doing so is to direct attention away from the task of working out principles of rightness and justification of treatment to the wholly secondary — and, if our moral intuitions vary, wholly unnecessary — task of trying to decide whether there are such rights in the first place and of what to make of the intuitionistic theses we encounter as a result?

On these bases, then, it seems doubtful that any light could be shed on moral qustions by positing the existence of a scheme of moral rights. For it is inevitably one's positing of the rights, not the questions, on which attention will be lavished; and when we come across the intuitionistic theses underlying their positing, with their attendant difficulty of being almost impossible to argue about if we disagree in intuitions, we are even further removed from the prospect of obtaining a surer grip on the issues. Would we not do better, therefore, to discard moral rights in order to forgo being side-tracked by them? We can still ask and debate whether our present treatment of animals is right and/or justified, only now the answer cannot be found in some appeal to moral rights. Perhaps even here we shall not have an easy time of it, but at least the diversions rights create can be avoided, and, so far as I can see, without loss to the debate on how animals should be treated.

Acquired and Unacquired Rights

I want to conclude with a few remarks on a distinction in respect of rights which I think points to a further reason why they are of little assistance in such discussions as the treatment of animals. I shall not father this distinction on any particular advocate of rights, if only because it is doubtless too crude to serve the purpose of developing a taxonomy of rights; but I think each of the writers earlier considered at least implicitly draws it. The distinction in question is that between acquired and unacquired rights.

Typically, acquired rights are acquired through a person's voluntary act. Property is typically acquired through purchase or exchange or through accepting an inheritance or gift, and, once acquired, its owner acquires rights in respect of it. Once a right to property has been acquired, it can be enjoyed, waived, possibly forfeited, recognized, relinquished, transferred, upheld, infringed, contested, lost, and so on.[29] Thus, something which has been voluntarily acquired can be voluntarily relinquished, as when I sell my shares in the firm; and subsidiary rights which I enjoy because of my initial voluntary act, such as the right to vote at the annual share-holders' meeting, can be waived, eventually relinquished, etc. In my view, we understand not only the right but also what it is to have such a right both by looking to its manner of acquisition and by locating (and eventually arguing about) it within the framework of those things which can be done with and to it.

Now McCloskey thinks there are intrinsic moral rights, Mackie that there are fundamental moral rights, and Dworkin that there is an absolutely fundamental moral right, and what is significant about these rights, I think, is that they are not acquired through any voluntary act of persons, such that failure to perform that act results in not having the right or rights in question. (Those concerned to extend moral rights to animals — or foetuses, or nature — will certainly believe this, since they will not want an animal's supposed right, e.g., to life to turn upon its 'voluntarily' doing this or that). Presumably, we have unacquired moral rights merely through having come into existence and through being the sorts of creatures we are. But what sorts of creatures are we? Rational? Language-users? Sentient? Persons? And once we pick and choose among the host of speculations which exist on the subject, we have to go further, into the endless speculations about the criteria of rationality or possession of language or sentiency or being a person. My point here, however, is not this very obvious one, that problems arise over what it is about us in virtue of which we have unacquired moral rights; it is something deeper.

We cannot use the case of acquired rights to shed any light upon unacquired rights, not only because acquired rights are typically acquired through voluntary acts, but also because those very activities which enable us to understand what it is to have an acquired right to, say, property, do not perform a similar function in the case of an unacquired moral right to, say, equal concern and respect. For, in a word, it is not clear these activities can occur, or, at least, are allowed to occur, by theorists of unacquired moral rights. For instance, can a fundamental right to equal concern and respect be forfeited or relinquished or waived? What does one have to do before one can be said to have relinquished all right to choosing how one shall live, or to life? These questions are sources of difficulty in arguing with rights-theorists; but this is not surprising, since the whole theoretical enterprise hangs by each theorist's initial positing of a scheme of unacquired moral rights in the first place, and each theorist is as free to posit that these rights cannot be relinquished, etc., as not.[30]

Argument about unacquired moral rights is severely constrained just because those activities within which we locate acquired rights and what can be done with and to them, activities and their upshots which are often argued in the courts, are themselves in doubt in the case of unacquired moral rights. If I say a person may waive or forfeit his right to life, and McCloskey's theory does not allow this, where am I left? If I say a person may give up or forfeit his fundamental right to equal concern and respect, and Dworkin denies this, what sort of argument could we have? So far as I can see, if Dworkin's theory does not allow that this right may be given up or forfeited, then that is the end of the matter; for nothing I can point to, no number of murders that the person in question may have performed, for example, will show this theoretical point false. In short, if a theorist of basic or fundamental moral rights posits such rights; if he also posits that these rights are possessed by all persons equally; and if he further posits that they cannot be relinquished, given up, or forfeited and cannot be ignored, infringed, or violated with impunity; then I just do not see how we can argue with him. And if we cannot argue with him, then I do not see how light is shed on moral problems by positings of this sort.

(Can a right to life be taken from one or forfeited? If one's model for understanding alleged moral rights is legal rights, then that model seems to incorporate as part of the nature of at least some rights that they can be lost. For example, in the United States, a right to vote can be waived by not registering, relinquished, by giving up one's citizenship, and forfeited, by being convicted of a felony. What, then, about some alleged right to life? I can well imagine someone replying in the affirmative, that such a right can be given up voluntarily, as in cases of voluntary euthanasia, and can be taken from one, as in cases of capital punishment. But the whole picture conjured up by the intrinsic, unacquired moral rights posited by our three theorists is of rights that cannot be lost or forfeited; and we must indeed allow that theorists are entitled to posit this to be the case. But where there is nothing we can do that results in our relinquishing, losing, or forfeiting them, can we not ask for some argument to show that what we have before us are indeed rights?)

In sum, I think the more we diverge from the case of acquired rights the more we lose our grip both on the nature and ground of rights and on our understanding of what it is to have a right. In the case of intrinsic or fundamental, unacquired moral rights, this divergence reaches a radical degree, and what grip we had on rights has, I think, been lost. Rather, we are at sea in a tide of theoretical claims and counter-claims, with no fixed point by which to steer. Such, I think, is, by implication, the case with the argument from moral rights, most especially if the rights are grounded in the ways I have canvassed.

Notes

1 See, for example, R. B. Brandt, *Ethical Theory* (Englewood Cliffs, New Jersey, Prentice-Hall, 1959), pp. 434 ff.
2 If one regards social institutions, wherein quasi-contracts are made, in a moral light, then institutional rights may be regarded as moral rights. Contractual arrangements of this sort are not at issue here, since no one to my knowledge defends an animal's supposed moral right to life on such an institutional basis.
3 For a discussion of some remarks by Charles Fried in this connection, see ch. 9, pp. 70–2.
4 Frey, *Interests and Rights*, ch. I.
5 A similar point is made by R. M. Hare in 'Abortion and the golden rule' (*Philosophy and Public Affairs*, vol. 4, 1975, p. 203), though not in these terms. For an extended discussion by Hare of moral conflicts, see his 'Moral conflicts', in S. M. McMurrin (ed.), *The Tanner Lectures on Human Value, 1980* (Cambridge, Cambridge University Press, 1980), pp. 169–93; and *Moral Thinking*, ch. 2, pp. 25–43.
6 Ronald Dworkin, *Taking Rights Seriously*, London, Duckworth, 1977.
7 H. L. A. Hart, 'Between utility and rights', in A. Ryan (ed.), *The Idea of Freedom* (Oxford, Clarendon Press, 1979), p. 97.
8 H. J. McCloskey, 'Moral rights and animals', *Inquiry*, vol. 22, 1979, pp. 23–54.
9 It seems clear that a good many humans do not share in this capacity either.
10 McCloskey, 'Moral rights and animals', p. 52.
11 Ibid.
12 Ibid., pp. 43–4.
13 J. L. Mackie, 'Can there be a right-based moral theory?', *Midwest Studies in Philosophy*, vol. III, 1978, pp. 350–9.
14 Ibid., p. 355.
15 Ibid., p. 356.
16 Ibid., p. 356. Notice the emphasis upon the equality of the rights, which, as I remarked earlier, explains why *prima facie* theorists are unable to form a hierarchy of rights.
17 Ibid., p. 356.
18 Ibid., p. 359.
19 Ibid., p. 357.
20 Ibid., p. 357.
21 Ibid., p. 352.
22 Ibid., p. 352.
23 His objection from preponderant external preferences *vis-à-vis* one's internal or personal preferences is, of course, a direct one.
24 Dworkin, *Taking Rights Seriously*, p. xii.
25 Ibid., pp. xiv–xv.
26 Mackie, 'Can there be a right-based moral theory?', p. 356.
27 Neil MacCormick, 'Dworkin as pre-Benthamite', *Philosophical Review*, vol. LXXXVII, 1978, pp. 585–607.
28 See Hare's 'A critical study of Rawls' *A Theory of Justice*', *Philosophical Quarterly*, vol. 23, 1973, pp. 144–55, 241–52.
29 In other words, I take these and other activities to constitute what is involved in having and using (acquired) rights.
30 On this score, see for example, McCloskey, 'Moral rights and animals', p. 28.

9

Rights, their Nature, and the Problem of Strength

If it is part of the nature of a right to show at least some resistance to appeals to utility, this is nevertheless a far cry from saying that rights, even allegedly fundamental ones, can never be overridden by utility. Many proponents of rights, in the heat of expounding their theories, often write as if (moral) rights resist utility completely; but, generally, if one reads closely enough, one finds that passage which concedes that this is not so. After all, almost no one thinks that the right to freedom of speech extends to causing panic among the passengers on an aeroplane, or that some right to privacy extends to precluding infringements by persons in great difficulty or danger, or that some general right not to be interfered with extends so far as to compel others to stand by and watch one die (e.g., because one holds some metaphysical/religious view about bodily evil). The general point, then, that individual (moral) rights *can* be overridden by appeals to utility, is normally conceded.[1]

Rights as Trumps

Occasionally, this point about utility is conceded only implicitly. This is the case with Dworkin's theory of rights in *Taking Rights Seriously*. D. N. MacCormick has remarked[2] of Dworkin's distinction between weak and strong rights that the closest Dworkin ever gets to characterizing strong rights is when he says 'a man has a moral right against the state if for some reason the state would do wrong to treat him in a certain way, even though it would be in the general interest to do so.'[3] Joseph Raz has picked up the same point[4] when he notices this passage in Dworkin: 'A successful claim of right, in the strong sense I described, has this consequence. If someone has a right to something, then it is wrong for the government to deny it to him even though it would be in the general interest to do so.'[5] Obviously, this strong sense of a right *is* the rights as trumps sense (noticed in the discussion of Dworkin in the last chapter), which is central to Dworkin's work as a whole and for which it has in part become well-known. It is a stipulated sense of a right. Dworkin himself speaks of this strong sense as his 'characterization' or 'description' or 'account' of rights, not as the analysis of the concept of a right, and I take these terms to be but different ways of saying that he is defining or stipulating a sense of rights as trumps. Indeed, in the second edition of his book, in his 'A Reply to Critics', one can find confirmation that this is the case:

> I do not claim (as I was careful to say) that my account of rights captures ordinary language exactly or completely. My account is in that sense a stipulation. . . . But it is a stipulation (or so I think) that isolates a distinctly important idea in political theory, which is the idea of an individual trump over decisions justified collectively.[6]

Dworkin's strong sense of a right, then, the anti-utilitarian sense, is a stipulation on his part, presented at least in part in order to capture some important idea in political theory, an idea which apparently demands, if utilitarians among others are to be kept at bay, that its adherents embrace some stipulated rights in the strong sense.

In fact, of course, the entire liberal political theory which emerges from *Taking Rights Seriously* depends fundamentally upon this strong sense of a right; resist the stipulation of this sense, and resist the stipulated right to equal concern and respect, and you resist that political theory. In his paper 'Utilitarianism and the vicarious affects', R. M. Hare speaks of rival doctrines to (act-) utilitarianism as 'usually based upon intuitions about rights and justice, which vary with the politics of their exponents',[7] and this seems to me essentially correct, capturing rather nicely, for example, a central difference between Robert Nozick's *Anarchy, State and Utopia*[8] and Dworkin's *Taking Rights Seriously*.

Rights in this strong sense for Dworkin trump background considerations, which in our society are not exhausted by, but centrally include, appeals to or justifications in terms of utility or the collective interest. But how strong a trump are these rights? The earlier quotations may possibly make them appear immune to considerations of utility, and there are a good many passages which foster this appearance. For example, Dworkin writes:

> No one has a political right (on my account) unless the reasons for giving him what he asks are stronger than some collective justification that normally provides a full political justification for a decision. Someone's strong preference for pistachio ice cream is, indeed, a reason for society's producing pistachio, and it is a stronger reason than others that can be found or invented for not producing it — like some one else's mild preference for vanilla. But it is pointless

to speak of a right to have pistachio (or a more general right to have strong preferences served) unless we mean that that preference provides a reason for producing pistachio even if the *collective* preferences for the community would be better served by producing vanilla.[9]

Clearly, then, to be a right in the strong sense requires *some* resistance to utility; for what in part it is to be a right in this sense is to exhibit just this resistance. But must resistance on this score be absolute? It seems not:

> No alleged right is a right (on my account) unless it overrides at least a marginal case of a general collective justification; but one right is more important than another if some especially dramatic or urgent collective justification, above that threshold, will defeat the latter but not the former.[10]

What this passage appears to mean is that, while rights must resist utility, some of them can be overridden by 'dramatic or urgent' collective justifications. So what about the rights which remain? Do not even 'dramatic or urgent' collective justifications override these? In fact, they do.

The picture Dworkin conveys is of rights in the strong sense being of greater or lesser importance: those of lesser importance show less resistance to utility than those of greater importance; and those of the very utmost importance show the greatest resistance of all. But not absolute resistance. For example, of what he calls human rights, Dworkin says only that their importance is such that they remain in force 'against any collective justification reasonably likely to be found in political society'.[11] This, however, is still not very forthcoming. In the notes to his paper 'Utility and rights',[12] however, David Lyons directs our attention to this passage in Dworkin:

> I must not overstate the point. Someone who claims that citizens have a right against the Government need not go so far as to say that the State is never justified in overriding that right. He might say, for example, that although citizens have a right to free speech, the Government may override that right when necessary to protect the rights of others, or to prevent a catastrophe, or even to obtain a clear and major public benefit (though if he acknowledged this last as a possible justification he would be treating the right in question as not among the most important or fundamental). What he cannot do is to say that the Government is justified in overriding a right on the minimal grounds that would be sufficient if no such right existed.[13]

Now in one sense this is more plain: strong rights, even of the utmost importance, can be overridden. In another sense, however, it muddies the waters; for it makes it appear that the Government cannot override important rights to secure any public benefit whatever, however sub-stantial. Thus, such rights can be overridden — they are not absolute — but not by utility. But then what is the nature of the 'catastrophes' which can override these rights or the nature of those 'dramatic or urgent' occasions when collective justifications justifiably override rights? These seem inevitably to be utilitarian in character, in the sense that the drama and urgency, the impending catastrophe, most likely take the form of a failure either to secure a major public benefit or to prevent a major public harm. When the members of the National Front in Britain are barred from exercising their rights to freedom of assembly and of speech in immigrant neighbourhoods, it is the threat to life, limb, and property that is the reason, in circumstances where, if the threat is realized, great harm would ensue. If this is correct, then the implication of Dworkin's remarks is that even rights in the strong sense, and of them, even those of the very utmost importance, are not completely utility-resistant.

The problem, of course, is that the meaning of such phrases as 'catastrophe' and 'dramatic and urgent' is so nebulous that it lies with Dworkin to give them substance, and this very fact in turn means that the precise degree of utility required to override some particular right remains in Dworkin's power to specify. He is perfectly free to lay down, on each occasion when we appeal to great public harm in order to override the right, that, say, the situation is not urgent enough or the gain in utility is not substantial enough or the harm to be prevented is not serious enough to warrant overriding the right. In this way, we can persistently fall short of the degree of utility required by Dworkin to override a specific right. I am not suggesting, of course, that Dworkin resorts to a series of *ad hoc* measures to cope with each case with which he is confronted, only that, if you posit a scheme of strong rights in the first place, you are equally free to posit whatever degree of utility you like and think appropriate to your intuitions, as the degree required to override some specific right.

Rights as Mirrors of Absolute Wrongs

If the point that individual moral rights *can* be overridden by appeals to utility is sometimes conceded only implicitly, only very occasionally indeed is it not conceded at all. Most theorists have not embraced absolute rights, particularly since they have been inclined to posit more than one right, something which, without some argument to the contrary, gives rise to the possibility of conflicts. But there is another aspect of absolute rights which, at least in the work of some theorists, makes them generally unattractive; this is their relationship to some extreme form of anti-consequentialism.

The view that rightness and wrongness are a function solely of an act's consequences may not be to everyone's taste, but the view that the rightness and wrongness of acts have nothing whatever to do with their consequences has, I should have thought, even fewer admirers. So to ground a scheme of absolute rights in some scheme of absolute wrongs is unlikely to make such a scheme of rights attractive in the first place.

A good illustration of this unattractive view is to be found in Charles Fried's *Right and Wrong*.[14] Fried espouses a theory of positive and negative rights. He ties this theory to our status as persons, which concept he in turn analyses for the most part in terms of rationality and freedom; so far as I can see, he then stipulates a connection between these attributes (but especially the second) and our possession of rights, particularly negative rights of non-interference, in the guise of respecting persons, which somehow is supposed to have acquired such immense importance as to have become a kind of absolute requirement of us.

Fried so defines rights that they become categorical and absolute, with the result that, so far as negative rights of non-interference are concerned, 'the violation of a right is always wrong.'[15] This is dressed up in the language of analysing the concept of a right,[16] and not the language of definition or stipulation; but the effect, whatever the language, is to bar appeals to utility, in order to make right or justify the infringement of a negative right.

At one point, Fried remarks that 'a claim of right blocks the appeal to consequences in justifying violations of a right', and he goes on to add, by way of summing up the first part of his book, that 'such an appeal is blocked in the case of wrongs' as well.[17] Now this is very significant, for it means that not even over right and wrong, let alone over rights, do consequentialists have a leg to stand upon. And this is Fried's view: rights are to him but another way of regarding moral wrongs,[18] and the discussion of right and wrong contained in the first part of his book, where his moral intuitions do much of the work, is anti-consquentialist in the extreme. He is convinced, for example, that it is never right intentionally to harm an innocent person or to lie to someone (such acts 'involve the agent's using the victim for his own purposes' and fail to respect 'attributes of the victims which it is essential to protect', essential, that is, 'to ensure the integrity of the person'),[19] and these absolute wrongs − there are others, of course − find their expression at the level of rights in absolute rights not to be intentionally harmed or lied to. Significantly, Fried remarks that 'it is wrong to harm an innocent person or to lie to someone, and this leads us to say that an innocent person has a right not to suffer intentional harm, not to be lied to'.[20] I for one, however, am not in the least led to say this; and I am not prepared to say that it would never be right to harm an innocent person or to lie to someone. In fact, the absolute and categorical nature of rights expounded and developed in the second part of Fried's book stems from and is based upon the absolute and categorical nature of wrongs expounded and developed in the first part; in this sense, it is Fried, not 'us', who needs the link of our being led from wrongs to rights. Without it, a big gap arises in his account of the bases of the negative rights he alleges we have.

In the case of Fried, then, absolute rights are but other ways of regarding absolute wrongs, and only someone enamoured of absolute wrongs is likely, therefore, to find Fried's rights attractive. Indeed, it is not at all clear to me that, confronted with Fried's option, most people would not move in the direction of consequentialism.

Absolute and *Prima Facie* Rights

Increasingly, anti-consequentialism/anti-act-utilitarianism takes the form of reliance upon rights, and the problem one faces, which is why definition and stipulation are so useful to a theorist, is to find a strength for rights (or certain rights) which provides more than token resistance to consequences/ utility but nevertheless not absolute resistance. Neither absolute nor *prima facie* rights appear to provide an answer to this problem.

Suppose it is alleged that a right to life is an allegedly fundamental, individual moral right: if this right is held to be absolute, then one ends up with a view which a vast number of people are likely to reject as too strong, as the lobbies in favour of abortion, euthanasia, infanticide, suicide, capital punishment, etc. illustrate. If some scheme of absolute rights is the only genuine competitor to consequentialism, then it is not obvious that the choice between the two is going to go against consequentialism. I am not suggesting that theorists of absolute rights cannot, as it were, wriggle off the hook and so purvey an absolute right to life as if it allowed us equally as much freedom in our acts as we should have if the right were not absolute; but a good deal of such wriggling is necessary, if absolute rights are going widely to be regarded as the vehicle of anti-consequentialism. If, however, the alleged right to life is held to be *prima facie*, then consequentialists/act-utilitarians may well argue that this amounts to the claim, as Jonathan Glover maintains in *Causing Death and Saving Lives*,[21] that there is a strong presumption against the rightness of killing; and no act-utilitarian has difficulty in accepting this, since naturally he will maintain, what appears not unreasonable, that presumptions (of this sort) can be overturned through considerations of utility. In other words, *prima facie* rights appear too weak to be the vehicle of anti-consequentialism, unless supplemented with arguments to show that they are more than mere (weak or strong) presumptions against such-and-such and/or that they do not yield to utility quite as readily as act-utilitarians appear to think.[22] On either score, such arguments are to the same end, namely, to posit for some or all *prima facie* rights a degree of resistance to consequences/utility which is not token. The intended effect is to build up the rights' strength and so enhance their anti-consequentialist/anti-act-utilitarian character.

The problem, then, is with the strength of rights: absolute rights are too strong, *prima facie* rights too weak to be the vehicles of anti-consequential-ism.

An Act-Utilitarian Account of Strength

Plainly, it is necessary to find a strength for rights that is neither absolute nor token. But this seems to allow the act-utilitarian an opening, if he wants to make use of it: he may seek act-utilitarian grounds for the admission of some scheme of individual moral rights into his theory; the question then becomes whether he can do enough to show that infringements of them on his theory will be relatively uncommon. How he will proceed is clear enough.

Of some scheme of individual moral rights, the act-utilitarian may argue that it has high acceptance-utility and, generally, a high observance-utility. With a high acceptance- and observance-utility, these individual rights will not be (allowed to be) easily infringed.[23] True, the act-utilitarian cannot concede *a priori* that these rights may never be infringed, no matter what the array of concerns allied against them; but, then, this is not so very damaging, unless one thinks of such rights as being absolutely immune to considerations of utility, which few theorists do.

The central worry of such theorists is not that *no* array of allied concerns, however extensive and weighty, can suffice to justify infringe-ments of individual rights; it is rather that they do not wish to countenance infringements for merely marginal increases in utlity. And *this* issue the act-utilitarian speaks to: the high acceptance- and observance-utility which the scheme of individual rights possesses, including the very important utility to be gained in fostering among people a feeling of personal security through these rights, is going to be offset only by a very substantial amount of increased utility. Moreover, a scheme of sanctions for infringement can be introduced, perhaps varying in degree of severity depending upon the human concerns at issue. Then, sanctions will not only help to produce behaviour which respects individual rights and reinforces people's expectations about other people's behaviour in this regard, but will also form an important source of disutility, which reinforces the utility of the rights and the feelings of personal security that these rights foster and which anyone contemplating infringement of one of them will have to weigh carefully. Thus in this way the act-utilitarian can move not only to find a place for rights in his theory but also to give them more than token strength. The charge of 'rights-worship' is not applicable to him, since he bases his case for rights upon the utility of accepting and observing those which make up the scheme of individual rights in question. Nor is the inclusion of a scheme of rights in an act-utilitarianism *on this basis* incompatible with the theory remaining a form of *act*-utilitarianism.

A further reason act-utilitarians will avoid cavalier treatment of these individual rights is not hard to find. Nearly everyone today who asserts that there is this or that moral right does so with one eye on the law; for whereas moral rights, even to their most ardent admirers, appear rather ethereal and elusive, legal rights are the very real stuff and substance of social life. By and large, proponents of moral rights to this or that seek legal acknowledgement of these rights; thus, for example, women who campaign for a moral right to abortion on demand would like nothing better than to see this right made into a legal one. As different pressure groups redouble their efforts, and as their views become increasingly widespread (assuming, of course, that they do become widespread), our laws may well in time be made responsive to those views. To the extent that this happens, to the extent, that is, that alleged moral rights are swept up by statute law, there arise very powerful sets of additional utilities connected with observing and fostering observance of the law which, combined with the further, powerful set of utilities that turn upon legal sanctions for infringement of the law, make it even less likely that act-utilitarians are going to justify frequent infringements of these (now legal) rights. Moreover, if observance of the law is part of the glue of society, as is often alleged, then there are the additional sets of utilities associated with the smooth running of society (e.g, predictability in human relations, co-operation among people, co-ordination of policies and activities, etc.) which open up to the act-utilitarian. In short, if and when the present campaigns for rights succeed in bringing some of them to the statute book, there will be even less reason to accuse the act-utilitarian of treating them in a cavalier fashion.

In sum, this act-utilitarian will seek act-utilitarian grounds for the admission of rights into his theory and for not justifying infringements of them for merely marginal increases in utility. What he has to be sure of is that he has done enough to endow them, or some of them, with a strength sufficient to put up more than merely token resistance to utility. Hence his search for additional sets of utilities, by which to make it even more unlikely that there will be many cases in which infringing the right maximizes utility overall.

Loosening Some Preconceptions about Rights

To this attempt on the part of the act-utilitarian to ground rights in utility and to give them more than token strength, some observations can be appended on his behalf. They are of different sorts, and I shall not try to ascribe them degrees of priority. They take the form of attempts to loosen certain preconceptions about rights.

Differing importance

If rights mark off human concerns, human interests, then some are bound to be more important than others. It seems quite likely that act-utilitarian theories can be made to reflect this fact, given that act-utilitarians are themselves concerned to protect, foster, and fulfil human interests. For example, the sanctions attached to infringing one right may be made considerably more fierce than those attached to another, and strong feelings of guilt may be inculcated for infringing the one; these things in turn seem likely to affect people's expectations and feelings of personal security, as well as their behaviour. Thus, if some scheme of individual rights is to be used to protect certain, very fundamental human interests, it seems likely that the act-utilitarian will find the acceptance- and observance-utility of such a scheme rather high. This does not mean, however, that these fundamental interests can never be set aside on behalf of the collective well-being; this is already agreed when we agree that there is *some* degree of utility which suffices to override some particular, individual right. Besides, it is easy to think of cases, serious cases, where many non-act-utilitarians would readily accept the sacrifice of some important interests of one individual for the well-being of an aggregate of individuals, e.g., compulsory conscription in Britain during the Second World War, which is almost universally regarded as a just war for the British to have fought.

Degree of utility to override

Since rights *can* be overridden by the exigencies of utility, the important question which remains, as we have seen, is the degree of utility required to override a specific right. Because of the varying degrees of importance of rights, the answer to this question may not be the same for all individual rights (contrast cases of freedom of speech with those of trivial promises), which means that the act-utilitarian may have to do less in one case than another to justify infringement; but there *is* an answer, which we might try to get at in particular cases by means of actual and hypothetical examples, comparing and contrasting different ranges of cases, arguments about what it would be rational to do if consequences are unclear, and so on.

It is a mistake to think that the infringement of a right is always serious; it depends upon the right and whether the context in which it figures is a serious one. Trivial promises and other such agreements are cases in point, as are cases where we think domestic peace and tranquillity have a high value, as when some right to be told the truth, if there really be such, is quickly infringed the moment one's daughter asks about the noticeable effects of her new diet.

(It must not be overlooked that seriousness is widely regarded as often partly a function of *who* holds the right. For example, at least in ordinary life, though perhaps not in a rights-theorist's classroom, rights often only really matter to us in any kind of deep sense, when they are held by individuals who, e.g., may suffer if we fail to honour the right. My landlord is a rich Oxford college, not a retired school teacher on an inadequate pension; and though the college has a right to a portion of my salary each month, it is not going to be any worse off if I pay only when the bailiffs threaten to throw me out of my rooms. In Britain, to people without much money, rights to money held against them by bodies of one sort or another are often not taken very seriously. Thus, in Liverpool each year, vast sums of money in rents, owed the city by people living in city-owned apartments and houses, are lost. These people, on lower incomes, could be evicted for not paying; but the city would then face an obligation to rehouse them, and the cycle would begin again. To tell these people that the city has a right to its money is not at all like telling them that the local newsagent has a right to his; the newsagent is paid, whereas the city is fobbed off with a few pennies on account. The right of the newsagent is altogether more momentous to them than the right of the city, and this in spite of the fact that the newsagent is far less likely to go to court and hound them.)

Exercising rights and right action

It is not having but exercising individual rights which ultimately matters, since, if such rights do mark off important human interests, it is their exercise which protects those interests. Plainly, therefore, it must be possible for us to exercise these moral rights rightly; if it were wrong to exercise them, they could not serve their protective role. This raises the question of what the relationship is between exercising moral rights and right action, and one rather popular view has been that to exercise one's rights *is* to act rightly or, slightly differently, in a way which requires no further justification.[24] This view is simply false. A husband acquires conjugal rights through marriage, but it is absurd to think he acts rightly no matter when he exercises or demands these rights. We make a wager in writing, whereby you pledge everything you own; if you lose, I acquire the right to bankrupt you. But it is quite untrue that no further justification on my part is necessary for taking your business, house, car, and money and rendering you and your family destitute. You promise your daughter a Rolls Royce, if only she will stop seeing some snivelling Hegelian; but it is quite untrue that she *ipso facto* acts rightly in exercising her right and compelling you to sacrifice your future and your retirement for this car. The literature of the 1930s in the United States is filled with examples of foreclosures on mortgages, with consequent harm, in circumstances where, through collapse of prices, crop failure, dust storms, or whatever, it was impossible that farmers should meet their (often rashly agreed-to) substantial mortgage payments.

Appeal to some other right to determine when a right can be exercised rightly simply raises the question of when that further right can itself be rightly exercised. Also, however, such a course commits one, in all sorts of contexts, constantly to search about for such a right, when the plain fact is that many people have made agreements the consequences of which they have lived to regret, when the right in question is pressed against them and goes unrelieved by their timely discovery of some other right which gets them off the hook.

If not by appeal to another right, how then *do* we determine when a right can be exercised rightly? Why not by appeal to the consequences, to the utility of exercising it in the circumstances? After all, when one goes back over the above and other similar examples, it is at least in part because of the appalling consequences that we think it was not right to exercise the rights in question. On this line of argument, appeals to utility have a role to play in deciding when rights may be exercised, and thus a role to play, if rights mark off human interests, in arbitrating both clashes between and the satisfaction of various human interests.

Might not the act-utilitarian, moreover, call the proverbial good man to his assistance here? For could the good man exercise his rights in cases such as the above ? If not, why is this not tantamount to saying, in the light of what I have said, that the good man could not bring himself either to exercise or to think it right to exercise his rights when really significant disutility would ensue? The only serious question would then be what counts in the various sets of circumstances as really significant disutility.

Constraints on freedom

There is another source of significant disutility here. In his well-known article 'Are there any natural rights?',[25] H. L. A. Hart writes generally of moral rights as moral justifications to limit the freedom of others and to determine how they should act. Plainly, if widely indulged, claims to moral rights run the risk of becoming, on Hart's thesis, a source of massive disutility: as the number of purported moral rights increases, the freedom and behaviour of other people is more and more constrained, and this is usually regarded by theorists of all stripes as a bad thing. Certainly, constraints of this sort must be a source of disutility, since people are prevented from behaving as they want to, which is true, of course, even when only one or a few moral rights are claimed. The point is obvious but its importance can be overlooked, as one focuses upon the interest to be protected by the right and not upon the loss of freedom for others which that protection entails. The interest in question is going to have to be of rather great significance, in order to justify the disutility in constraining the freedom of others which concession of a right entails;[26] and I should have thought this consideration likely to militate against some present claims to moral rights.

The non-interference view of rights

The extension of W. N. Hohfeld's analysis of legal rights — the talk of claim-rights, liberties, immunities, liabilities, powers, privileges[27] — to morals and the analysis of alleged moral rights has had, I think, some unfortunate results.[28] Nevertheless, Hohfeldian analysis has been responsible for what might be called the minimal view of alleged moral claim-rights, namely, that if A has a moral claim-right to X, then some or certain specified or all other people have a moral duty not to interfere with A in his pursuit of X. This minimal, non-interference view is widely embraced today, yet, without some careful account of what counts as not interfering, it seems open to an obvious abuse even so far as legal claim-rights are concerned.[29]

Suppose some group proposes to hold a demonstration in furtherance of its political aims, and appeals to some legal (and moral) right to freedom of assembly: quite how is my duty not to interfere to be interpreted? For, consider: I may justifiably organize a counter-demonstration at the same time and place; I may bring sound equipment that completely drowns out that of the demonstrators; I may barrack any and all of their speakers and sue for assault if I am manhandled by their marshals; I may take steps, so long as they are not violent and likely to incite to riot, to disrupt the planned demonstration; and I may take vociferously active steps to bring about a boycott of the demonstration and, so long as I avoid slander and libel, to impugn the integrity of its organizers. I can refuse to print, circulate, or exhibit the demonstrators' posters and flysheets, to allow them use of or movement across my property, even to provide them with the barest necessities (food, drink, toilets) which a long march may require. In what sense, then, am I not to 'interfere' with them? True, I cannot murder the lot of them, or beat them senseless, or throw acid upon them, but then no one ever thought, with or without rights, that I could do these things.

In fact, in Britain today, the above is a recipe not infrequently resorted to in order to compel the authorities to cancel the demonstration in question. By threatening, promising, and, in some previous cases, following through on the above, the counter-demonstrators force the Chief Constable and local authorities to consider whether the march should be allowed to take place; and if the cost/benefit analysis comes out one way rather than another, if the threats and prospect of violence and injury are dire enough, the march is banned.[30] The demonstrators have had their legal (and moral) rights to freedom of assembly and freeodm of speech set aside in the interests of civil order, and the people who have brought this to pass are (part of) those who, presumably for Hohfeld, are under a duty not to interfere with the demonstrators in the pursuit of their rights.

The act-utilitarian, then, if he is to have moral rights, must seek act-utilitarian grounds both for admitting individual moral rights into his theory and for not justifying infringements of them for merely marginal increases in utility. I have sketched one way he might set about these tasks and presented some of the arguments and observations by which he might try not only to make his theory amenable to individual rights but also, as it were, to make individual rights amenable to his theory.

Rights and the Duty to Compensate

Finally, there is an argument for rights that has come to have a certain prominence, and I want to append a few words about it. It has not so much to do with the strength of rights as with how to tell whether rights are present, though, of course, if rights are present, the issue of their strength immediately arises.

In her paper 'Rights and compensation',[31] Judith Jarvis Thomson, developing some earlier work of her own in her lecture 'Self-Defense and rights'[32] and of Joel Feinberg's in his paper 'Voluntary euthanasia and the inalienable right to life',[33] speculates on some link between a duty of compensation and an infringed right. Precisely what form the link takes is not very clear: to say that the duty of compensation *shows* that a right has been infringed is far too strong, whereas to deny any link whatever leaves one more or less unable, I think Thomson would say, to deal with the example around which her paper is formulated. She concludes, therefore, that 'the duty to compensate is at best a sign of an infringed right — and probably not even a very good one at that.'[34] I am not certain that even this is the case; at least, the cases which seem to me most amenable to supporting the kind of link Thomson describes are those involving property and property rights, of the kind she and Feinberg discuss. In other sorts of cases, I seem to be able to account for my duty to compensate in the absence of any alleged, infringed rights, in the sense that, in order to understand why I am under that duty, I can provide an account which does not go through some one or other infringed right. And this can be done, I suggest, even in cases where compensation will be widely agreed to be owed.

Consider this example: I invite you and your wife to dinner. You accept, but only after the two of you rearrange your plans, cancel another engagement, and arrange for a baby-sitter. On the day of the meal, I call and cancel the evening, truthfully giving as my reason urgency of work. Virtually everyone would agree that, morally, I am under some obligation to compensate you for this cancellation (for example, by having you to dinner another evening); but I cannot see that this obligation on my part either betokens the existence of some infringed moral right of yours or is to be accounted for only by arguing through some such right or other. What it betokens, what I argue through, is my realization of your disappointment, your own and possibly other people's frustration and annoyance, your loss, say, in not having a night out or through not realizing your other plans, etc., not some shadowy moral right on your part to a meal at my house. Significantly, moreover, you yourself do not take the duty to compensate in this way; most certainly, you do not call me up and demand your meal or discuss the situation between yourselves in terms of when I will honour your right to a dinner or contemplate calling me publicly to book for this meal or give my colleagues a blistering statement of my moral inadequacies. It might be suggested that you *could* do these things, that is, you would be entitled to, but embarrassment and good breeding prevent you. If, however, you think about the case, I do not think you will concede yourself such entitlements. For we do not think of situations of this sort as giving someone a hold over someone else, though we certainly do think of them as contexts in which talk of compensation is appropriate.

Again, consider this more pointed and poignant example: the youngest of three children stays at home to look after her aged mother, and she carries on doing so for many years. The mother eventually dies and leaves her money and possessions equally among her three children. One may want to say that the mother had some sort of duty to compensate her youngest child for that child's care and attention, and one may even want to say that the other children have some sort of duty to compensate the youngest child for that care and attention; but I doubt very much if the youngest child has some moral right to a greater share of her mother's money and possessions, which the terms of the mother's will infringes. In part, this doubt reflects the fact that we do not think that care and consideration somehow become transformed into a moral right, for example, to a greater share of goods; virtue and self-sacrifice may warrant a reward, but they are not tickets to a moral right to the Cadillac. Indeed, the thought that, if only one looks after one's mother long enough, one slowly but surely (or quickly but surely) acquires a moral right to a greater share of her pots and pans than one's sister has a certain squalid look after it. The squalor, such as it is, stems not from some worry that the prospect of increased gain will take over as the motivating concern of one's care for one's mother, but rather from the view that care and consideration for one's mother gives one a hold over her and/or her possessions and their disposal. (More than once, I have come across this argument among feminists: because women bear, care for, and raise the child the foetus will become, they have a moral right to choose whether the foetus will be born. Care and consideration are here made to do a good deal of work. But consider: I have sole care of my old father and discharge it faithfully, over a great many years. Do I *thereby* acquire moral rights over the old man, if not in respect of his life, then in respect of his pipes, parrots, and plants? What the feminist is asserting is a hold over the life of the child the foetus will become, as if (prospective) care and consideration somehow *ipso facto* cede one this hold.)

I am strongly inclined to think that the duty of compensation is not even a sign of an infringed right, unless we are prepared to think of the case to hand, unlike those above, already as one in which we might characterize the relationships in which people stand to each other in terms of rights. In the case of property or property rights, in cases of commercial transactions generally, and in cases of institutional structures (where one can treat another as the occupant of an office, rather than on a personal basis), we do think of the relations in which we stand to others in terms of rights. In these cases, my duty to compensate you for taking and using something of yours in an emergency may well betoken an infringed right on your part, and with your hold over me you can demand your due or restitution. But I find it almost impossible to think of my relationships with family, friends, colleagues, and neighbours in these terms and, therefore, to think of these relationships in terms of rights; yet, I have no difficulty at all in seeing these relationships as sometimes requiring compensation of me. Of course, nothing in all this shows Thomson's contention wrong, nor is it intended to; but the scope of that contention is seriously affected, if, as I suggest, accounts of my duty to compensate would serioulsy jar with how we think about a great many cases if those accounts went through talk of rights.

Notes

1 One might argue that it is not utility but other people's rights which overrides the particular right in question. Many people will be unhappy with this way of trying to avoid allowing utility a role here, since it commits us, in each and every case where we normally justify infringement on the basis of potential harm or damage or loss in utility, to the timely discovery of other rights, in sufficient number and of sufficient strength, to override the particular right in question. When an injured person violates your rights to privacy and freedom from trespass in order to ring for a doctor, it seems very far-fetched indeed, in order to try to keep appeal to utility out of the picture, to begin, as it were, to search about in that person for just enough rights of just enough strength to override your rights.

2 MacCormick, 'Dworkin as pre-Benthamite', pp. 585–607.

3 Dworkin, *Taking Rights Seriously*, p. 139.

4 Joseph Raz, 'Professor Dworkin's theory of rights', *Political Studies*, vol. XXVI, 1978, pp. 123–37.

5 Dworkin, *Taking Rights Seriously*, p. 269.

6 Dworkin, *Taking Rights Seriously*, p. 366. Dworkin goes on to say that this stipulated sense of a right is one which 'captures the idea of individual rights used in American constitutional practice'. It is not clear to me that this sense of a right can be fully extrapolated to English law, where there is no written constitution containing a Bill of Rights and where constitutional practice as a result cannot so readily be assimilated to the American model. In this sense, 'standing on one's rights' strikes me as something of an American phenomenon, which in turn leads me to remark that *Taking Rights Seriously* strikes me as very much an American book.

7 R. M. Hare, 'Utilitarianism and the vicarious affects', in E. Sosa, (ed.), *The Philosophy of Nicholas Rescher* (Dordrecht, Holland, D. Reidel, 1979), p. 146.

8 R. Nozick, *Anarchy, State and Utopia*, Oxford, Basil Blackwell, 1974.

9 Dworkin, *Taking Rights Seriously*, pp. 365–6; italics in original.

10 Ibid., p. 366.

11 Ibid., p. 365.

12 In *Nomos XXIV*, 1982. This is a revised version of his paper 'Utility as a possible ground of rights', *Noûs*, vol. 14, 1980, pp. 17–28.

13 Dworkin, *Taking Rights Seriously*, pp. 191–2.

14 C. Fried, *Right and Wrong*, London, Harvard University Press, 1978.

15 Ibid., p. 108.

16 Ibid., e.g., p. 134.

17 Ibid., p. 81.

18 Ibid., p. 81.

19 Ibid., pp. 132–3.
20 Ibid., p. 81.
21 J. Glover, *Causing Death and Saving Lives*, Middlesex, Penguin Books, 1977, pp. 83–5.
22 As we saw in ch. 8, there is no obvious reason why, when *prima facie* rights clash, that a principle of utility, either alone or in conjunction with other principles, should not be used to resolve the conflict.
23 See R. M. Hare, *Moral Thinking*, ch. 9; and Jan Narveson, 'Rights and utilitarianism', in *New Essays on J. S. Mill and Utilitarianism, Canadian Journal of Philosophy Supplementary Volume V*, 1979, pp. 137–60.
24 I put the matter this way, in terms of justification, in order to allow for the fact that, in law, acting upon one's legal rights may well be to act legally rightly.
25 H. L. A. Hart, 'Are there any natural rights?', *Philosophical Review*, vol. LXIV, 1955, pp. 175–91.
26 Narveson has an argument designed to show that the disutility of forcing me to do something other than what I want will be a sizeable disutility for the utility of your doing what you want (because of your right) to overcome; Narveson, 'Rights and utilitarianism', pp. 144ff.
27 W. N. Hohfeld, *Fundamental Legal Conceptions* (New Haven, Yale University Press, 1919).
28 Among these has been the incredible proliferation of alleged moral claim-rights, on the basis of Hohfeld's correlative thesis of claim-rights and duties, simply by thinking up moral duties. For example, it is not at all uncommon to see animals endowed with moral rights in quick order as follows: we have a moral duty not to do X to an animal; therefore, animals have a moral right not to have X done to them. On this argument, which was once rightly characterized to me as 'vulgar' Hohfeld, there is no restriction whatever on the number and variety of rights an animal may possess, except that of human ingenuity in thinking up additional duties on our part.
     Another time, I should also want to argue that the application of Hohfeldian analysis to morals often has the effect of making the moral case much more clearly delineated than it is; that is, such a neat classificatory scheme, if applied assiduously, has the effect often of tailoring moral phenomena to fit the scheme.
29 In this regard, see Glanville Williams, 'The concept of legal liberty', in R. S. Summers, (ed.), *Essays in Legal Philosophy* (Oxford, Blackwell, 1968), pp. 121–45.
30 Such a decision is not taken lightly, of course, in Britain or anywhere else, where a thriving, participatory democracy is valued.
31 J. J. Thomson, 'Rights and compensation', *Noûs*, vol. 14, 1980, pp. 3–15.
32 J. J. Thomson, 'Self-Defense and rights', *The Lindley Lecture*, University of Kansas Press, 1976.
33 J. Feinberg, 'Voluntary euthanasia and the inalienable right to life', *Philosophy and Public Affairs*, vol. 7, 1978, pp. 93–123, (especially pp. 101–2).
34 J. J. Thomson, 'Self-Defense', p. 14.

10

Rights, Consequentialism, and Act-Utilitarianism

Not surprisingly, the present enchantment with moral rights[1] has led to (further) disenchantment with act-utilitarianism. Because of its purported failure to cope with such rights, as their alleged number has increased prodigiously, and as they have come to occupy a prominent place in much recent moral, legal, and social theorizing, act-utilitarianism has fallen (further) into disfavour.

In a sense, of course, this outcome is no surprise. Even in the very recent past, first duties, then rules, then absolute prohibitions have been seen as the instrument of the act-utilitarian's demise; and moral rights appear to be but the latest, currently most fashionable candidate for this role. Presumably, there is some perpetual need to kill off act-utilitarianism; all that varies, from period to period, is the precise instrument of death.

In the face of such onslaughts, act-utilitarians have not stuck together, and it is one aspect of a split in their ranks over moral rights that I want to discuss in this chapter. This split can be seen, I think, as a difference in the spiritual legacies of Mill and Bentham.

Mill and Bentham: Accommodation and Hostility towards Moral Rights

In its most general form, the argument for the rejection of act-utilitarianism on the basis of moral rights is this: (a) there are fundamental, individual moral rights that are absolutely essential for the protection of persons; (b) act-utilitarianism cannot accommodate these rights; (c) therefore, act-utilitarianism is either an inadequate normative ethical theory or, more weakly, less adequate than one that can accommodate such rights. The argument is made specific, obviously, by formulating (a) and (b) around some (alleged) specific right, such as a right to life, or to autonomy, or to equal concern and respect.

We can distinguish between two sorts of act-utilitarian replies to this argument, depending upon whether it is (b) or (a) that draws the fire of the act-utilitarian. The former is a reply in the spirit of Mill, the latter a reply in the spirit of Bentham.

The Spirit of Mill This is essentially a spirit of amenability and accommodation, and in the present context these take the form of trying to ground some scheme of individual moral rights in utility, and so of purveying a utilitarian theory of moral rights, on the order, for example, of what was briefly sketched in the last chapter. The above argument turns out not to work, then, because (b) turns out not to be true; it is not true that act-utilitarians cannot accommodate individual moral rights within their theories.

The Spirit of Bentham This is a spirit of hostility and scepticism towards moral rights, in part the legacy of Bentham's treatment of natural rights and of the absence in his work of anything approaching chapter 5 of Mill's *Utilitarianism*. In this context, hostility and scepticism can take different forms. For example, one form they took in chapter 8 was an attack on the claim that there is this or that moral right.

I do not deny that there are, for instance, legal and, more generally, institutional rights; and if one wants to maintain that the law and social institutions generally can be and, perhaps typically, are regarded in a moral light, then I am happy to speak of these institutional rights as moral rights. But this is not what rights-theorists today normally have in mind when they write of fundamental, individual moral rights, and for a particular reason. The point is not that, say, a right to life, or to autonomy, or to equal concern and respect is not typically regarded by them as an institutional right. It is that the fundamental rights of rights-theorists do not come into and go out of existence with this or that institution; rather, they antedate such institutions and serve as constraints on which institutions we should have. In the broad sense, in the sense of holding that there are pre-institutional moral rights, such theorists are natural rights theorists. It does not follow, however, that all such theorists are condemned to being natural rights theorists in the narrow sense, since they do not all offer an account of the ground(s) of the rights they purvey in terms of (nature or) human nature. For instance, in *Taking Rights Seriously*, it is a tenet of Dworkin's position that our absolutely fundmental right to equal concern and respect is not brought into existence by community decision, social practice, or public legislation, and survives contrary decisions, practices, legislation, and adjudication. Indeed, it constrains our decisions, practices, and legislation. But he does not ground this right in (nature or) human nature; he simply affirms, as we have seen, that it is 'fundamental and axiomatic'. From it, from its positing, other dependent rights are derived. Whereas stipulation may enable this right to evade the charge that it is nothing more than an alleged natural right in the narrow sense, stipulation is not something that will endear it, or any right, to sceptics. When one probes the ground(s) of alleged rights and finds stipulation, recommendation, moral intuition, self-evidence, obviousness, or natural law, the sceptic is not going to be satisfied.

My position on moral rights in chapter 8 was two-pronged. On the one hand, I raised queries about whether there are any moral rights, and I sketched a beginning to argument for this thesis by probing and exposing the way these rights are put into existence. As I say, the rampant use of stipulation, recommendation, intuition, self-evidence, obviousness, and appeals to natural law in order to ground rights, is open to attack. On the other hand, even supposing there are moral rights, I argued that they are superfluous to and distracting from argument about substantive moral issues. I supported four theses in these regards. First, rights do not have a fundamental role to play in ethics; they are utterly superfluous, in the face of a fully developed theory of right and wrong, which is all we need in order to decide how we will act. Second, we gain nothing in clarity, precision, and understanding by trying to discuss moral issues in terms of rights, among other reasons, because we lack a method of arguing about rights, certainly, with any degree of finality. Third, rights actually get in the way of the issues: our attention is diverted from the important business of working out principles of rightness and justification of treatment in cases of the sort at hand to the wholly speculative tasks of making something of (competing) rights-claims, of their (often many) alleged grounds, and of the vast number of competing criteria for rights-possession currently on offer. Fourth, the only value of rights-talk in ethics, certainly at the present juncture in the development of rights-theory, is to place one's opponents on the defensive. Rights-claims have become, as it were, devices for shifting the burden of argument on to those who will not otherwise cede one what one wants.

In short, if we take the start made on a position in chapter 8 as illustrative of one possible Benthamite approach to moral rights, then the above anti-act-utilitarian argument turns out not to work, because (a) turns out to be objectionable; (claims to) moral rights are themselves suspect, and, accordingly, we have no reason to reject act-utilitarianism on their basis.

For different reasons, then, the Millian and Benthamite approaches to rights both reject the argument from moral rights. But whereas one camp seeks to carve out space in its theories for some scheme of individual moral rights, the other seems bent upon eliminating rights-talk altogether from ethics. In a word, natural allies are in conflict.

I believe there is much to be said for the Benthamite approach to moral rights; but I shall not pursue the matter here, at least not directly. Rather, I want to point to a problem at the very centre of the Millian approach, to the pressure this problem creates for the act-utilitarian seriously to complicate his theory, and to the particular form this complication seems likely to take, namely, a bifurcation in our moral thinking between theory and practice, with act-utilitarianism confined to the level of theory.

Consequentialism and the Place of Rights in Act-Utilitarianism

There is a problem at the very centre of the Millian approach to rights: if the Millian keeps his rights away from his consequentialism, he will fail to be an act-utilitarian; if he brings them into contact with his consequentialism, then the rights he incorporates into his theory are going to be shadows of full-blooded rights.

Rights and consequentialism: no contact By consequentialism, I understand the view that acts are right or wrong solely in virtue of their (actual) consequences. This view is the subject of many alleged (and some real) difficulties, among which some have wanted to include the charges that it places its adherents in the hands of evil men and that it betokens a corrupt mind; but I do not want to argue over these or other alleged difficuties here.

One may be a consequentialist without being an act-utilitarian, as is the case with ethical egoists; one may be a utilitarian without being a consequentialist, as is the case with the various types of rule-utilitarians; but one may not be an act-utilitarian without being a consequentialist. Consequentialism is not the whole of act-utilitarianism, but it is an integral part of it, and one cannot give up consequentialism without giving up act-utilitarianism.

The inclusion of consequentialism within his theory compels the act-utilitarian to treat moral rights, provided the case for there being some is made, in exactly the same way as he treats moral rules. The view that acts are right or wrong in virtue of their (actual) consequences is *incompatible* with any view of moral rules or rights that allows them even partially to determine the rightness of acts. At bottom, act-utilitarianism is a conjunction of (a) consequentialism, (b) some standard of intrinsic goodness by which to evaluate consequences, and (c) a range component, to the effect that it is the consequences as affecting everyone that count towards determining rightness; and there is simply no provision in the theory as a theory of rightness for moral rules or rights to play a role in opposition to consequentialism.

Rights and consequentialism: contact It does not follow from the above, however, that an act-utilitarian cannot find some place in his theory for rules and rights. Indeed, in the case of rules, it is now known that he can argue for the inclusion in his theory of the very general rules of ordinary morality, on the ground that their utility, particularly in the face of general human weaknesses, such as succumbing to pressures, bias, and temptation, and of the possible lack of a clear view of the consequences of acts, is far too high for them in practice to be easily set aside. Not *easily* set aside: when factors such as the above are absent or present only to a minimal degree, and when utilities so work out, the rules will be broken.[2] Nevertheless, an act-utilitarian can concede these rules a role in moral thinking even if they play no role in his account of what makes right acts right.

It should be apparent, however, that the role he concedes rules and rights is restricted. It is not just that they do not make right or wrong the acts falling under them or that they are not absolutely immune to utility; two further matters are at issue. First, rules and rights do not figure at the most basic level of act-utilitarianism. At that level is to be found utility, or, more accurately, consequentialism, a standard of intrinsic goodness for evaluating consequences, a range component, and the particular theory's principle of utility (in which 'utility' is interpreted in the light of the theory's standard of goodness). Unlike rule-theorists or rights-theorists, for whom rules or rights are basic at the level of theory, act-utilitarians can have rules and rights in their theories only at levels above the basic. Second, while rules and rights, at the level of practice, are not unimportant, their importance is a function of their utility, and their utility is a function of our human situation. That is, because of our human situation, rules and rights acquire an importance in act-utilitarianism which they otherwise would not have, and, indeed, do not have, if our particular situation is not characterized by or improves with respect to the factors noted earlier.

Now the combination of these points makes of moral rights mere shadows of the rights of rights-theorists. To the rights-theorist, it is not finding a place in one's theory for individual moral rights but the place that is found for them that is crucial. On the one hand, to ground rights on the shifting sands of utility is to place them in jeopardy, since, under the right conditions, they will be set aside or violated. Possibly such conditions will obtain only infrequently; but that is a contingent affair, dependent upon how utilities work out, and an act-utilitarian can give no *a priori* guarantee in the matter. On the other hand, to rest the utility of rights on our human situation is obviously to make their utility subject to something which may well change.

But this way of putting the matter does not go deep enough. The real point is this: this combination of the above factors makes moral rules and rights *at best* mere appendages to a theory of right and wrong. If moral rules and rights are not basic in the theory, and so do not form part of the theory's account of what makes right acts right, they are dispensable. All that prevents this happening are the practicalities of our human situation, which can and often do alter.

Rights that are theoretically non-basic in a theory of rightness are shadow rights, at least if we think in terms of the widely fashionable, Dworkinian view of at least some moral/political rights as trumps. That is, I take the claim that some individual moral/political rights are trumps to be the claim that there are certain things that other individuals or groups may not do to one (for example, in pursuit of the collective good), and what makes it wrong to behave in these ways is that such behaviour infringes one or more of one's individual moral/political rights.

The situation, then, is this: consequentialism prevents the act-utilitarian from allowing moral rights a hand in deciding the rightness of acts, but anything less than this will mean that the rights which an act-utilitarian incorporates into his theory will be shadow rights.

Consequentialism and Rights Compartmentalized

The most obvious way an act-utilitarian will move to take rights seriously (as described in chapter 9), is in fact of use to the Benthamite, should he wish to incorporate a scheme of rights into his act-utilitarianism, but not the Millian. I used to think that any attempt to incorporate a scheme of individual rights into an act-utilitarianism was a move in the Millian direction, but I now see this as a mistake; to incorporate rights but to make them subject to consequentialism is in fact not a Millian but a Benthamite move.

Consider some scheme of individual moral rights of the scope that is fashionable today: if this scheme possesses the gravity and centrality for moral/political life which its supporters declare, then the act-utilitarian may argue that it has a high acceptance-utility, and, in view of the seriousness with which many people invest such rights as protectors of important human concerns, generally a high observance-utility. The high acceptance and observance utilities, including the utility to be gained in fostering among people a feeling of personal security through these rights, are going to be offset only by a very substantial amount of increased utility through infringing a right in the particular case, and the number of cases where this occurs is likely to be few.

The problem here, should the Millian try to make use of this argument, is not the usually made-up claim that cases where rights can be infringed will be few (after all, it is long, hard work to think through and calculate the utilities of a situation), but rather that the rights incorporated into the theory remain subject to consequentialism. All this argument does is make it more difficult for consequentialism, on a case by case basis, to override a right; it remains true that it is right to override rights if utility reaches the required magnitude (obviously, the argument is partly designed, as we saw, to prevent infringements of rights for merely marginal increases in utility), and true as well that it is a purely contingent affair whether in a particular case utility reaches that magnitude.

In fact, then, it is the Benthamite, not the Millian, act-utilitarian who can make use of this argument; and if he does, then it follows that, because rights remain subject to consequentialism, the Benthamite can still have at best only shadow rights in his theory. And this is true, I want to emphasize, even if the act-utilitarian were to accept one of the traditional ploys, such as that we will always give in to temptation, or that we never command a clear view of the consequences of acts, by which to argue that it would never be right to depart from rules or to infringe rights. For the truth is that even this position retains moral rules and rights as subject to consequentialism; all it does is exploit some facet of our human situation in order to ground a claim that we shall stand a better chance of maximizing utility *under these conditions* by adhering to the rules or rights. Even this move, then, even the move to exploit our human situation in order to have a scheme of rights that, because of that situation, never give way in the face of consequences, is a move a Benthamite, but not a Millian, might make use of. For rights remain shadow rights: consequences make acts right or wrong, and it is only because we sometimes or often have difficulty calculating these or difficulty calculating them in a detached manner, that we do not use, or are reluctant to use, consequences to make right infringements of the rights.

It seems perfectly clear that, in order to escape the problem at the centre of his approach to moral rights and to have in his theory something more than mere shadow rights, the Millian must find some way of keeping his consequentialism and scheme of rights apart; and the way he finds of doing this, I stress, must be such as to be consistent with his consequentialism and with the non-basic character of rights in his theory. So far as I can see, there is only one way a Millian can move to achieve his ends under these constraints: he must radically complicate his theory by compartmentalizing our moral thinking and assigning consequentialism and his scheme of individual rights to different compartments.

To urge the Millian to adopt, on act-utilitarian grounds, some scheme of rights that bars direct appeals to utility with respect to them will not, as I have indicated, be of much use to him; but it also will not capture what he actually wants. It makes it appear as if what is at issue between the Benthamite and Millian is simply how many infringements of rights the act-utilitarian will justify, and this is to miss the point. It is not the number of infringements justified, but the fact that consequentialism can justify infringements at all which matters; for so long as it *can* justify infringements, act-utilitarianism will contain mere shadow rights. To avoid this, consequentialism and rights must be assigned different compartments so that they do not interact; it will then be true that consequentialism will not justify infringements of rights (except, if at all, at the limit of catastrophe) but this will have nothing to do with some worry about keeping the number of infringements small. (If *this* were the central worry, then a Benthamite who was prepared to have a scheme of rights in his theory would resort to the device sketched in chapter 9, namely, the appeal to additional sets of utilities by which to make it more difficult to infringe a right on a particular occasion.)

Now the sort of complication of act-utilitarianism that will have to occur is at least clear in general outline; almost certainly, it will take the form of a distinction between theory and practice, with appeal to consequences occurring at the level of theory but not at the level of practice. But this *per se* is not enough; for, as we have seen, depending upon how the claim about practice and appeal to consequences is argued, a Benthamite can have good reason for not appealing to consequences in the particular case. What must be added is that appeal to consequences is not appropriate at the level of practice, by which I mean that, at that level, what it is right to do will not be determined by appeal to consequences in this case, even if there is nothing whatever to impede our assessing consequences. And what will render appeal to consequences in the particular case inappropriate will almost certainly be the claim that utility will be maximized by foregoing case-by-case utilities.

Hare's Two-Level Account of Moral Thinking

An example of the sort of complication I have in mind is to be found in Hare's *Moral Thinking*. Hare distinguishes two levels of moral thinking, critical and intuitive, embraces act-utilitarianism at the critical level, and finds a place for substantive moral rights at the intuitive level.[3] For our purposes here, the crucial part of this split-level account of moral thinking is this: one uses act-utilitarianism at the critical level in order to select those guides at the intuitive level by which to conduct one's life, and the guides selected will be those whose general acceptance (Hare chooses between guides on the basis of their acceptance-utilities) will maximize utility. Thus, given that these guides have been selected with an eye to the situations in which we are likely to find ourselves, action in accordance with them is likely to give us the best chance of doing the right, that is, the optimific thing.

At one level, then, we have act-utilitarian critical thinking, at the other, guides for living selected by that thinking. If the guides selected take the form of principles, then most of our moral thinking at the intuitive level will take the form of trying to decide what it would be right to do, on the basis of these principles. (Occasionally, to be sure, particularly when principles conflict, we are forced even in the practicalities of the situation to do some critical thinking, in order to decide what it would be right to do.) In other words, given the principles selected by act-utilitarianism, what is right is what is in accordance with the principles; and if our principles at the intuitive level confer some rights upon us, then, unless we have a conflict of principles or are confronted with a situation our principles cannot readily deal with, an act is wrong if it infringes one of these rights. In this way, at the intuitive level, Hare's split-level account of moral thinking is not directly consequentialist.

It is for this reason that Hare is able to draw the sting of the charge that act-utilitarianism conflicts with ordinary morality. He appeals to consequences at the theoretical or critical level, but at the practical level, on grounds of utility, he bars any extensive use of such an appeal. Since the guides he gives examples of in his book as selected by utility are much of a piece with ordinary morality, and since action in accordance with these guides is nearly always right (the theory at the practical level typically bars consequentialist appeals), the clashes with common opinion, of which so much has been made in the anti-act-utilitarian literature, effectively disappear.

In the past, act-utilitarianism was differentiated from other theories by its results. What Hare has done is to construct an argument for act-utilitarianism that, in terms of what the agent does, more or less removes the sharp, distinctive results with which the theory has been identified and puts in their place results which do not distinguish act-utilitarians from rival theorists. Indeed, on Hare's position, there is no reason *in theory* why one cannot be an act-utilitarian at the critical level and a Kantian at the intuitive level; all that is required is that the guides selected by utility at the critical level be of Kantian character and of Kantian ferocity with respect to the appeal to consequences. It is not difficult to meet these requirements, if one plays up our inclination to bias and temptation, our weakness in the face of pressure, our inability to be detached and clear-headed in thinking through moral problems, our lack of complete factual information about the various alternatives open to us, our lack of a clear view of the consequences of acts, etc. If one bears in mind that the thinking of which the split-level thesis is an account is supposed to take place in a single agent, then one can see that Hare's account of moral psychology is going to have to be sufficiently flexible to allow the agent to be comfortable with this bifurcation in his moral thinking and the act-utilitarian/Kantian dichotomy that in principle can issue from it.

The Two-Level Complication as the Model for Compartmentalization

Something like the Harean complication of act-utilitarianism can give the Millian what he wants over rights, namely, moral rights that are not shadow rights. On the split-level view, appeals to consequences and substantive moral rights occur at different levels; and what is right at the intuitive level is determined by applying those principles selected by act-utilitarianism at the critical level as giving us the best chance of maximizing utility in the situations we are likely to encounter.

But will an act-utilitarian be attracted by this complication? There are a great many strengths to Hare's account of moral thinking; but will an act-utilitarian avail himself of them? This is not the place to fill out Hare's views and to undertake a detailed discussion of them; but I do think we can see a possible source of difficulty any act-utilitarian may have in embracing the split-level thesis.

Consider any case where a reasonable amount of utility can be produced in this instance through the agent doing other than what his relevant guide directs him to do: on the split-level approch, where the agent is using consequences or utility not as a means of deciding what it would be right to do but rather as a means of selecting guides, the application of which at the intuitive level determine what it would be right to do, the agent has to look that particular dollop of utility in the face. He does so in the name of overall utility; that is, where the agent uses consequences or utility as the means of selecting guides which overall, if accepted, will maximize utility, the agent has, in the name of overall utility, to look in the face the particular utility to be derived from doing other than the relevant guide directs. As cases mount, in which a reasonable amount of utility can be gained through doing other than his guide directs, the agent continues to foresake particular utilities on behalf of overall utility.

The problem, I think, is whether the act-utilitarian is really ever in a position to make this more global determination of utility.

At some point, of course, it may well occur to the agent that by adopting slightly different guides, ones which increase the incidence of direct appeal to acts' consequences, but which still serve the role his initial guides were designed to serve, he can capture more of these case-by-case utilities while still preserving overall utility more or less as it was. To respond that such guides would not in fact maximize utility is simply not something that can be pronounced upon in advance of actually doing the calculations. And this is the point: it is not that there is one principle to choose from, but rather that there are many, and what we must do on the split-level approach is to select that principle with at least as high an acceptance-utility as any other. But to determine this is by no means an easy task, even if we leave aside the uninviting prospect of our having to determine it constantly, as first one candidate and then another for greater acceptance-utility is presented.

For example, does a principle of the form 'keep promises' have a greater acceptance-utility than one of the form 'keep important promises'. One can see how the issue is joined: if the determination of importance is left up to each of us, it is easy to see how disutility might ensue; if we are enjoined simply to keep promises, it is easy to see how disutility may ensue through overly rigorous observance of the principle. Disutility, then, might ensue on either principle. But will it? If this is asking us to make a judgement about actual loss of utility over all promise-keeping situations we are likely to encounter, then I do not see that such a judgement is possible. Surely, then, the question is asking us to *estimate* over the promise-keeping situations we are likely to meet with the difference in acceptance-utility between the two principles. But consider how complicated making such an estimate will be, and the numerous factors that may affect it. I must ask myself the question of whether, for all the types of promise-keeping situations I am likely to find myself in, the one principle or the other has the greater acceptance-utility. Again, I must ask myself the question of whether, for all the types of speaking situations I am likely to find myself in, the principle 'tell the truth' has more acceptance-utility than some other principle or set of principles. The number of speaking situations I find myself in daily, however, is vastly numerous and widely varied, and the factors which affect them, as any reader will realize upon reflection, multifarious. So what am I to do? Am I to think of only a few types of situations in judging acceptance-utility? Then, however, I will not be able to affirm that one principle has greater overall acceptance-utility, since I will not have looked over all the types of speaking situations and all the types of contingencies that arise within them that I am likely to encounter. Or am I to think of all the types of speaking situations I am likely to be in, all the various principles that are on offer with respect to them, all the various factors that are likely to affect them, and so on. Then, however, there must be real doubt that I can do this, at least in a sense which makes estimating acceptance-utility something other than merely guessing at it. And if estimating comes down to guessing, it is by no means an open-and-shut affair that an act-utilitarian will pass up particular utilities in the cases at hand on behalf of guesses at overall utility.

Notice how a ploy the split-level account may use at the intuitive level, in order to contend against setting aside a principle, can feed the above doubts at the critical level. Playing up the shortcomings of our human situation, in order to cast doubt upon our utility-calculations in particular cases, creates the problem that these same shortcomings can be played up at the level of designing principles. If utility-calculations are suspect at the one level, why not at the other? This question will have particular force, if the aspect of our situation which is played up is our not infrequent lack of a clear view of acts' consequences.

Notice, too, how the matter of confidence enters. It is far easier for me to estimate utilities in the particular case (I do not imply that this is an easy task in itself) than it is for me to make the more global estimates of acceptance-utilities of different principles over cases of sorts I am likely to encounter. For this reason, I seem far more likely to have greater confidence in my judgement in a particular case than in the broader, more global judgement. In other words, when I am told to forsake the particular utilities of breaking the principle in this case because the principle overall maximizes utility for cases of this type, I will not have all that much confidence that the principle does maximize utility overall, unless I am capable of performing feats of utility-calculation that I am not simply licensed in assuming I can perform. And if I lack confidence in this regard, including less confidence than in my judgement of utilities in this case, am I likely as an act-utilitarian to pass up these case-by-case utilities?

I must emphasize that the problem is not one of being able to say, on utilitiarian grounds, that having some guide or other for cases of this sort is obviously more utile than having no guide at all; a Benthamite act-utilitarian, with his rules of thumb, can say this. The problem is to be able to say, and with confidence, that *this* guide maximizes utility overall for cases of this type. Whether we are reduced to guessing at acceptance-utilities, because of the pressure to take into account all the various contingencies, or reduced to not being able to determine greater overall acceptance-utility, because of the pressure to take into account no contingencies, we seem unlikely to have the requisite confidence.

Nor does this problem disappear, the more we flesh out the Harean complication of act-utilitarianism. To give but a single example, Hare interprets the maximization of utility in terms of the maximization of the satisfaction of desires or preferences, and this means that, in deciding among guides at the critical level on the basis of acceptance-utility, we are looking for guides that maximize the satisfaction of desires or preferences. This refers not, or not exclusively, to our own desires and preferences, but to everyone's desires and preferences; that is, what we are seeking are guides whose general acceptance would enable us to maximize the satisfaction of the desires or preferences of those in and affected by the situation. Furthermore, to recall, we are not selecting guides for this case but for cases of this type, so feats of imagination — of contingencies, of people's desires and preferences, of the desires and preferences of all those in and affected by situations of this sort — are once again required. It seems to me pressure will inevitably move us in one of two directions, to judge acceptance-utility on the basis of relatively full knowledge of the above factors, or to make this judgement on the basis of relatively incomplete knowledge of these factors; and the problem set out above arises again. In other words, utility-calculations on something like the split-level complication of act-utilitarianism either require us to know more than we are ever likely to know about factors that affect situations of that type, including different people's different desires and preferences, or else judgements of overall acceptance-utility are going to have to be made under conditions where the danger exists that such judgements will amount to guesses. Either way, the issue of confidence is a real one.

Curiously, then, a standard demand issued to act-utilitarians — that they not merely assume utilities turn out one way rather than another, but actually present the detailed calculations that make their case — seems even more pressing against the split-level complication of act-utilitarianism than against the more traditional theory, since it requires more global calculations of utility.

Consequentialism and Practice

Compartmentalization of consequentialism and rights is only going to attract the Millian if the model of compartmentalization is attractive, and a split-level model is only going to be attractive to act-utilitarians if the utility-calculations it requires are feasible and can be realized, and if we have at least as much confidence in more global calculations as we do in the calculations in particular cases. It is still open to one to make an act-utilitarian case for not being an act-utilitarian in practice (whereby I mean not appealing to consequences), but I should have thought this rather curious defence of the theory would need to be especially clear-cut in its utility-calculations, if it is to attract act-utilitarians. Otherwise, one attracted in the first place to a consequentialist ethic is unlikely to be especially enamoured of a complication to his theory, the outcome of which is virtually to give up appeals to consequences at the level of practice.

Notes

1 It is still relatively uncommon in Britain, both among people at large and among philosophers, to argue moral questions in terms of rights. The seeming inevitability with which rights-talk is injected into moral issues in the United States is missing here. Of course, the hue and cry about rights in the United States has not gone without its effect in Britain, and it would be a foolish person who prophesied that that effect will not grow. Nevertheless, it has reached nothing like the gargantuan proportions it has in the United States, nor is there any sign at the moment that it is going to.
2 Put differently, an act-utilitarian is not required to say of these rules that it would never be right to break them, in order to appreciate the case for their utility.
3 I speak of 'substantive' rights here, since, for Hare, a right, say, to equal concern and respect is a purely formal right. Hare, *Moral Thinking*, ch. 9.

Part IV

11

The Appeal to the Wrongness of Killing

I do not believe that the argument from killing is likely to prove substantially effective in the cause of negative moral vegetarianism. As we saw in chapter 6, the argument does not really gain renewed life from the introduction of the distinction between negative and positive moral vegetarianism. The claim that what is wrong with painful farming practices is that the animals are eventually killed (a) overlooks the painful character of those practices (therefore, it has nothing specifically to say to factory farming), (b) makes the wrongness of those practices dependent upon somewhat esoteric and difficult questions about the value of animal life (if it has no, or only slight value, then killing animals is not obviously wrong), and (c) is consistent with the condemnation of the killing but not the harsh treatment of animals. Alternatively, moral vegetarians who adhere to the argument from pain and suffering avoid these difficulties, and we saw in chapter 6 how this is of advantage to them.

Moreover, basing one's moral vegetarianism on the argument from killing is most unlikely to bring about a wholesale change in society's eating habits. The reason is obvious, though perhaps it requires some brief elaboration in its statement.

(So much has recently been written about the morality of killing, in connection with abortion, euthanasia, infanticide, suicide, capital punishment, war, and the like, that even to begin to do justice to the subject and its wealth and complexity of detail would consume many more pages than I am allowed. Besides, in the face of such a massive outpouring, it is difficult to say anything very fresh, and especially difficult to do so in a way which does not amount to tidying up and perhaps supplementing some already, thoroughly well-canvassed view. Accordingly, my discussion of killing will be in rather broad terms.)

At the Mercy of Competing/Conflicting Theories

Plainly, it is impossible to discuss the morality of killing without bringing in the case of humans, and the moment one does the central problem in the case of animals becomes strikingly apparent. For if we cannot agree about the morality of taking human life, then how likely are we to agree about the morality of taking animal life? And we do not agree in the human case, as is obvious from the present, rather heated controversies over, say, abortion, euthanasia, and capital punishment. Indeed, so intractable have these disagreements become that the parties to them often regard themselves as implacable opponents.

At a deeper, philosophical level, this clash over killing humans typically represents, as is the case with so many issues in substantive ethics, a clash between (act-) utilitarians and their opponents; and because we are talking about the wrongness of killing, it seems inevitable, if moral vegetarianism is made to turn upon this issue, that one side or the other is going to object, depending upon whch side the moral vegetarian has embraced.

When one objects to killing, one must go on to say why killing is wrong, and discussion of this issue quite naturally divides into two parts, depending upon whether one urges utilitarian or non-utilitarian considerations against killing. As is well-known, whichever one resorts to, there are problems, and each camp tries to exploit these to the detriment of the other.

I think the upshot of these problems is that we have reached an impasse, so far as the morality of killing is concerned.[1] The fact is that neither side has vanquished the other. In the face of such internecine warfare, the moral vegetarian who bases his case upon the wrongness of killing seems bound to be caught up in the impasse, with consequent effect upon his case.

It is quite clear how this may occur. For example, if you argue against killing animals that they have an absolute right to life, no (act-) utilitarian will accept your case. If you argue that they have a *prima facie* right to life, then (act-) utilitarians may well maintain, as we saw in chapter 9, that these rights are, for example, presumptions of greater or lesser strength, which can be overturned, if not easily, nevertheless eventually by considerations of utility. And if you argue that animals have neither an absolute nor a *prima facie* right to life but merely some sort of claim or demand not to be killed, then (act-) utilitarians will maintain that there is even less reason to think either that utilitarian considerations are beside the point or that they cannot carry the day.

As for the act-utilitarian side to the dispute, if you argue against the killing of humans on the basis of the consequences or side-effects of killing them, then you are likely to get absolutely nowhere with non-utilitarians. After all, it does seem odd to try to get at what is wrong with killing someone by focusing upon the effect this killing will have, for instance, on the person's employer and drinking companions; and it better have some negative effect upon them, or else it becomes increasingly likely that killing that person is not wrong. In the case of killing *animals*, not even this type of argument is usually available, since the presence of side-effects on other animals or on us (except for pets) is very questionable.[2] If, therefore, you are forced back upon maintaining that what is wrong with killing animals is that it reduces the amount of pleasure in the world, as is Peter Singer in his *post-Animal Liberation* paper 'Killing humans and killing animals',[3] then I strongly suspect that you are simply going to bewilder non-utilitarians. For I really do not think that a person not already of utilitarian sympathies would know what to make of someone who objected to killing anything on this basis; I think they would be entirely at a loss to see what diminution in the amount of pleasure in the world had or had essentially to do with killing and its wrongness.

Historically, of course, act-utilitarians have had considerable difficulty in showing why killing is wrong, armed as they have been only with the argument from side-effects;[4] and the argument from side-effects, precisely because it provides no direct reason against killing, has had little success with non-utilitarians generally.

In short, by avoiding the argument from killing in favour of the argument from pain and suffering, one avoids just this impasse, just this clash of entrenched views and theories. One avoids what utilitarians will see as the shortcomings of non-utilitarian accounts of killing, without having to take on board what non-utilitarians will see as the shortcomings of utilitarian accounts. In this way, one's case for vegetarianism is not weakened at the outset, by relying upon what to one camp or the other will be an objectionable account of killing. In turn, this fact seems likely to extend the influence of that case, since it almost certainly has a better chance of gaining acceptance with each camp than does some case resting upon a suspect account of the morality of killing. And if one truly hopes to change society's diet, it surely makes sense to try to reach as many people as possible with one's arguments.

More generally, if one bases moral vegetarianism upon the argument from killing, it is necessary to say what is wrong with killing, and this raises such a diverse range of questions, whether one urges utilitarian or non-utilitarian considerations against it, that probably only a fairly complete normative ethical theory could provide answers to even half of them. Even then, the answers are likely to clash with those given by competing theories. In fact, killing is and always has been a battlefield of competing utilitarian and non-utilitarian ethical theories, and in the midst of this turmoil, as these theories are explored and assessed, the case for moral vegetarianism falls prey to the relative success or failure of one's ethical theory (something which in turn raises those questions about criteria of adequacy in ethical theory which I touched upon in chapter 8). Accordingly, unless the moral vegetarian can bring us round to the ethical theory upon which his argument from killing is based, he has not a hope of changing our eating practices; and it is precisely because of widespread and fundamental disagreement in ethical theory that his hope in this regard must be faint indeed. In this way, his aim of changing our eating habits has been caught up in the impasse we have reached over the morality of killing, which is nothing less than an impasse of theories.

By contrast, there is the argument from pain and suffering: condemn the infliction of undeserved pain and suffering, maintains Singer, and you must become a vegetarian. The vast theoretical baggage required in the cases of rights and killing is, it seems, missing here. This is not to say, of course, that Singer's own argument from pain and suffering is theory-neutral; it is not, and parts of the theory behind it I have criticized in *Interests and Rights*.[5] But this kind of argument must surely stand the best chance of all of reaching the overwhelming majority of people, whatever the particular niceties of their views on rights and killing, whatever the particular niceties of their ethical theories. For all the argument requires to get underway and allegedly to be effective is that they condemn the infliction of undeserved pain and suffering. Such economy of argument is simply impossible in the case of appeals to rights and to the wrongness of killing.

Notes

1 Compare, e.g., Jonathan Glover's *Causing Death and Saving Lives* with Germain Grisez's and Joseph M. Boyle, Jr's *Life and Death with Liberty and Justice* (London, University of Notre Dame Press, 1979).
2 I put the matter thus ('not . . . usually available'; 'very questionable'), in order to allow for those cases where the killing of an animal is sometimes alleged to have an effect on other animals, say, because of pair-bonding or because of a parent-offspring relationship.
3 *Inquiry*, vol. 22, 1979, pp. 145–56.
4 Some recent act-utilitarians, including Singer, have a further weapon in their armoury, at least so far as killing persons is concerned; see below, ch. 15, pp. 159–65.
5 Frey, *Interests and Rights*, especially chs 4 and 11.

12

The Value of Life

If life has no value, then it is hard to see why taking it is wrong. So what do we think of the value of animal and human life? Obviously, this is a vast and multi-faceted issue, and I want in this and the next few chapters to comment upon some widely different facets of it, ones which are presently of great interest to philosophers and laymen alike.

Life Principles

The views which may be summarized by the rubrics 'reverence for life' and 'respect for life' do not emerge from the conflict with (act-) utilitarianism unscathed. Each partakes of the same central difficulty

If such rubrics are regarded as having no exceptions and so as explicitly barring any taking of life, then they are likely to find little favour in contemporary Anglo-American society. For example, if they are restricted to human life, then, apart from not helping animals, they rule out, for instance, abortion and euthanasia; if they are held to encompass all life, they rule out picking flowers, removing plants, cutting trees, etc.; and if they are restricted to human and animal life, then they rule out not only killing agricultural pests, mosquitoes, and flies, but also killing animals when the aim is to benefit or assist them, as when they are killed (a) to eradicate or control the spread of diseases which, even if no threat to man, are harmful to them, or (b) because of severe physical injury or (c) to control numbers and thereby to help foster some sort of equilibrium between food resources and population size. If, however, these 'life principles' do have exceptions, then they do not slam the door on killing. How, then, do we determine which are the exceptions to the principles? Obviously, utility is the (act-) utilitarian's answer; and every time it is mooted whether *this* is an exception, the danger exists that the (act-)

utilitarian will come up with good (act-) utilitarian grounds for claiming that, indeed, killing is justified in this case.

To people who are in favour of, say, abortion or euthanasia, these 'life principles' simply must be more flexible than those who wield them usually allow. Their problem, however, is to achieve this flexibility without either achieving too much flexibility and so eroding the principles as *life* principles (they will then allow too much killing), or achieving flexibility by appeal to the utility of killing in the particular case and so infecting the very core of these principles, usually held in opposition to consequentialist/act-utilitarian positions, with precisely the kind of appeal they were intended to ward off.

As for a 'sanctity of life' rubric, it traditionally has been reserved to human life only,[1] largely, I suppose, because it was earlier regarded as having a theological underpinning; and even quite a few of those who rely upon it today may not be prepared to see it extended to animal life, possibly because they have reason to think animal life far less valuable than human life. Certainly, orthodox Christians on the whole seem to think this.

If what all these life principles amount to, once they are regarded as having exceptions, is a plea to think carefully and compassionately about taking life, *any* life, then (act-) utilitarians will have little difficulty in accommodating them. For there is no inconsistency whatever between thinking carefully and compassionately and taking life; it happens constantly, when one reaches the conclusion about some person suffering from a very painful terminal illness that killing him is the right and compassionate course.

Nor is anything achieved by some such claim as 'life is life', an incommensurable value, incapable of being traded-off against any other. For the whole question of whether there are any incommensurable values is itself presently a bone of contention, not merely between (act-) utilitarians and their opponents, but also between these opponents and those laymen who do not exclude taking life in some cases of, say, abortion, euthanasia, or infanticide.

Kinship and Reverence for Life

I have never seen a rigorous defence of a 'reverence for life' principle. What attempts I have seen, all of which have sought to include more than human life within the scope of such a principle, have failed both to make out a very strong basis for the principle and to be very clear about why it is the *lives* of creatures that I am to revere. Perhaps a single example can suffice to illustrate what I have in mind here.

In his book *Returning to Eden: Animal Rights and Human Responsibility*,[2] Michael W. Fox deplores our harmful effect upon and treatment of wildlife, pets, and food and research animals, and he endorses a reverence for life position — what he calls a 'biospiritual ethic' — by which to come to terms with and to do something about this effect and treatment. The ground of this ethic is, according to Fox, the kinship of all living things, and kinship, he assures us,[3] can be scientifically established. What then follows, without analysis and differentiation, is a jumbled series of claims, over all of which, presumably, Fox detects the warming glow of science. Animals can experience pain, fear, anxiety, pleasure, and satisfaction; they can experience jealousy, guilt, embarrassment, sadness/depression, love/devotion, and altruism;[4] they can experience the emotional loss of loved ones; they perhaps have a psychic mechanism which enables them to conceptualize death; they can be empathetic, possessive, and emotionally insecure; they can know the difference between right and wrong and can develop a conscience;[5] they can experience remorse; they have a sense of self in relation to others; they can communicate their intentions and possibly even concepts and ideas to other animals; they can develop psychosomatic disorders and succumb to anorexia nervosa and paranoia; and so on. I shall leave it to readers to enquire after the truth of these matters.

Now this hodgepodge of unanalysed, undifferentiated claims would seem to betoken on Fox's part a desire to establish kinship by sheer adumbration of similarities. In fact, however, this is not the case. And it is just as well; for even if we do not question (some of) Fox's claims on other grounds, they seem most unlikely to underpin a reverence for *all* life. Again, in common with others, Fox at one point cites as 'one proof of our kinship with animals' similarities in brain structure and function;[6] this, too, however, would estabish our kinship only with some other mammals and so is not a broad enough base to support a reverence for all life, which is Fox's position.

Plainly, then, the basis of kinship has to be so widely encompassing that everything Fox wants to include within the class of our 'kin' can get in, and this seems to require a search for some lowest common denominator linking all species. Fox finds what he is seeking:

> When we go back in time, to study fossil records of past epochs, or when we compare the structure and components of our body cells with those of slime molds, fish, and prairie grass, we find that we all converge. . . . All existing species come from common ancestral family roots which can easily be traced; for example, bears, raccoons, ferrets, cats, and wolves all share the same ancestors.[7]

If I am to revere everything with body cells just so or with common ancestral family roots, then, presumably, I am to revere slime molds and prairie grass. To many, however, the kinship thesis will now underpin too much. Indeed, if we go along with the factual claim, which I do not know the truth of, about body cells and ancestral roots, what is excluded? Not even rocks and dirt can be counted out, since Fox seems prepared to be .

very generous with the notions of 'convergence' and 'common ancestral family roots'; in any event, he writes of 'our kinship with animals and with earth as a whole (for the earth is indeed our flesh) . . .'[8] But this is by the way.

Surely even a tepid supporter of a life principle must be somewhat dismayed at having to advance a kinship thesis, and so having to defend a reverence for life position on the basis of fossils, body cells, or distant ancestors? Possibly whales and Japanese fishermen had a common ancestor; but this seems a rather weak basis on which to demand that the Japanese stop hunting and begin revering whales. And that basis is not obviously strengthened through speculations about whether whales have a conscience, can experience remorse or guilt, can love and hate, and can succumb to anorexia nervosa or some other disorder. Appeal to pain may succeed, but only up to the point that a painless way of killing them is devised (e.g. explosive harpoons with a paralysing drug on the tip).

The kinship thesis, then, does not appear very well grounded, and it is the basis of Fox's reverence for life position. In addition to this, however, Fox must contend with other issues. First, how are we supposed to get from similarities between a gorilla's brain and our own, or from similarities in structure and components between our body cells and those of fish, to morals? How are supposedly scientific facts about brains and body cells and ancestral roots supposed to yield moral conclusions about, say, treatment? All Fox has to say on the matter is this: 'The evidence that there is kinship beneath the apparent diversity of all life is now irrefutable. Surely this fact is an injunction to mankind to think and act differently and to work towards a unity of all nations and races and of the rest of creation.'[9] The word 'surely' in this passage betokens a plea, not an argument, however, and the injunction Fox sees certain facts as representing has no more firm basis than that. Yet, he proceeds as if it did, as if, when he writes of wolves in their natural environment killing deer that 'to intervene would be ecologically and therefore ethically unsound', [10] that he has demonstrated the 'therefore'.

Second, it is simply not clear why or how my learning that a creature has certain similarities to myself is supposed to induce in me a reverence for its life. If I learn that frogs have eyes and legs and other similarities to myself, why am I supposed to begin to revere their lives?

Third, why should what I revere about a creature, if I come to revere anything, not be it similarity to me? It is tempting to think of kinship in terms of degrees: I see a closer bond between myself and dogs than between myself and frogs, and I do so because of the number of similarities in the one case to myself. If I then revere dogs at all, it is because and in so far as they are like me, which, in effect, is to erect similarity to myself as the standard for revering things. Of course, this way of proceeding is harmful to Fox's enterprise, since, before I have descended the evolutionary scale very far, let alone reached slime molds and prairie grass, I either run out of similarities to myself or find I can posit them only in some tenuous sense, which means, obviously, that I am most unlikely to revere all life.

Fourth, Fox's notion of kinship far outstrips the range of our natural sympathies, which typically are extended to creatures like us in important respects, such as being able to suffer. Yet, forests, flowers, plants, and the ecological systems in which they figure; the 'lower' animals; these comprise a large part of creation. Unless our sympathies are extended to include them, a curious disharmony will lie at the bottom of Fox's reverence-for-life position: it will instruct us to think one thing, while our natural sympathies will either pull us in another direction or not exert any pull on us at all. It seems most unlikely indeed, however, that talk of fossils, body cells or common ancestral roots is going to suffice to bring this portion of creation under our sympathies.

Many of those who might be expected to find Fox's position attractive will not do so; for he is prepared to allow, in the guise of destruction 'as part of an essential act of compassion',[11] a rather generous amount of killing (and other things). For example, compassion includes maintaining the balance of nature in a well-managed ecosystem, and this allows, provided we behave humanely, culling animal populations, the destruction of animal habitat, some trapping,[12] and some hunting.[13] Fox is also not an antivivisectionist,[14] and (some) killing is allowed in medical and scientific research. Nor are we barred from moving against animals purely and simply to secure our own advantage: 'A more open farm system may necessitate destruction of wildlife habitat if present farmland cannot be used more effectively through crop rotation, diversity of products, and so on.'[15]

Thus it seems that Fox is trying simultaneously to have an expanded reverence for life ethic, expanded to encompass all of creation, while at the same time trying to distance himself from any absolute bar on killing. But there is a tension in this, a tension between his biospiritual ethic and the notion he uses when he comes to discuss particular cases, namely, humane stewardship.[16] We are, according to Fox, the stewards of our natural environment, not its masters, and we must discharge our stewardship humanely. Humane stewardship, however, is compatible with killing; indeed, it may, he thinks, demand killing, as when the population of one species of animal grows too large for its food resources. It allows other killing as well, all in the name of efficient animal management, provided the killing is carried out humanely. I suspect that many of those who might otherwise be expected to endorse Fox's position may well find that they cannot bring themselves to adopt his attitude of a reverence for all life, while exercising in full measure his view of our stewardship over the remainder of creation.

Lastly, since this chapter began with a question about the respective value of animal and human life, I cannot forbear pointing out one obvious and very damaging implication of Fox's particular, reverence-for-life position. We are licensed to cull animal populations when serious overpopulation and, therefore, a disruption in the balance of nature is threatened. Why, then, are we not licensed to cull our own species, which in many parts of the world has long since outstripped its food resources? If a reverence for life is compatible with culling animals, why is it not compatible with culling humans? If I can kill animals in the name of an efficient, well-managed ecosystem, why not humans? Is the reason ultimately that, though we are to revere all life, we are to revere the lives of members of our own species above all others? If so, then Fox's reverence-for-life ethic has a systematic bias in our favour built into it.

The Value of Animal and Human Life

If we do not hold a reverence for life position or if we hold such a position but of Fox's variety (i.e., which allows killing), then I suspect most of us, when we reflect on the value of animal life, have only vague intuitions about it and then only if we think in the most general of terms. In such terms, these intuitions can perhaps be captured in three theses.

Animal life has some value We do not think that animal life has no value and that, therefore, we need not trouble ourselves morally about taking it. It is significant, however, that nearly all of us think here in terms of the 'higher' animals; for I doubt if it is very meaningful to speak of our 'intuitions' about the lives of animals well down the evolutionary chain, or, if it is meaningful, that it captures anything but the very roughest guesses of what we take these creatures' lives to be like.

Some creatures, however, are not valued in the least: most people do not value the lives of ordinary worms and would have little hesitation in killing them; and they would be hard-pressed, I suspect, to think of some human end which, because it involved killing worms, was for that reason impermissible or should for that reason be thought as having morally something against it.

Not all animal life has the same value While we place a reasonably high value on the lives of cats and dogs, we place a much lower value on the lives of mice and rats, and a still lower value on the lives of flies. Of course, reasons can arise for our valuing what up to now we have not: if a strain of worm were faced with extinction, we might place a very high value indeed on preserving it; and this is perfectly consistent with our otherwise valuing that strain of worm scarcely at all.

Animal life is not as valuable as human life We value human life far above animal life; in the end, I think this is why the use of animals in *serious* medical research would receive most people's support. Of course, it may be possible to think up cases where we might prefer to save some animal at the expense of some human, for example, where a dog is normal and healthy but where the human is terminally ill or irreversibly comatose or, possibly, morally corrupt. Nevertheless, confining ourselves to ordinary men and ordinary dogs, we value the former well above the latter. Nor is this an instance of speciesism or species discrimination, if we can cite, as we think we can, reasons for our view which are more than mere window-dressing for preferring our own kind.

Why do we think human life more valuable than animal life? One way of putting the answer is briefly to spell out what we might say, in the light of the above theses, about a major food animal, such as chickens. For example, the mere fact that we think the lives of chickens have some value will not show that it is wrong to kill them for food. For we place a very high value indeed upon our present, meat-based diet, upon the obvious ease and quickness with which that diet can be satisfied, upon the ease and convenience with which that diet enables us to meet our nutritional needs, and upon the livelihoods of all those involved in the diverse industries which directly and indirectly touch upon the commercial farming of chickens. Accordingly, we appear to be confronted with a conflict of values, of a sort not unlike that sketched in connection with rights in chapter 8.

What if the value we place upon the lives of chickens, however, is in fact exceedingly minimal? This is the case, I think, with the overwhelming majority of us. For chickens are mass-produced in their billions, rarely achieve any individuality in our eyes, are not noted for their behavioural, let alone intellectual, affinities to ourselves, are rarely, if at all considered to be self-conscious, are rarely contemplated for inclusion in the class of persons, and, in general, lead us to believe that, for most purposes, one is pretty much as good as another. If, then, the value we place upon the lives of chickens is minimal, this conflict is not going to be resolved in their favour. Accordingly, if one's case for moral vegetarianism turns upon the argument from killing, and if the wrongness of killing is correlated with the value of the life taken, then one's moral vegetarianism, if it is to have any claim upon us at all in this case, hangs upon argumentation to convince us that we are mistaken to value the lives of chickens at the level we do. This is no easy task, to say the least.[17]

This way of indicating why we think human life more valuable than animal life, however, is less direct than simply affirming that it is the quality of human life which makes it valuable. In turn, it is the sheer richness of human life, and in what this richness consists, which gives it its superior quality. Some of the things which give life its richness we share with animals; there are other things, however, which can fill our lives but not their's. For example, falling in love, marrying, and experiencing with someone what life has to offer; having children and watching and helping them to grow up; working and experiencing satisfaction in one's job; listening to music, looking at pictures, reading books, and so becoming acquainted with our cultural past and present; wondering where we have come from, where we are going, and what explains what happens around us; experiencing humour, delight, and fantasy; making plans and striving to realize them; striving to make something of one's life, in terms of one's purposes and goals; seeking through years of training and hard work excellence in some athletic, artistic, or academic endeavour; these are the sorts of things, more in some lives, less in others, which give them their fullness and texture. The list is varied and lengthy, and it includes the tears of sorrow as well as the tears of success. By comparison with animals, our lives are of an incomparably greater texture and richness, and when we say of a dying man that he has led a rich, full life we allude to something incomparably beyond to what we would allude, were we to say the same of a dying chicken, cat, or chimpanzee. There is nothing speciesist about this: we find human life to have a much higher quality than animal life, not on the basis of species, but on the basis of richness; and the very high value we place on human life is a function of its quality.

It is sometimes remarked that the chicken's life is as valuable to it as a particular man's life is to him; it is the only life either has. To say only this, however, is not as yet to say that the chicken's life has any value. All this remark amounts to is the claim that, if the chicken and the man are dead, they have no life which they can carry on living, at whatever quality. That is, being alive is a precondition for having a life, of some quality or other; but this *per se* does not confer on the life of that creature which is alive any value as such.

This distinction between being alive and having a life, which I borrow from James Rachels,[18] helps here. To say of someone that he 'has not much of a life' is not to say that he is not alive; rather, being alive is a precondition for not having much of a life, and this amounts, in part, to saying something about the quality of his life. In other words, being alive is a precondition for both the chicken and the man having a life, but the lives they have are of vastly different qualities. The man has considerably 'more of a life' than the chicken.

Diminution in Value

Obviously, when I note that we place a high value on human life, I have in mind the lives of ordinary human beings. It should be apparent, however, that if the value of a life is a function of its quality, then as its quality diminishes, its value diminishes. This gives rise to (at least) three interesting results.

First, as we deviate *radically* from ordinary human lives, whether through severe mental and physical deformity or an irreversibly comatose state or whatever, the quality and, therefore, the value of human life plummets drastically. To a great many people, who include but are by no means confined to (act-) utilitarians, a life whose quality is so drastically at odds with ordinary human life ceases to be or, in any event, can cease to be a life worth living. We are all familiar with the sorts of lives of which this is not uncommonly said today, and discussions of euthanasia of whatever stripe — voluntary, involuntary, non-voluntary — and, indeed, of infanticide not infrequently occur because we say it. Of course, it is doubtless true that no precise determination may be given of the quality of life below which life is not worth living; but that does not mean that we cannot mark off, say, the short lives of spina bifida children and the lives of the irreversibly comatose as of a quality massively below that of ordinary children and of ordinary people.

Second, as the value of human life plummets drastically, it would seem to become amenable to trade-offs with other values. One can come to think this, I must emphasize, quite independently of coming, formally, to learn something about and to embrace some form of utilitarianism. Once one comes to think that the value of life is a function of its quality and that some lives are of a radically diminished quality; and once one is confronted with a conflict, say, between using money and resources to keep very severe cases of encephalitis alive, or using them in some other and worthwhile way; then one will almost inevitably be led to take into account — and to think it right to take into account — the quality of life being lived, in order to help decide the conflict.

Third, as the quality and value of human life plummets and continues its downward course, it can approach and even fall below the quality of life of some quite ordinary animals. In cases of the latter sort, if we are confronted with the choice between saving the human or saving the animal, then we should be bound in terms of consistency to regard the animal's life as of greater value and to act accordingly. This point has serious implications in the matter of vivisection.

The Value of Life, Vivisection, and the Appeal to Benefit

Most people are not antivivisectionists and for a particular reason, namely, they think that some benefit or range of benefit can justify experiments, including painful ones, upon animals. Increasingly, there are some things these people do not think, such as that they are committed (a) to regarding simply anything — another floor polish, another eye shadow, for which animals have suffered — as a benefit, (b) to approving of simply any experiment on animals, in the hallowed name of research, (c) to forgoing criticism of certain experiments as trivial or unnecessary or a PhD. exercise, (d) to halting the search for alternatives to the use of animals or to refraining from criticism of scientists who, before commencing their experiments, conduct at best a perfunctory search for such alternatives, (e) to approving of (extravagant) wastage, as when twenty rabbits are used when five will do, and (f) to refraining, in the case of some painful experiments, from a long, hard look at whether even *this* projected benefit is important and substantial enough to warrant the infliction of *this* degree of pain.

Who benefits? Sometimes animals do, and sometimes both humans and animals do; but, not infrequently, indeed, perhaps typically, the experiments are carried out upon animals with an eye to human benefit.

Some antivivisectionists appear to reject this appeal to benefit. I have in mind especially those who have, as it were, a two-stage position, who begin by objecting to painful animal experiments and eventually move on to objecting to animal experiments *per se*. Among other reasons for this move, two are noteworthy here. First, vivisectionists may well seek to reduce and eliminate the pain involved in an experiment, e.g., by redesigning it, by dropping parts of it, by adopting different methods of carrying it out, by the use of drugs and pain-killers (and by fostering new developments in drugs and pain-killers and genetic engineering), by painlessly disposing of the animals before they come to feel post-operative pain, and so on. The point, of course, is not that the vivisectionist must or will inevitably succeed in his aim but rather that, if he did, or to the extent that he does, the argument from pain would, or does, cease to apply. Thus, it may well be the case that giving up painful experiments is not the only or the only effective way of dealing with the pain they involve. So, it is tempting to shift to a condemnation of animal experiments *per se*, which at once reduces the manoeuvrings of the vivisectionist over pain to nothing. Second, and, to a great many antivivisectionists, possibly even more importantly, the pain argument has nothing to say to the countless millions of painless and of relatively painless animal experiments performed each year throughout the world; and these, I should have thought, vastly outnumber the painful ones. So, in order to encompass them in one's antivivisectionism, it is once again tempting to shift to a condemnation of animal experiments *per se*.

The above in no way denies, of course, that the antivivisectionist may want to deal first with painful experiments, before turning to look at any others; but turn he will, if those I have talked to are representative. For, in the end, it is the use of animals as experimental subjects at all, not just or possibly even primarily their use as subjects of painful experiments, that I have found lies at the bottom of their antivivisectionism.

To the vivisectionist, the antivivisectionist would appear to think that *no* benefit is important and substantial enough to justify painful animal experiments and, eventually, that *no* benefit is important and substantial enough to justify animal experiments. And this position, the vivisectionist will think, is very unlikely to recommend itself to many people. It is obvious why. Would your view of Salk vaccine simply be turned on its head, if it came to light that it was tested on monkeys or that some monkeys suffered pain (perhaps even intense pain) in the course of testing it or that it is made by cultivating strains of a virus in monkey tissue?

It would be silly to pretend that all animal experiments are of vast, stupendous importance; it would be equally silly, however, to deny that benefit has accrued to us (and sometimes to animals) through animal experimentation. (Often, the problem is that a series of experiments, at different times, by different people, enable still someone else to build upon those experiments to yield a benefit; for this reason, it is not always easy to tell of a particular experiment what its ultimate significance will be.) If informed, concerned people do not want animal research carried out without guidelines as to animal welfare, since animals are not merely another piece of equipment, to be manipulated however one will, neither do they want our laboratories closed down until, assuming such a time comes, all experiments can be carried out on bacteria or, more generally, on non-animal subjects.

There is a feature to this appeal to benefit that is not widely appreciated. When, in the work I discussed earlier, Michael W. Fox rejects antivivisectionism, he does so in these terms: 'Some antivivisectionists would have no research done on animals. This is a limited and unrealistic view since in many cases it is the only way to test a new vaccine or drug which could save many lives — human and animal. Often the drugs being tested will treat or alleviate disease in both animal and human.'[19] Fox might have posed a sterner test for himself if he had drawn the example so that the vaccine benefited only humans but was tested, and tested painfully, only on animals; but this is by the way. The important point is Fox's entirely false presumption that the only alternative to not testing the vaccine and reaping the benefit is to test it upon animals; it could, of course, be tested upon human beings. There is absolutely nothing about the appeal to benefit which precludes this; so far as it is concerned, if securing the benefit licenses (painful) experiments on animals, it equally licenses (painful) experiments on humans, since the benefit may be secured by either means. Moreover, we must not forget that we already have a powerful reason *for* human experiments: we typically experiment upon animals with an eye towards benefiting humans, and it seems only sensible, if we want to find out the effect of some substance upon humans, that we test it upon humans. This is especially true, as increasing doubts arise about whether extrapolations from the animal to the human case are not very prone to error and to the effects of in-built differences between animals and humans. (The saccharin controversy is sometimes cited as a case in point.) In some cases, such extrapolations may be positively dangerous; I have in mind cases where a substance has far less marked or severe effects in animals than in humans. (I have heard thalidomide, and what testing was done with it, cited in this connection.)

Someone who relies upon the appeal to benefit to justify (painful) experiments on animals, then, needs one more shot in his locker, if he is to prevent the appeal from justifying (painful) experiments upon humans. Specifically, he needs some reason which demarcates humans from animals, some reason which shows that, and why, we are not justified in doing to humans what we in our laboratories do to animals. If this individual is, as I am, non-religious, then specifically religious doctrines, such as the sacredness of human life and the dominion of man over the beasts, are not available.

A great many things could be said at this point, but I think it will be widely held that the reason to allow the appeal to benefit in the animal but not the human case is to be found in the value of the respective lives. Human life, in a word, is more valuable than animal life. (Notice that someone who appeals to some non-religiously grounded principle of reverence or respect for life, where the principle does not cede human life greater value than animal life but rather enjoins us to revere life or living things *per se*, still has no reason for thinking the benefit may only be secured through animal and never through human experiments.)

But now we must confront the fact that not all human lives have the same enrichment or scope for enrichment. (There are babies, of course, but most people seem happy to regard them as leading lives which have the relevant potentialities for enrichment.) Some people lead lives of a quality we would not wish even upon our worst enemies, and some of those who lead these lives have not the scope for enrichment of ordinary human lives. If we regard the irreversibly comatose as living human lives of the lowest quality, we must nevertheless face the fact that many humans lead lives of a disastrously lower quality than ordinary human lives, lives which lack enrichment and where the scope, the potentialities for enrichment, are severely truncated or absent.

If we confront the fact that not all human life has the same quality, either in terms of the same enrichment or the same scope for enrichment, and if we are thinking of the value of life in these terms, then we seem compelled to conclude that not all human life has the same value. And, with this conclusion, the way is open for redrawing Fox's vaccine example in such a way that makes it far less apparent that we should test the vaccine on animals. For, as opposed to testing it on quite ordinary and healthy animals, with a reasonably high quality of life, the alternative is to test it on humans whose quality of life is so low either as to be exceeded by the quality of life of the healthy animals or as to approach their quality of life. On the former alternative, and it is as well to bear in mind that a great many experiments are performed upon healthy, vigorous animals, we would have a reason to test the vaccine on the humans in question; on the latter alternative, we would again find ourselves in need of a reason for thinking it justified to test the vaccine on animals but not on humans.

Where does this leave us? If we are not to test the vaccine on humans, then we require some reason which justifies testing it on animals but not on humans. If we purport to find that reason in the greater value of human life, then we must reckon with the fact that the value of human life is bound up with and varies according to its quality; and this opens the way either for some animals to have a higher quality of life than some humans, or for some humans to have so low a quality of life as to approach that of some animals. Either way, it is no longer clear that we should test the vaccine on the animals.

So, in order to make this clear, what is needed, in effect, is some reason for thinking that a human life, no matter how truncated its scope for enrichment, no matter how low its quality, is more valuable than an animal life, no matter what its degree of enrichment, no matter how high its quality. I myself have and know of nothing with which to satisfy this need; that is, I have and know of nothing with enables me to say, *a priori*, that a human life of any quality, however low, is more valuable than an animal life of any quality, however high. Perhaps some readers think that they can satisfy this need; I am receptive to suggestions.

In the absence of something with which to meet the above need, we cannot, with the appeal to benefit, justify (painful) animal experiments without justifying (painful) human experiments. We seem to have, then, two directions in which we may move. On the one hand, we may take the fact that we cannot justify animal experiments without justifying human experiments as a good reason to re-examine our whole practice of (painful) animal experiments. The case for antivivisectionism, I think, is far stronger than most people allow: so far as I can see, the only way to avoid it, if you are attracted by the appeal to benefit, is either to have in your possession some means of conceding human life of any quality greater value than animal life of any quality, or to condone experiments on humans whose quality of life is exceeded by (or possibly equal to) that of animals. If you are as I am and find yourself without a means of the required sort, then the choice before you is either antivivisectionism or condoning human experiments. On the other hand, we may take the fact that we cannot justify animal experiments without justifying human experiments as a good reason to allow some human experiments. Put differently, if the choice before us is between antivivisectionism and allowing human experiments, can we bring ourselves to embrace antivivisectionism? For, consider: we find ourselves involved in this whole problem because we strongly believe that some benefit or range of benefit can justify (painful) animal experiments. If we choose antivivisectionism, we may very well lose the many benefits obtained through vivisection, and this, at times, even if we concede, as we must, that not every experiment leads to a Salk vaccine, may be a serious loss indeed. Scientific research and technological innovation have completely altered the human condition, occasionally in rather frightening ways, but typically in ways for which most people are thankful, and very few people indeed would look in the face the benefits which medical research in particular has conferred upon us, many of which benefits we owe to vivisections. If the appeal to benefit exerts its full attraction upon us, therefore, we may find ourselves unable to make the choice in favour of antivivisectionism, especially if that meant a good deal of serious research in serious affairs of health had either to be stopped until suitable, alternative experimental subjects were developed for a full range of experiments or, if nothing suitable for a full range of experiments were developed, to be stopped entirely.

Accordingly, we are left with human experiments. I think this is how I would choose, not with great glee and rejoicing, and with great reluctance; but if this is the price we must pay to hold the appeal to benefit and to enjoy the benefits which that appeal licenses, then I think we must pay it.

I am well aware that most people will find my choice repugnant in the extreme, and it is easy to see how I can appear a monster in their eyes. But I am where I am, not because I begin a monster and end up choosing the monstrous, but because I cannot think of anything at all compelling that cedes human life of any quality greater value than animal life of any quality. It might be claimed by some that this shows in me the need for some religious beliefs, on the assumption that some religious belief or other will allow me to say that any human life is more valuable than any animal life. Apart from the fact that this appears a rather strange reason for taking on religious beliefs (i.e., believing in the existence of God and of God's gifts to us in order to avoid having to allow experiments on humans), other questions about those beliefs, such as their correctness and the evidence for this truth, intrude. I may well find that I cannot persuade myself of the beliefs in question.

Is there nothing, then, that can now be cited which, even if we accept that we are committed to allowing human experiments, would nevertheless serve to bar them? There are, of course, the likely side-effects of such experiments. Massive numbers of people would be outraged, society would be in an uproar, hospitals and research centres would come under fierce attack, the doctor-patient relationship might be irrevocably affected, and so on. (All of us will find it easy to carry on with the list.) Such considerations as these are very powerful, and they would have to be weighed very carefully, in deciding whether actually to perform the experiments. Perhaps their weight would be so great that we could not proceed with the experiments; certainly, that is possible.

It must be noted, however, that it is an utterly contingent affair whether such side-effects occur, and their occurrence is not immune to attempts – by education, by explaining in detail and repeatedly why such experiments are being undertaken, by going through yet again our inability to show that human life is always more valuable than animal life, etc. – to eliminate them. It is this last fact especially, that such things as outrage and harm to the doctor-patient relationship can be affected by education, information, and careful explanation, that poses a danger to those who want actually to bar human experiments by appeal to side-effects. So, I do not play down the importance of side-effects in deciding whether actually to perform human experiments, I only caution that they do not provide a once-and-for-all bar to such experiments, unless they survive any and all attempts to mitigate and eliminate them.

Notes

1 See, for example, Owsei Temkin, 'The idea of respect for life in the history of medicine', and W. K. Frankena, 'The ethics of respect for life', in Stephen F. Barker (ed.), *Respect for Life* (Baltimore, Johns Hopkins University Press, 1976).

2   M. W. Fox, *Returning to Eden: Animal Rights and Human Responsibility*, New York, Viking Press, 1980.

3   Ibid., p. 2.

4   I am not sure what it means in this context to 'experience' altruism.

5   Fox writes: 'a dog and a child both learn what is socially acceptable behavior and, in knowing the difference between right and wrong, develop the sense of conscience and guilt' (M. W. Fox, *Returning to Eden*, p. 5).

6   Ibid., p. 10.

7   Ibid., p. 18.

8   Ibid., p. 34.

9   Ibid., p. 18.

10 Ibid., p. 19.

11 Ibid., p. 20.

12 Fox writes: 'to ban all trapping is impractical', M. W. Fox, (*Returning to Eden*, p. 18); see also p. 60.

13 Fox writes: 'to ban *all* hunting is illogical since some, for management of ecosystems, is essential' (ibid., p. 168; italics in original).

14 Ibid., p. 116.

15 Ibid., p. 169.

16 Ibid., e.g., pp. 97–8, 140–2, 159–64, 167–70.

17 With the argument from pain and suffering, of course, it is an unnecessary task; for even if we assign the lives of chickens an exceedingly minimal value, they can still suffer.

18 See his paper 'Do animals have a right to life?', in H. B. Miller, W. H. Williams (eds), *Ethics and Animals* (Clifton, New Jersey, Humana Press, 1983). See also his paper 'Medical ethics and the rule against killing: comments on Professor Hare's paper', in S. F. Spicker, H. T. Engelhardt, Jr (eds), *Philosophical Medical Ethics: Its Nature and Significance* (Dordrecht, D. Reidel, 1977).

19 M. W. Fox, *Returning to Eden*, p. 116.

13

Killing and the Doctrine of Double Effect

As we have seen, certain problems attend life principles depending upon what the compass of such principles − humans, animals and humans, all living things − is taken to be. Even when restricted solely to human life, such principles produce what will be widely seen as unacceptable results, such as the prohibition of abortion and euthanasia. But this, it may be urged, is too quick: it assumes in such cases that nothing more may be said, and this has yet to be determined.

Inevitably, those who hold principles barring the taking of (innocent) human life must contend with difficult cases, cases in which, for instance, an especially tragic outcome will ensue (e.g., mother and foetus will die) through a rigorous adherence to such principles (e.g., not aborting the foetus). On the other hand, these principles do not envisage a less than rigorous adherence to them. Plainly, therefore, what adherents to such principles require is some means, as it were, of avoiding the tragic outcome consistent with not deviating from their principle. In some cases, the doctrine of double effect can appear to constitute one such means.

The doctrine has figured most commonly in Catholic moral theology, but it would be quite wrong to think that only Catholics embrace it. Increasingly, it has come to figure in the work of normative theorists opposed to (act-) utilitarianism, such as Thomas Nagel,[1] as part of their development and defence of a deontological normative ethic. On the other hand, not surprisingly, (act-) utilitarians have been in the vanguard of those unhappy with the doctrine. (And they are not alone there: I have found students and laymen generally rather hostile to the doctrine, mostly because it strikes them as a means of trying to obtain in a roundabout way what one simultaneously insists may not be obtained directly.)

I want to examine several features of the doctrine which are in part the source of my own unhappiness with it, features which attend several conditions for its (successful) employment.

Conditions for Employment

The doctrine (hereafter abbreviated to DDE) is a principle of conduct that allows it adherents in certain difficult cases, provided certain conditions are satisfied, to bring about an effect indirectly that they are forbidden to bring about directly. By 'indirectly', I mean that the effect in question is aimed at neither as end nor as means. In terms of Bentham's distinction between 'olique' and 'direct' intention,[2] DDE may be characterized as the thesis that, in certain difficult cases, provided certain conditions are satisfied, one may bring about (it is permissible to bring about) by oblique intention, as the merely foreseen consequence of an act, what one may not directly intend, either as end or as means.

The conditions in question are four, and failure to satisfy any one of them ensures the inapplicability of DDE to a particular situation. Condition One is that the act to be done, considered in itself and apart from its consequences, must not be intrinsically wrong. So far as the rightness or wrongness of acts is concerned, DDE does not itself specify *what* makes acts right or wrong, *which* acts are right or wrong, or *how* one knows or finds out which acts are right and which wrong; it is assumed, in order even to consider whether DDE is applicable to a particular case, that one knows whether the contemplated act is intrinsically wrong. Plainly, therefore, DDE will form part of a larger, normative ethical theory, almost certainly of an anti-consequentialist, deontological stripe. For DDE does commit its adherents to a partial rejection of consequentialism. They need not reject consequentialism out of hand; indeed, they may accept it as the account of what makes the vast majority of acts right or wrong. But at least for some acts (or kinds of acts), if DDE is to be invoked, adherents must regard these acts (or kinds of acts) as right or wrong independently of their consequences. How numerous such acts (or kinds of acts) are, remains for them to indicate. Because, then, DDE only makes sense against a backcloth of acts which are intrinsically right or wrong, it follows that no consequentialist can embrace DDE; and from this it follows, because all act-utilitarians are consequentialists, that no act-utilitarian can embrace DDE. As for the various types of rule-utilitarians, since they are not consequentialists, they are not similarly debarred from adopting DDE. I shall not explicitly concern myself with this first condition for the employment of DDE.

Condition Two is that, given both a good and an evil effect of an act, the evil effect must not be intended, but simply tolerated or permitted. Here, we encompass the distinction between direct and oblique intention: one aims at the good effect and merely foresees the evil effect as a by-product of one's act. It is this distinction which has monopolized discussion of DDE; and while I, too, will be concerned with it, I shall argue that it plays a subsidiary role in determining what we say in several important cases in which DDE is thought applicable, subsidiary, to be specific, to what I shall call *control responsibility*. I shall develop this notion in the course of arguing that the distinction between direct and oblique intention is not the index of character or goodness that the defenders of DDE take it to be.

Condition Three for the employment of DDE is that, given both a good and an evil effect of an act, and given that the evil effect may only be permitted, the good to be obtained must be desirable enough to offset permitting the evil effect. Essentially, this condition requires weighing up what is to be gained against what is to be permitted; and the former must compensate for the latter. I shall not consider this third condition explicitly; therefore, I will not inquire after the principles by which this weighing operation is to be carried out or after the standards for adjudging (adequate) compensation.

Condition Two has so dominated discussion of DDE that Condition Four has scarcely received an airing; yet, it is both important and interesting enough to warrant one. This condition is that the evil effect of the act must not be a means of bringing about the good effect, or, as it is sometimes put, that the good effect must be produced directly or immediately by the act and not by the evil effect. I shall consider briefly whether the order of causation between the evil and good effects of an act is morally significant, and I will argue that it is not.

In short, I shall be concerned with Conditions Two and Four, though much more with Two, not least because, relying upon the distinction between direct and oblique intention to draw moral differences between cases, adherents to DDE reach conclusions in cases of killing which a great many others, who include but are not confined to those with utilitarian sympathies, find unacceptable.

Direct and Oblique Intention

Adherents to DDE, as I have said, use the distinction between direct and oblique intention to draw moral differences between cases. For example, a doctor who has been administering a drug to relieve his patient's pain now finds that an ordinary dose no longer brings relief; he, therefore, proposes giving his patient the minimum dose necessary to relieve the pain, in the knowledge, however, that this amount will in fact prove fatal or at least hasten death. Is the doctor's act permissible? It is, according to DDE; for the doctor directly intends the relief of pain, not his patient's death, and only foresees as a by-product of his act that death will in fact result or be hastened. If, however, in exactly similar circumstances, another doctor were to directly intend his patient's death, then his proposed act would not be permissible; it would, adherents to DDE would say, be murder. So they will want to distinguish morally between these two cases, between one in which the patient's death is obliquely intended and one in which the patient's death is directly intended, even though the final result is the same in each case, viz., the patient ends up dead.

In recent years, this use of the distinction between direct and oblique intention, not to separate our two drug cases into one of intentionally killing and one of knowingly bringing about or hastening death, but, once the cases are thus separated, to draw a *moral* difference between them, has come under fire.[3] In his paper 'Intention and punishment', H. L. A. Hart argues that neither the verbal differences in characterizing the two cases nor their differences in causal structure 'are correlated with moral factors'; in his view, there is between the cases 'no relevant difference . . . on any theory of morality.'[4] He concludes:

> It seems that the use of the distinction between direct and oblique intention to draw the line as Catholic doctrine does between what is sin and what is not sin, in cases where the ultimate purpose is the same, can only be explained as the result of a legalistic conception of morality as if it were couched in the form of a law in rigid form prohibiting all intentional killing as distinct from knowingly causing death.[5]

What Hart fails to add is that, in examining DDE, talk of sin serves only to obscure matters. Specifically, it obscures the distinction between the rightness or wrongness of acts and the goodness or badness of agents, and the considerations relevant to each. What is at issue is whether DDE's use of the distinction between direct and oblique intention can establish a difference in the goodness or badness of our two doctors, one of whom intentionally kills his patient, the other of whom knowingly brings about his patient's death. The adherent to DDE thinks it can, whereas Hart, rightly, I believe, thinks otherwise. So far as the rightness or wrongness of acts is concerned, we have already seen in connection with Condition One that in order even to consider whether DDE is applicable in a particular case, it is assumed one knows whether or not the proposed act is intrinsically wrong.

Just as talk of sin may obscure matters, so may use of the label 'murderer'. It may, for example, fail to pick out one of our two doctors. Even if we define murder (unless suicide by definition is murder) as 'the intentional taking of another, innocent human life', we are still left with the question of whether the doctor who knowingly brings about or hastens his patient's death, not as his aim or part of his aim, but as a foreseen and certain consequence of his act of administering a quantity of drug, is guilty of murder. Since the law may not recognize any distinction between intention and foresight, use of the label 'murderer', as a way of marking off the goodness of the one doctor from that of the other, may be inapposite.[6] Then, too, use of the label 'murderer' can make it appear that the only kind of responsibility, the only sense of 'responsible' germane to assessing the goodness of our two doctors is the sense in which guilt (and/or blame) is ascribed to an agent. This is not the case, as I hope to show.

In his book *The Sanctity of Life and the Criminal Law*, Glanville

Williams also attacks the use of the distinction between direct and oblique intention to try to establish a difference in the goodness of the two doctors.[7] His complaint is clear enough:

> It is altogether too artificial to say that a doctor who gives an overdose of a narcotic having in the forefront of his mind and the aim of ending his patient's existence is guilty of sin, while a doctor who gives the same overdose in the same circumstances in order to relieve pain is not guilty of sin, provided he keeps his mind off the consequence which his professional training teaches him is inevitable, namely, the death of his patient. . . . If [DDE] means that the necessity of making a choice of values can be avoided merely by keeping your mind off one of the consequences, it can only encourage a hypocritical attitude towards moral problems.[8]

Now one important issue this passage touches upon indirectly, and quite independently of the perhaps overly contentious description of the doctor in the one case as trying to keep his mind off a consequence he knows will occur, is whether one can withhold intending or willing an evil effect of one's act, if one knows that that effect will in fact occur.[9] What view one takes is in many cases likely to depend upon just how certain one is that the evil effect in question will occur; and one is likely to be quite certain if the evil effect is inevitably or inseparably connected with the proposed act. For example, if late at night, I set fire to a dwelling-place on my land, in order to rid myself of this shack, then even if I claim to be directly aiming at or intending only to rid myself of an eyesore, I must realize that the people asleep in the shack will very likely die as a consequence. Death seems *inevitably* linked with setting fire to a dwelling-place in the middle of the night; so, if I set fire to the shack, it seems doubtful that I can withhold intending the ensuing deaths. In other cases, withholding intention appears doubtful because of the evil effect's *inseparable* link with the act. If I drop a cannister of napalm into the midst of a village in order to deter snipers from firing at ground troops, it must be doubtful that I can withhold intending the villagers' deaths. For napalm is an anti-personnel weapon, and killing and maiming are the very functions it was perfected to fulfill; so that, to withhold intending to kill and/or maim the villagers, I should have to think both that the function and developed use of the weapon are other than I know them to be and that the napalm itself, once dropped, will be selective in alighting only upon snipers and not upon villagers. Now our case of the doctor who knowingly brings about or hastens his patient's death appears of this sort, since the doctor both knows and admits that death is inseparably linked causally with this quantity of this drug. Must it not be doubtful, therefore, that he can withhold intending his patient's death? Nor is he helped by one's agreeing that there are degrees of foresight, for instance, that consequences may be foreseen as certain, probable or merely possible, and that intention may be withheld from consequences foreseen as only slightly probable or merely possible; for, of course, the doctor foresees as a certainty that death will result or be hastened through administering this dosage of this drug. It is tempting to conclude, then, that the degree to which one cannot withhold intending an evil effect is a function of the degree to which one foresees this effect as a certain outcome of one's act: the more certain one is, the more doubtful one can withhold intending it.

Responsibility

An adherent of DDE may try to establish a difference in the goodness of our two doctors by trying to make out a difference between them in respect of the responsibility which each bears for the death of his patient. His aim will be to show that the doctor who only foresees his patient's death and does not directly intend it is not responsible for that death. Three ways come to mind in which this might be attempted.

(1)   The question of whether an agent can withhold intending an effect he foresees as certain to occur should be kept quite distinct from the question of whether an agent is responsible for what he foresees as a certain and inevitable or inseparable consequence of his act (as well as for what comes about through a direct intention of his). If he is responsible for such a consequence, then it is beside the point whether he can successfully withhold intending that consequence, since he will be responsible for it whether or not he directly intends it. On this view, our doctor who knowingly brings about his patient's death, who foresees as a certainty that this dosage of this drug will prove fatal, will be on all fours with the doctor who intentionally kills his patient, so far as responsiblity for a death is concerned. If, however, an agent is only responsible for what comes about through a direct intention of his, then a difference between our two doctors in their responsibility for a death will be established and thereby, perhaps, a difference in their goodness. Quite ordinary examples can be used to show, however, that one is responsible for more than one directly intends. To adapt a familiar example, Bill and Bob are walking to work when simultaneously they see a wallet bulging with money; both dash forward for the wallet. Bill gives Bob a terrific push which he intends to knock Bob over and which he foresees as likely to cause Bob injury. He does not intend to injure Bob but only to get the money. Nevertheless, when Bob goes down and sustains serious injury, Bill seems clearly responsible. Why should the same not be true of the doctor who knowingly brings about the death of his patient, viz., that he who knowingly brings about a consequence does not escape responsibility for it merely because he did not directly intend it? Of course, the degree of responsibility an agent incurs for foreseen consequences may depend upon his assessment (or perhaps an assessment by the proverbial 'reasonable

man') of the likelihood of those consequences coming to pass. But if this is so, then at one extreme will surely fall the napalm and drug cases, where the consequences in question are foreseen, whether by the agent himself or by the 'reasonable man', as certain to occur; and we may assess degree of responsibility accordingly.[10] The doctor's degree of responsibility, therefore, is not diminished through his having assessed the likelihood of death resulting from this dosage of this drug as very slight.

(2)   One might try to draw a difference between our two doctors in the responsibility each bears for the death of his patient by suggesting that one is not responsible for those consequences which one foresees but does not want. Thus, the doctor who knowingly brings about his patient's death, though he foresees that death as a certain consequence of his act of administering the drug, nevertheless does not desire it, and, therefore, is not responsible for it. This view may possibly be twisted out of the case of *Director of Public Prosecutions v. Smith*, in which attention was focused on the question of whether an agent intends the foreseen though unwanted consequences of his acts.[11] In commenting on this case, Anthony Kenny noted that, on the ordinary meaning of 'intends', 'an agent intends an action only if (a) he knows he is doing it and (b) wants to do it either for its own sake or in order to do some other action.'[12] If this is correct, if a man who foresees but does not want a certain consequence has not intended it, then it may be suggested he is not responsible for that consequence. Kenny himself rejects such a suggestion,[13] and quite ordinary examples render it doubtful. Bob shoots at Bill, knowing himself to be an excellent shot and intending only to frighten him; he foresees that Bill could be killed but neither intends nor wants that he should be (nor thinks that he will be, given his marksmanship); in fact, Bill is killed. Bob seems clearly responsible for his death. The point holds good, whether we consider a case involving a positive act or one involving negligence. Thus, a man who leaves his kerosene stove burning when he goes out foresees that it could explode and that fire could result both in his and other apartments, though he neither intends nor wants such an explosion (nor estimates its likelihood as very high, as his stove is new); nevertheless, if an explosion occurs, and the apartments burn, he seems clearly responsible. Thus, the suggestion that one is not responsible for foreseen but unwanted consequences is doubtful, and our doctor who knowingly brings about his patient's death but who neither intends nor wants that his patient should die does not thereby escape responsibility for that death.

(3)   It might be claimed that an agent is responsible only for his acts and not for the consequences of his acts. On this view, the doctor who intentionally kills his patient is responsible for an act of murder, whereas the doctor who knowingly brings about his patient's death is merely responsible for an act of administering a drug, of which the death of his patient is a consequence. This suggestion, however, assumes that the

act/consequence line is both fixed, that is, it can only be drawn at one place in the causal chain and in one way, and moral in kind, that is, it separates the morally relevant from the morally irrelevant features of a case. Both assumptions, I think, are mistaken. I think it can be shown, though to do so here would divert us from our immediate purposes, that the act/consequence line can be drawn at different places in the causal chain of act and consequences and in different ways, and that, by redescribing an act, what was previously the act or part of the act can be rendered a consequence. More importantly, it is a mistake to think that the act/consequence line separates the morally relevant from the morally irrelevant features of a situation; for, as all of the examples in this section have shown, an agent can be held responsible for bringing about a particular set of consequences. In his dash for the wallet, Bill injured Bob; even if his act were described as 'seeking money', responsibility for bringing about Bob's injury remains his. So far as our doctor who knowingly brings about the death of his patient is concerned, then, even if he is described as 'administering a drug' or 'relieving pain', responsibility for bringing about that particular set of consequences which includes the patient's death is his.

In short, these three attempts to forge a difference in the goodness of our two doctors, through establishing a difference between them in respect of the responsibility each bears for the death of his patient, come to nothing.

Control Responsibility

It is necessary to sharpen and develop these remarks on responsibility, and I shall do so in the context of examining a case that has come to have a permanent place in the literature on DDE.

A woman in labour will die unless a craniotomy is performed on the foetus, while if the operation is not performed, the child can be delivered by Caesarian section after the mother's death. To (Catholic) adherents to DDE, craniotomy is impermissible and may never be performed, whether the mother's life alone is threatened, or whether the lives of both mother and foetus are at stake.[14] Operating on the foetus in this way is a case of 'direct' killing, in that the doctor directly attacks the foetus with the intention of killing it, whereas by not operating and delivering the child after the mother's death, the doctor only foresees or obliquely intends the death of the mother. Hence, if he operates, the doctor is said to have committed murder, whereas if he does not operate, the mother is said to have been 'permitted to die'. Put differently, while it is forbidden the doctor to directly intend the death of the foetus, it is not forbidden him to 'permit' the death of the mother. (The use of 'permits' in these contexts appears standard practice among Catholic thinkers.[15] The reader must be careful, therefore, because of the expression 'permitted to die', not to confuse the act/omission distinction with DDE, which applies equally to acts and omissions.) To adherents to DDE, then, there is an alleged moral difference in this case between operating, and intending a death, and not operating, and permitting a death; and the doctor who performs the operation is to be judged wicked. In this way, we should have established a difference in the goodness of two doctors, one of whom performs the craniotomy, the other of whom, in exactly similar circumstances, does not.

In the drug case, I have argued that the alleged difference in goodness between two doctors, one of whom intentionally kills his patient and the other of whom knowingly brings about his patient's death, is not to be found in the fact that one patient's death is directly intended while the other patient's death is merely foreseen and unwanted. Unless, that is, the distinction between direct and oblique intention is correlated with some difference in the responsibility each doctor bears for the death of his patient, as would be the case, for example, if an agent were only responsible for what comes about through a direct intention of his; and I found no such correlation. Likewise, in the craniotomy case, I think the claim that the alleged moral difference between operating (and intending a death) and not operating (and permitting a death) consists in the fact that on the former but not the latter course the doctor is responsible for the outcome is equally suspect. But, here, use of the phrase 'permitted to die' can possibly lead one to think that, if the doctor does not operate, he is no longer a causal factor in effecting the mother's death; so to speak, events are left to run their natural course. As a result, it may be suggested that he is removed from responsibility for her death. And by their talk of the mother's death as 'unavoidable', some adherents to DDE encourage me to think that they have adopted this line.[16] In my view, it is mistaken; but to show this requires me to specify the sense in which I think the doctor who does not perform the craniotomy *is* responsible for the mother's death.

I wish to say of this doctor that he is responsible for the mother's death, because I wish to say that he is responsible *whatever* the outcome of his intervention or action in her case, though not, of course, if, out of the blue, through no fault of his own, she dies, say, of cholera. But what are we suggesting when we say that he is responsible whatever the outcome? The concept of responsibility would appear to oscillate among (at least) three meanings. On one meaning, perhaps the most common, to be responsible for X is to be the cause of X; on a second, to be responsible for X is to be guilty of having done X. On a third meaning, however, to be responsible for X is to say that there is a case to be put and so a case to be answered; while guilt is not ascribed, there is present the implication that we shall look into the answer that is forthcoming. It is a variant of this third sense I am using when I suggest that the doctor is responsible for the mother's death. That variant is, that while we are not labelling the doctor an evil man or a murderer, we are saying something about his control over what happens in the woman's case. In that it is his decision whether or not to operate, the situation is one within the doctor's control; and whatever results in her case — and here and elsewhere I exclude circumstances of the kind where, out of the blue, the mother dies of cholera — cannot be said to be independent of the exercise of that control.

Of course, some men lose control of a situation. It seems probable in the case of *Director of Public Prosecutions v. Smith*, for example, that Smith became excited and angry and lost control of the situation; events, so to speak, took charge of him rather than vice versa. This is why it is perhaps unjust to ask what an unexcited, reasonable man would foresee in Smith's situation; for the question assumes the very control of a situation which through excitement or anger or whatever Smith has lost. Nothing like this exists in the case of the doctor, however, so that, even if excitement, anger, etc., are defeating conditions of control, he cannot make use of this fact. This is why talk of the mother's death as 'unavoidable' must not be allowed to pass: the doctor has not lost control of the situation, and her death becomes unavoidable only if he exercises his control one way rather than another, viz., by deciding not to perform the craniotomy. This, too, is why the phrase 'permitted to die' must be treated carefully: to say that by not operating the mother is 'permitted to die' is to say that the doctor has decided to exercise his control in this way. She is not, therefore, simply 'permitted to die'; she is 'permitted to die' by the doctor. Of course, the woman need not have died; but then the foetus need not have had its skull crushed. Whichever of these unhappy alternatives comes about, however, nothing is achieved by refraining from saying that the doctor 'permits' the woman to die or that the doctor kills the foetus.

In my view, then, control of a situation ensures responsibility for the eventualities that ensue, in the sense that one is answerable for them; accordingly, the doctor in the craniotomy case is responsible whichever course he adopts, since he is the one confronted with the choice between operating and not operating. By not operating and 'permitting' the woman to die, he does not remove himself from responsibility for her death.

Several matters must be guarded against. First, it might be said that, in operating, the doctor intervenes and exercises his control, whereas in not operating, he does not intervene and so pointedly refrains from exercising control. It is a mistake, however, to think that the doctor's control of a situation can manifest itself only through acting and never through not acting. How he exercises control is his responsibility; the woman need not have died, if he had decided differently, had decided to operate. As for intervention in the flow of events, it is true that by operating the doctor intervenes whereas by not operating he does not. But the important element is not whether he intervenes, but that the decision whether to intervene is his; for the woman is 'permitted to die' by the doctor only if he decides not to intervene. Second, I do not think the doctor escapes control responsibility for the outcome in the craniotomy case by surrendering his control over the decision to operate to some moral authority, whether to the pronouncements of some person or body, or to some hierarchy of increasingly absolute or exceptionless duties or rules. This is the first step towards the plea that the doctor is but a minor link, a non-decider, in a great chain of decision-making, so that his hands are clean simply because he transmits decisions from higher to lower links in the chain. For obvious reasons, I think we should all, before accepting this plea, want to look rather carefully into the decisions being transmitted, to satisfy ourselves that they are above reproach.

Moreover, in the craniotomy case, the doctor is not merely the transmitter of a decision of some moral authority; he is also the instrument of that decision's implementation. We can distinguish the doctor's surrender of his control over the decision to perform the craniotomy from his willingness to act upon the decision that that authority provides in this case: the decision to act upon the authority's decision remains the doctor's.

Finally, the decision to surrender his control over the decision to operate or not is itself within the doctor's control, and he bears control responsibility for it. Since what ensues in the mother's case will be a result of how *this* decision is made, the doctor does not obviously evade control responsibility for the outcome in her case.

What, therefore, turns upon establishing control responsibility? The answer, so far, is, first, that because talk of the mother's death as 'unavoidable' or of her being 'permitted to die' are not *per se* defences to control responsibility, in deciding not to perform the craniotomy, the doctor does not escape responsibility for the resultant death; and second, that in deciding not to operate and so allowing events 'to take their course', the doctor does not remove himself as a causal factor in effecting the mother's death, since she is only 'permitted to die' and events are only allowed 'to take their course' if he decides to exercise his control in this way, her death coming as a direct result of this decision. But this is only a partial statement of the importance of control responsibility; to provide a more complete statement, a fuller inspection of the doctor's position is necessary.

Attempts to Render Control Responsibility Superfluous

I shall provide this fuller statement of control responsibility, in the course of examining several accounts of the doctor's position in the craniotomy case by opponents of DDE, accounts which might be thought to render superfluous the notion of control responsibility. These accounts, I believe, are mistaken.

Immoral omissions

In the craniotomy case, by not performing the operation, it might be argued that the doctor is guilty of an immoral omission. The case can appear in this light, that operating is acting, is a doing or a doing-something, whereas not operating is not acting, is a not-doing or a doing-nothing; and the former may be regarded as acts of commission, the latter as acts of omission.[17] Since by not operating the doctor does nothing, and since we are responsible for our omissions, the doctor is guilty of an immoral omission. I think this view of the doctor's position is mistaken.

What are the necessary and sufficient conditions for a not-doing or a doing-nothing to amount to an immoral omission? If we suppose that several men stood by and watched a non-swimmer drown, then to say that they 'did nothing' at the very least means that they did nothing about the particular event in question, since they may well have been doing something, e.g., exercising or playing football. But failure to act is not an omission; it is necessary to add that the men had the ability to do something to save a drowning man, i.e., could swim (no other way will save the man), and that they had an opportunity or occasion to save a drowning man. A non-swimmer does not omit to save our drowning man, and swimmers who lack the opportunity to save a man do not omit to save one either. Thus far, then, the following conditions are necessary for an individual's failure to act to amount to an omission:

(a) A does not X
(b) A has the ability to X
(c) A has the opportunity to X.

In addition, I think we need also some indication that the swimmers on shore are or were expected to take action to save the drowning man, so that they took no action in a situation in which they were expected to:

(d) A is expected to X.[18]

Suppose the swimmers on shore admit all this (but admit afterwards that they did not want to become involved): are they guilty of an immoral omission? Their failure to act may amount to an omission but it does not amount to an immoral omission because, so far, there is no suggestion that they either ought or were required to act. Whereas, for example, a life-guard who satisfied conditions (a)—(d) would be guilty of an immoral omission, since he is required to act in such a situation. Therefore, to be guilty of an *immoral* omission, I think a fifth condition is necessary:

(e) A ought or is required to X.

Now what is it that requires one to act? The most obvious candidate for this role is that of duty. If one of the swimmers is the son of the drowning man, and if there is no raging sea to impede rescue, then we may think that the son is required, by some duty to his parent, to attempt the rescue; certainly, knowledge of the family tie will lead others to expect the son to plunge in. Again, even if none of the swimmers on shore is related to the drowning man and neither know him nor anything about him, we may still think they are required, e.g., by some duty to render mutual aid, to undertake the rescue. (Clearly, it is problematic whether we are under any such duty, which may help to explain the common failure to act in this sort of case.) The life-guard's case, however, is different: the reason we expect him to plunge in is our knowledge that he is required to do so by his job; and he knows he is required to, since the post of life-guard is defined by its duties. (In this case, condition (e) above may be regarded as a stronger version of condition (d).) This requirement is not in disregard of circumstances, for instance, of the raging sea variety, and the life-guard may have cause for not jumping in. But it is important that he show cause for not acting in such a case; otherwise, we shall take his job and its functions, where these are defined in terms of duties, to require him to act.

What, then, of the doctor in the craniotomy case? By not operating, is he guilty of an immoral omission? I think not. In nearly all respects, it is true that the doctor's situation is the same as the life-guard's: conditions (a)—(d) are satisfied, and he seems clearly required to save life. The reason we expect him to 'do something' is because we know his job or profession requires him to. The crucial difference between the two men, however, is that, while the doctor is under a duty to save life, that duty does not specify in the craniotomy case *which* life, the mother's or the foetus's, he is to save. The decision of which it is to be is his, and he bears control responsibility for that decision. Plainly, were he to make no effort to save either mother or foetus, then he would be guilty of an immoral omission; but if he saves the foetus/child, though we may complain on behalf of the mother, he can nevertheless be said to have done what he is required to do, that is, to save life.[19]

Acting and refraining

Another, though very similar, account of the doctor's position, which, if correct, would likewise render the notion of control responsibility superfluous, exploits a distinction between acting and refraining. The craniotomy case can appear in this light, that operating is acting while not operating is not acting, is a not-doing or a doing-nothing; and it may be suggested that a not-doing or a doing-nothing by the doctor amounts to refraining from acting or 'letting the mother die'. Since refraining or 'letting die' implies doing wrong, the doctor does wrong in not operating.[20] I think this characterization of the doctor's position is mistaken, and for the same reason as the previous one. The necessary and sufficient conditions for a not-doing to amount to a refraining are, I think, as follows:

(a)   A does not X
(b)   A has the ability to X
(c)   A has the opportunity to X
(d)   A considers Xing but rejects it.[21]

The important difference between refraining and omitting is that to refrain from Xing one must consider or deliberate Xing: if I do not turn out the lights or feed the baby, I may in certain circumstances omit to do so; but there is no suggestion that I considered turning out the lights or feeding the baby and decided otherwise. Now in the craniotomy case, it is true that the doctor *does* consider saving the mother; if he then saves the foetus, he clearly refrains from saving the mother. Importantly, however, from the fact that the doctor refrains from saving the mother, it does not follow that he has, *ipso facto*, done wrong. If I debate the merits of each but decide to stay inside to practise the piano and refrain from going walking, I have not done something wrong or something I ought not to have done. Why should the same not be true of the doctor? The only reason I can see why one might want to treat him any differently is because one goes on to construe refraining in his case as failing in his duty; and if he has failed in his duty, he has done wrong. But he has not failed in his duty. Once again, the doctor's duty does not indicate which life he is to save:[22] so long as he undertakes to save either the foetus or the mother, he will have done what he is by his profession required to do, namely, to save life. Since the decision as to which life to save is his, control responsibility remains his.

Duty and moral criticism

In the craniotomy case, I have accepted 'to save life' as a characterization of the doctor's duty; but I do think it can be seriously misleading to characterize it thus. For so long as the doctor attempts to save either foetus or mother, he will have done his duty, with the result, it may be thought, that his decision as to which life to save is, morally, immune to criticism. I suggest that this is not the case.

The doctor's decision as to which life to save is not made *in vacuo*, but in a particular situation, with attendant circumstances and consequences; and in order to reach his decision about what he ought to do, we may expect and urge him to take into account as many of these circumstances and consequences as he can, or, at the very least, as many as he thinks (and we think) likely to be morally relevant. Such factors as the mother's mental and physical health, the already existing family relationships of which she is a part, the capabilities of the parents to have additional children, the dependence of the present children of the marriage upon the mother, the husband's inability to afford another child, his inability to look after the present children properly if his wife were to die, etc., may all be drawn to the doctor's attention. In deciding not to perform the craniotomy, should the doctor leave out or exclude a good many or all of these attendant circumstances and consequences in reaching his decision on which life to save, though he will not have failed in his duty, he may well have made the wrong decision. He ought to have decided the other way, and talk of his having 'done his duty' *whichever way* he decides can obscure this matter.

The point has application elsewhere. In her note 'Who is wronged?',[23] G. E. M. Anscombe argues that it is not clear, in a case in which a doctor can save the many or the few, that he must save the many: his duty is to save life, which he does by saving the few, and she queries which of the many is entitled to complain of his act. Leaving aside the questions of whether the doctor's duty is to save life or to save as many lives as possible, and of what difference number makes, I think talk of the doctor's having 'done his duty' in saving the few may mislead us into thinking that, *therefore*, he reached the right decision on what to do. This need not be so: perplexed by such a decision, we may enquire after those considerations the doctor took into account and those he left out in reaching it; and on the strength of what this enquiry reveals, we may come to think the doctor made the wrong decision. Even *prima facie*, it is difficult to grasp what considerations there were (he did not lack medicines, etc.) that could have led him to such a decision;[24] and even to one who adheres rigidly to a characterization of the doctor's duty as simply 'to save life', an explanation may be required as to why he chose to do his duty so narrowly and not more broadly and so more generously. (Nor is it difficult to conceive explanations that point to defects in the goodness of the doctor.)

In the craniotomy case, then, the doctor's decision as to which life to save can be open to criticism, morally, through an inspection of the considerations that he included and excluded as morally relevant to that decision. A situation in which such criticism may be considered appropriate is easily imagined. For example, suppose the doctor knows that the foetus will almost certainly die anyway or will be born with a very serious and ultimately fatal malady: the point is, and this is where control responsibility matters, that should the doctor not take this factor into account, should he simply exclude it in reaching his decision on which life to save, then he could leave himself open, not only to the charge that he came to the wrong decision in saving the foetus and ought to have saved the mother, but also, *because* he enjoys control responsibility over the decision, to the ascription of responsiblity for her death in the guilt sense as well.[25] This explains why it is important to establish firmly in cases like this one where control responsibility over the operative decisions lies. In Professor Anscombe's example, where a doctor can save the many or the few, the operative decision on the fate of the many is in the doctor's hands: the many would not have perished if he had decided differently. Control responsibility is firmly established, and because this can be a ground for the ascription of guilt responsibility, our investigation into those considerations the doctor included and excluded in deciding to save the few becomes vitally important. What turns upon establishing control responsibility, then, is not simply (a) that talk of the mother's death as 'unavoidable' and talk of her being 'permitted to die' are not *per se* defences to responsibility for the outcome in her case, and (b) that the doctor's 'permitting' the mother to die does not remove him as a causal factor in effecting her death, but also (c) that the possibility exists, as a result of establishing the doctor's control responsibility even in the case where the mother is 'permitted to die', of holding him guilty of the death in question. This conclusion would seem to accord well with the conventional wisdom that what a person is prepared to permit, allow, or see happen, is as much a part of his moral make-up as what he does.

Bringing Aid and Avoiding Injury

In the previous section, the line taken on the craniotomy case did not revolve around the distinction between direct and oblique intention. This distinction, I have suggested, is not an index of the doctor's goodness unless it can be correlated with some difference in his responsibility for the deaths in question, i.e., for the foetus's death, should he operate, and the mother's death, should he not; and I find no such difference. Because the doctor is responsible (in the sense outlined) whatever the outcome, the distinction between direct and oblique intention has little part to play in determining what we say in this case.

In her paper 'Abortion and double effect', Philippa Foot also turns away from the distinction between direct and oblique intention in her treatment of DDE.[26] Instead of emphasizing the notion of control responsibility, she discusses the craniotomy case in terms of a distinction between positive and negative duties,[27] which she characterizes broadly as the distinction between bringing aid and avoiding injury; and it is this distinction upon which her discussion of DDE turns. Presumably, we are to regard the doctor in the craniotomy case as confronted with a conflict of duties, between, on the one hand, the duty to bring aid by performing the craniotomy and, on the other, the duty to avoid injury by not performing the craniotomy; and it seems to be Mrs Foot's view that the duty to avoid injury, at least generally or in the broad run of cases, is more stringent than the duty to bring aid.[28] Apparently, then, she thinks the conflict is to be resolved in favour of not performing the craniotomy, the conclusion, of course, reached by adherents to DDE by a different route. The usefulness of the distinction between bringing aid and avoiding injury is, however, not to be confined to cases involving abortion. It also seems to be Mrs Foot's view that the distinction fits or is applicable to the usual run of cases in which DDE is employed: 'My conclusion is that the distinction between direct and oblique intention plays only a quite subsidiary role in determining what we say in these cases, while the distinction between avoiding injury and bringing aid is very important indeed.'[29] I doubt, however, that this distinction will bear the weight Mrs Foot puts upon it.

First, Mrs Foot is mistaken in thinking that the bringing aid/avoiding injury distinction is applicable to that range of cases to which DDE is applicable; indeed, it seems quite easy to generate cases to which DDE is applicable but which cannot easily, if at all, be framed in terms of bringing aid and avoiding injury. For example, a student in order to get his degree in literature must read an erotic text; he foresees that he will be aroused but neither directly intends nor wants to be aroused. DDE may be invoked to show that his reading the text is permissible. I do not see how to characterize this case in terms of bringing aid and avoiding injury, since to speak of reading as bringing aid and not reading as avoiding injury hardly makes sense; and, in any event, it is not clear what we are to make of 'bringing aid to oneself'. Again, suppose a woman of great beauty but modest reputation comes to our small village: she foresees that when she goes about the streets she will evoke feelings of lust in the villagers, but she neither directly intends nor desires that they should have those feelings. DDE will support the view that her walking through the streets is permissible; but is her walking through the streets bringing aid to the villagers? In a sense, of course, it is, viz., it may satisfy their lusts; but this is not the sort of thing I think Mrs Foot had in mind. Because the distinction between bringing aid and avoiding injury may fit abortion cases, we should be wary of going on to assume that it fits others as well.

Second, and more importantly, I think the bringing aid/avoiding injury distinction is unhelpful, even in the abortion cases. Let us suppose in the craniotomy case that the doctor is confronted with a conflict between positive and negative duties and that by performing the craniotomy he brings aid whereas by not operating he avoids injury: where have we got by this reformulation? Our concern has been with what the moral difference is, if any, between operating and not operating. If we are unsure of what this difference is, will we not be equally unsure what the moral difference between bringing aid and avoiding injury is, since these are but different ways of referring to operating and not operating? In other words, I think we shall not have gained anything by this reformulation, *unless* one of the two conflicting duties is always overriding. For if this is not the case, then in each instance the doctor will have to deliberate whether the duty to bring aid is more or less stringent than the duty to avoid injury; and I fail to see how he is any better off weighing these two duties than in weighing the merits of operating against those of not operating, especially in view of the fact that what he includes and excludes as factors morally relevant to deciding the more stringent of the two conflicting duties will be the same factors he includes and excludes as morally relevant in deciding between the merits of operating and not operating. On the other hand, if one of the conflicting duties, for example, avoiding injury, is always overriding, then the circumstances in which acts are contemplated and performed and the consequences in which they issue will once again be ignored or put aside. Thus, in the craniotomy case, is the duty to avoid injury (by not operating) overriding even when the doctor knows the foetus will die anyway? Even when he knows that the foetus will almost certainly suffer from serious malformation and malfunctioning of both internal and external organs? In these cases, I should have thought the more plausible course was to go the other way, to favour the duty to bring aid as overriding.[30]

My conclusion, then, is that the reformulation of the craniotomy case in terms of a conflict of duties between bringing aid and avoiding injury is unhelpful, that for it to be otherwise, we should have to assume − what is implausible − that one of the two duties is always overriding, and, therefore, that the notion of control responsibility is not rendered superfluous to the craniotomy case by the distinction between bringing aid and avoiding injury.

The Order of Causation between Effects

The discussion of DDE so far has been in terms of Condition Two for its successful employment. To conclude, I want briefly to consider Condition Four. It, too, encompasses an important aspect to DDE, though one all too frequently ignored.

Condition Four is that the evil effect of the act must not be a means of bringing about the good effect. Phrased in this way, it may be regarded as a reformulation of the traditional (Catholic) belief that moral evil may never be done that good may come. Two points require immediate attention. First, if the good effect comes through or as a result of the evil effect, then the evil effect as means is willed to achieve the good effect as end; in which case, the agent directly intends the evil effect, and his goodness is held thereby to be affected. Second, it can be misleading to characterize this fourth condition by saying that the good effect must 'come before' the evil effect, since what is important is *causal* and *not temporal* sequence. To repeat, the act and not the evil effect must be the cause of the good effect, which has sometimes been expressed by saying that the good effect must be produced 'directly' or 'immediately' by the act and not by the evil effect.[31] Both these points may be seen at work in the craniotomy case. The good effect, the saving of the mother, is not produced directly or immediately by the operation but by the evil effect, the killing of the foetus, and Condition Four for the successful employment of DDE is, therefore, violated. Since the evil effect is killing, and since this killing is directly intended as means to the end of saving the mother, the doctor who performs the craniotomy is said to be guilty of murder, and his goodness is held thereby to be affected.

In saying that the good effect must be produced directly or immediately by the act and not by the evil effect, it is assumed that the order of causation between the effects is morally significant. Specifically, should the order of causation flow from the act to the evil effect to the good effect, then Condition Four is violated and DDE cannot be employed to render permissible the act in question. Now to decide whether the order of causation is morally significant in the way described, we must decide whether the position of an effect, in particular, the evil effect, has any bearing upon the permissibility of the act in question. For I take it as obvious that the position of an effect in the causal series of act and consequences can have no bearing upon the goodness or badness of that effect. In the craniotomy case, for example, the goodness of saving the mother is not contingent upon the position of this effect in the causal order. Saving life is saving life: if the mother is saved, a life is saved, and that, *ceteris paribus*, we typically think of as a good thing, wherever it may fall in the causal series. Likewise, the badness of taking the life of the foetus is quite independent of the position of this effect in the causal series: a life is lost, and that, *ceteris paribus*, we typically think of as a bad thing, wherever it falls in the causal series of act and consequences.

But what about acts? Does the position of an effect, in particular, the evil effect, have any bearing upon the permissibility of the act in question? I incline to the view that it does not, that where the evil effect falls — indeed, where any of the effects of an act fall — in the causal series is of no significance whatever to the permissibility of acts. A number of cases may be cited to support this view; the ones I have chosen all exhibit the order of causation of the type to which adherents to DDE object, namely, where causation flows from the act to the evil effect to the good effect.

First, in a state comparable to Nazi Germany, suppose I am arrested on completely fabricated charges, and during the course of my trial am asked to name the leader of those members of the University I know to be soft on democracy. I know that a particular minion in the Ministry of Interior is the individual who in practice though not in title is directing operations in universities aimed at stamping out democratic ideas, that this minion has informers within university groups, and that other members of the Government know him to have these informers. At my trial, then, in response to the demand to name the leader of the democratic group, I decide to perjure myself, not by making up some fictitious name or through stretching credulity by naming some high official in the Government, but rather by naming this minion in the Ministry of Interior, in the knowledge that his known contacts with university people will incriminate him and in the hope that he will be discredited. My ploy works: discredited, the minion commits suicide and so ceases to persecute my friends. The good effect, that my friends are no longer persecuted, comes through the evil effect, the minion's suicide, which in turn is a bad effect of my act of perjury. So far as the permissibility of my act of perjury is concerned, I think that, to anyone who accepts that a rule (or duty or whatever) proscribing perjury has exceptions, whether the cessation of the persecution of the University democrats comes before or after the minion's suicide in the causal order is of no significance. For if they had ceased to be persecuted without his suicide but because, under a cloud of suspicion as the result of my perjury, he had had to tread more lightly, my act of perjury would not suddenly have altered and become permissible.

Of course, the Catholic defender of DDE will reply that perjury is a kind of act that he thinks intrinsically wrong, so that the question of whether a particular act of perjury is permissible never arises. Here, Condition One for the successful employment of DDE, that the act to be performed must not be intrinsically wrong, is used to try to block a counter-example to Condition Four. This is why the case is addressed to anyone who thinks that there are no absolute proscriptions or that perjury is not among such proscriptions.

Second, consider a variation on the case of Jan Palach (the Czechoslovakian student who burned himself to death as a protest against the invasion of his country by Soviet forces), or the Buddhist priests of South Vietnam: a foreign army has invaded one's homeland and is proceeding to stifle most freedoms. An individual decides to protest against this loss of freedoms and in a powerful way, in the hope of rallying the people either to throw out the invaders or to keep the heritage of their freedoms firmly before their minds and so make them intractable and rebellious to government. Suppose, then, our individual sets himself alight: his act of protest has the evil effect of his death or suicide and, through the evil effect, the good effect of rallying the people to defend their freedoms. Where his suicide occurs in the causal order seems irrelevant to the permissibility of this individual's act of protest. To anyone who thinks that a rule (or duty or whatever) proscribing suicide has exceptions, the place of suicide in the causal order seems irrelevant to its permissibility.

It may be thought, however, that perjury and suicide are so wrong that the possibility of a particular act of perjury or suicide being permissible simply cannot arise; so let us take as a final example another case of an act that Catholic adherents to DDE regard as intrinsically wrong but which most other people do not, an act, these people would think, which is far less seious or important than perjury or suicide.

Suppose a prisoner has been released into the care of a social worker, who knows that the man has gone to prison three times for violent sexual assaults on women. The social worker begins to realize that the sexual tensions that precede the onset of the man's violent sexual passions have begun, and so to realize that something must be done quickly to prevent further women from being attacked. He decides (the use of drugs to lessen sexual desire has not yet been discovered) to give the man pornographic literature, in the hope that the man will masturbate and so perhaps dissipate his sexual energy. The ploy works. In this case, the act of giving the man pornographic literature has the evil effect of inducing masturbation, through which comes the good effect of preventing further sexual assaults. To the permissibility of giving the man such literature, the place of masturbation in the causal order appears totally irrelevant. Condition One will be invoked, for to Catholics masturbation is intrinsically wrong (and so on a par with murder and perjury), and it is the means in this case to achieving the good effect; but to anyone who thinks that masturbation is not intrinsically wrong or that a rule (or duty or whatever) proscribing masturbation has exceptions, the place of masturbation in the causal order will have no moral significance to the permissibility of the act.

The supposition, then, that the place of the evil effect in the causal order bears upon the permissibility of the act in question is doubtful. What does seem important to the permissibility of acts, as in our examples, is that they *have* this or that consequence, be that consequence good or evil, temporally and/or causally near or remote. But this is likely to represent far too much of a concession to suit adherents to DDE, since it appears to make consequences either the arbiter or the partial arbiter of the permissibility of acts.

Notes

1   See Thomas Nagel, 'The limits of objectivity', in S. McMurrin, *The Tanner Lectures on Human Value, 1980* (Cambridge, Cambridge University Press, 1980), p. 129 f.

2   H. L. A. Hart characterizes the distinction thus: an oblique intention refers to the 'mere foresight of consequences', whereas in the case of direct intention 'the consequences must have been contemplated by the accused not merely as a foreseen outcome but as an end which he set out to achieve or as a means to an end, or constituted at least part of his reason for doing that he did' ('Intention and punishment', *The Oxford Review*, no. 4, Hilary Term, 1967, pp. 10–11). See also J. Glover, *Causing Deaths and Saving Lives*, pp. 86–91.

3   See, e.g., Jonathan Bennett, 'Whatever the consequences', *Analysis*, vol. 26, 1966, pp. 83–102.

4   Hart, 'Intention and punishment', p. 13.

5   Ibid., pp. 13–14.

6   One might, of course, argue that there was such a thing as moral murder, and that not all cases of moral murder were cases of legal murder. One could then argue that a distinction between intention and foresight was germane to moral murder, even if not to legal murder. In this way, even if both of our doctors were guilty of legal murder, one would not be guilty of moral murder, and a difference in their goodness would thereby be established. What counts as moral murder, what the necessary and sufficient conditions are for an act to amount to moral murder, I shall not go into.

7   Glanville Williams, *The Sanctity of Life and the Criminal Law*, London, Faber & Faber, 1958.

8   Ibid., p. 286.

9   For an attempt by a defender of DDE to come to grips with this problem, see J. Ford, SJ, 'The morality of obliteration bombing', *Theological Studies*, vol. 5, 1944, 261–309.

10   There is also point to the remark, of course, that one ought to have foreseen the likelihood of certain consequences coming to pass.

11   *Director of Public Prosecutions v. Smith* (1961) AC 290. Driving a car containing stolen property, Smith was told to pull over by a policeman, whereupon Smith accelerated and drove away, with the policeman clinging to the car. The car hit three others, after which the policeman fell off, directly in front of a fourth, and received fatal injuries. In essence, three things were at issue in the Smith case: (a) the maxim that a man intends the natural and probable consequences of his acts, (b) the maxim (law) that if a man intentionally inflicts grievous bodily harm, then if death results, he is guilty of murder, and (c) objective and subjective tests of intention. It was agreed by all that Smith did not directly intend to kill the policeman, but as a result of the objective test of intention, the jury (in the court of first instance) was instructed that it could reasonably consider Smith

to have *had* this intention, since a reasonable man would in the circumstances have foreseen the likelihood of grievous bodily harm befalling the policeman. (This anomaly brought out another peculiar aspect to the case: while everyone agreed that Smith did not directly intend to kill the policeman, they were also agreed that Smith *did* intend to shake the policeman from the car, and drove in such a way as to bring this about; and if the maxim that one is guilty of murder if the intentional infliction of grievous bodily harm results in death is applied, then Smith is guilty of murder — in spite of the fact that he did not intend to kill the policeman.) The Law Commission (*Imputed Criminal Intent, D.P.P. v. Smith*, London, Her Majesty's Stationery Office, 1967) has now come out in favour, not of an objective test of intention, i.e., one which raises the question of whether a reasonable man in the circumstances would or would not have foreseen consequence X as a consequence of his act, but of a subjective test, which concerns itself with the actual state of mind of the accused, not with any hypothetical state of mind of any hypothetical individual.

12   A. Kenny, 'Intention and purpose', *Journal of Philosophy*, vol. LXIII, 1966, p. 647. An important issue arising out of Kenny's paper is whether the law *should* distinguish between foresight and intention, i.e., whether the legal use of 'intends' should be construed as entailing 'foresees and wants', a development Kenny favours.

13   '. . . Consequences which are foreseen but which the agent is indifferent to or rejects are not intended. Of course, it may well be correct to hold the agent responsible for these consequences, but that only means that we can be held responsible for more than we intend.' (Ibid., pp. 648–9.)

14   Cf. Holy Office Decree, 28 May 1884. This decree sets out clearly the ban on craniotomy. This ban is reiterated in the Holy Office Decree of 19 Aug 1889, and there widened to include any operation which involves a direct attack upon the life of the foetus.

15   Cf. G. Kelly, SJ, *Medico-Moral Problems* (London, Burns Oates Ltd, 1960), pp. 73, 75; E. Healy, SJ, *Medical Ethics* (Chicago, Loyola University Press, 1956), p. 196.

16   For example, Kelly, *Medico-Moral Problems*, p. 75.

17   See E. D'Arcy, *Human Acts* (Oxford, Clarendon Press, 1963), pp. 40–57. This section on avoiding control responsibility draws on D'Arcy's work.

18   See F. Siegler, 'Omissions', *Analysis*, vol. 28, 1968, 98–106.

19   The same reasoning will hold if it is the mother who is saved.

20   See P. J. FitzGerald, 'Acting and refraining', *Analysis*, vol. 27, 1967, pp. 133–9; J. Bennett, 'Acting and refraining', *Analysis*, vol. 28, 1968, pp. 30–1.

21   G. H. von Wright, to whose work this section on avoiding control responsibility is indebted, treats omissions as either identical with or a species of forbearances (*Norm and Action*, London, Routledge & Kegan Paul, 1963), pp. 45–54). If, and in so far as, to forbear doing X is identical with a species of refraining from doing X, there would seem to be a difference not only between omitting and refraining but also between omitting and forbearing.

22   A case might be devised in which the doctor's duty did indicate which life he was to save, e.g., a case in which he had the choice between saving *his* patient or another doctor's and could not save both.

23   *The Oxford Review*, Trinity Term, no. 5, 1967, pp. 16–17.

24   If a doctor treats individual life as valuable, and if he thinks — what he is taught — that no individual life is beneath his craft, then in a case where he can choose between saving five or fifty persons, number will make a difference *to him*. Since he regards each life as valuable, the saving of fifty valuable lives is preferable *to him* to the saving of five. We must not overlook the effects of the doctor's training and of what he has been taught on his decision between the five or the fifty. Of course, I do not wish to imply that what is his duty depends upon what he has been taught, only that what he has been taught will bear upon how he interprets his duty in particular cases.

25   Obviously, all sorts of cases can be envisaged, where what the doctor takes into account horrifies us; but in these as in all cases we rely upon the doctor's good judgement and, in the last analysis, upon his character. The point here is simply that knowledge of the fact that the foetus will almost certainly die anyway seems obviously relevant to the doctor's decision as to which life to save.

26 Philippa Foot, 'Abortion and double effect', *The Oxford Review*, Trinity Term, no. 5, 1967, pp. 5–15.

27 By a positive duty, Mrs Foot means such things as looking after the welfare of children or of aged parents, though she extends the notion to include acts of charity; by a negative duty, she means such things as refraining from killing and robbing (ibid., p. 12).

28 She notes of an example that 'one does not *in general* have the same duty to help people as to refrain from injuring them' (ibid., p. 12, italics in original). She goes on: 'it is interesting that, even where the strictest duty of positive aid exists, this still does not weigh as if a negative duty were involved' (ibid., p. 12).

29 Ibid., p. 13.

30 It is not clear to me in these sorts of cases that there is not a point beyond which any duty to avoid injury is extinguished.

31 See, for example, A. Fagothy, *Right and Reason* (St Louis, C. V. Mosby Co., 1959), p. 154; S. Windass, 'Double think and double effect', *Blackfriars*, vol. 44, 1963, p. 257; W. Conway, 'The act of two effects', *Irish Theological Quarterly*, vol. XVIII, 1951.

14

Value in Nature: On the Alleged Possibility of an Environmental Ethic

To speak of the value of human and animal life, but to stop short of speaking of value in nature or non-sentient creation is, increasingly, to court objection. A human-centred or a human- and animal-centred ethic is held to be an impoverished ethic, one with an impoverished notion of the moral community, and, as I noted in *Interests and Rights*,[1] criteria for admission to this community that bar non-sentient creation from membership have brought environmentalists and animal liberationists into conflict. In that earlier work, I must admit that I seriously underestimated the depth of this conflict, not least because I failed sufficiently to appreciate (a) just how extensive had been the influence among environmentalists of Aldo Leopold and his 'land ethic' and (b) the pressure this influence in turn created even among non-Leopoldian environmentalists and others to find in nature an inherent value that owed nothing to shared capacities with humans and/or animals. As well as the depth, I also underestimated the vehemence of the conflict,[2] largely because I did not then fully grasp just how profoundly mistaken Leopoldians would see the way animal liberationists and other environmentalists were going about the question of membership in the moral community.

What, then, about this larger issue of value in nature? Can there be a *genuine* environmental ethic?[3]

I am not persuaded that there can be. There are a number of reasons for this, but here I shall develop only one. This reason is not more fundamental than others I might present, but it does centrally feed an overall scepticism about the possibility of an environmental ethic, as well as more closely cohere with the questions of value discussed in this Part.

Moral Standing and Inherent Value

There is an argument one often encounters among environmentalists, by
which they hope to demonstrate the possibility of an environmental ethic.
It runs as follows:

    (1)   If a genuine environmental ethic is to be possible, it must be the
case that, in addition to humans and animals, at least some
natural objects have moral standing in their own right.

    (2)   If something is to have moral standing in its own right, it must
have value in its own right.

    (3)   At least some natural objects do have value in their own right
and, hence, possess moral standing.

    (4)   Therefore, a genuine environmental ethic is possible.

In this argument, possession of moral standing is treated as a necessary,
not a sufficient, condition for an environmental ethic, and possesion of
intrinsic or inherent value is treated as a necessary (and, possibly by some
writers, a sufficient) condition for moral standing.

Plainly, the difficulty comes over premiss 3; for some argument is
needed to show that (some) natural objects have value in their own right.
So far as *that* argument is concerned, some writers are cautious. Thus, in
his essay 'The nature and possibility of an environmental ethic', Tom
Regan observes that 'if I am right, the development . . . of an
environmental ethic requires that we postulate inherent value in nature';[4]
but when the questions of what makes something inherently valuable and
how we can know which things are inherently valuable are raised, Regan
observes: 'I now have very little to say about these questions, and what
little I do have to say concerns only how not to answer them.'[5] Fair
enough; but others have not been so cautious. Today, there is a plethora of
suggestions as to the value or values natural objects possess; and an
industry of sorts seems certain to turn out more. Indeed, I think the very
number of suggestions may, to some people, create suspicions that what is
in fact going on, to use Regan's term, is postulation of values on a rather
substantial scale, where the only restriction on what can be postulated is
the inventiveness of the author in thinking up further bases of postulation.
In any event, I do not wish to become enmeshed in this thicket of
suggestions, so I am simply going to assume that all parties appreciate
some of the obstacles that must be overcome in defending premiss 3.

Epistemologically, if an environmental ethic is to be usable, we must be
able to tell whether or not something has inherent value. A good many
people, myself included, would want to dissociate themselves from
Christopher Stone's suggestion in *Should Trees Having Standing?* of a kind
of universal consciousness inhabiting things;[6] but one can see the
advantage of this kind of cosmic suggestion. For one faces the demand of
differentiating among existent things those which have inherent value

from those which do not, and something like Stone's suggestion gets round this demand by conferring upon everything in the natural world an inherent value. Without some cosmic suggestion or other in this matter, the environmentalist's task becomes very much more complicated, since, presumably, what confers inherent value upon trees may well not be the same as what confers inherent value upon rock formations or bodies of water. In other words, if different kinds of things have different sources of inherent value, and if we could find out that different kinds of things have different sources of inherent value and what, precisely, those sources are, then a good deal of time and effort is going to be required of the environmentalist to put himself, epistemologically, into a position even to address the question of developing an environmental ethic.

One cosmic suggestion, formerly much more common in Eastern societies but increasingly found in our own, solves the epistemological problem in a rather novel way: it simply concedes inherent value to what exists because it exists. This seemingly eliminates the problem about telling whether something has inherent value. Such a cosmic suggestion may strike us as odd, since we do not think, e.g., hair, or, if this be objected to, volcanic ash and mud have inherent value. On the other hand, it is not difficult to see a problem that pushes many environmentalists in the direction of such a suggestion.

If you go into a forest, you see a good many trees that are not only not flourishing but also appear altogether mediocre specimens beside others. Do even these mediocre trees have inherent value? To the extent that flourishing and being a hardy specimen go with inherent value, they do not; but this seems to leave such trees liable to the axe, which we may presume, among environmentalists, is an unwanted outcome. In order to avoid this outcome, therefore, the link between flourishing/being a hardy specimen and inherent value is severed. Now even mediocre or miserable specimens can have inherent value (or some inherent value, if we think in terms of degrees); but that value cannot consist in flourishing or being good of their kind, so the search is on once again for the source of their inherent value. If even mediocre or miserable trees can have inherent value, and if we exclude something like Stone's suggestion as the source of this value, then sheer existence can seem a possible alternative source.

Thus, at least if one is an environmentalist, the real reason, which is not Regan's, for rejecting his earlier suggestion of identifying inherent goodness with being good of its kind,[7] is that it renders all specimens not good of their kind ripe for the axe. In order to protect them, therefore, the environmentalist must find a source for their inherent value which is compatible with their being mediocre or miserable of their kind, and sheer existence can seem a tempting answer.

The point may perhaps be made more clearly with regard to human children: there are many children who are not good of their kind and who, for physical and mental reasons, lead lives of very low quality; if you are nevertheless going to endow their lives with inherent value and so protect them, say, from the wielders of utilitarian arguments for killing, you have got to find a source of their inherent value that is compatible with their being poor specimens of their kind. If we reject religious analogues to Stone's suggestion, the fact that these children are actually in existence can seem to matter. After all, most non-Catholics would almost surely find contraception far less morally repugnant than infanticide.

I have alluded, so far, to three clusters of problems that must be faced in trying to draw up an environment ethic: these are (a) problems with actually assigning inherent value to natural objects, (b) problems with specifying precisely what that value is, and (c) problems with knowing that some natural object actually has that value.

Conflicts in Values

I want briefly to mention two further sets of problems that help to fill out the picture of inherent value which seems required by an environmental ethic.

Regan remarks in his essay that the 'case of the survival of caribou versus the economic development of wilderness' involves 'two incommensurable kinds of good, the inherent good of the caribou with the non-inherent good of economic benefits', and he observes that 'the inherent value of the caribou cannot be cashed in terms of human economic benefit'.[8] I think I understand the point Regan is making, but I am unclear on two matters.

First, how important to his case is the *survival* of something? For instance, suppose a developer wants to cut down part of a forest to put up a factory: there will still be trees in the world, even in his part of the world, if he cuts *these* down, and we might demand of the developer, in any event, that he plant some trees for those he cuts. In this case, does Regan mean that absolutely no scale of human economic benefit, however important and substantial, can justify cutting down part of the forest? This seems extreme, and, if applied rigorously, for instance, to trees, dirt, and land mass, might prevent us from building anything which brings economic gains to people.

Second, if a natural object's inherent good is incommensurable with a human's non-inherent good, is it nevertheless commensurable with a human's inherent good? If so, and if there is a conflict, which will triumph? So far as I can see, for there to be a genuine environmental ethic, there must be cases in which the natural object wins; otherwise, we shall have an essentially human-centred ethic, which says that, whenever our inherent good conflicts with the instrumental or inherent good of anything else, our good predominates. But, then, which are the cases in which the natural object wins? I do not believe these can be only trivial cases, in the sense that the cost to our inherent good in allowing that of the natural object to predominate is trivial; surely, if an environmental ethic is to amount to anything, the natural object will win in some cases where the cost to a human's inherent good is non-trivial? What are these cases like?

Consider a far-fetched example: you have only a bit of water left, and you can give it either to your plant or to your child. Do you really give it to your plant? Complicate the example: your child is going to die anyway and the water will keep him alive only a short while longer, whereas the plant, if given the water, will live on for some time. Would you really deprive your child of the water? It is unlikely. I admit the example is far-fetched; but precisely what do the cases look like in which we sacrifice or impair our own or some other human's inherent good for that of a natural object? I can imagine a sort of case where one might be tempted to say this, where, say, the alternative to giving the bit of water to the plant is to give it to a person who is, morally, utterly corrupt. I doubt myself that I could give the water to the plant but, in any event, the case is a very difficult one. For how exactly are a human's moral transgressions supposed to erode his inherent value? I am not very clear on what sort of answer an environmentalist will want to give to this question.[9]

Conflicts, then, both between inherent and non-inherent values and between inherent values, pose difficulties which must be overcome by the environmentalist. And it is important to bear in mind, in the course of trying to overcome them, that an ethic needs a theory of motivation as well as a theory of value: if the ethic tells us to give the bit of water to the plant instead of the child, one has to believe that good, conscientious environmentalists will decide to do just that, even if it runs strongly counter to their moral intuitions. One sees here a mirror image of the act-utilitarian's alleged albatross, that of producing harsh results which must be implemtned even at the cost of one's deepest moral intuitions.

Feelings and Attitudes

A fifth and final set of problems that must be overcome in the development of a theory of value with which to endow an environmental ethic concerns our feelings and attitudes. In common with others, Regan claims that the fitting attitude toward inherent value is admiring respect, but he also claims that we cannot discover what is inherently good simply by cataloguing those things which we, so to speak, admiringly respect. The reason is this: we can 'be as mistaken in our judgment that something is inherently good as we can be in our judgment about how old or how heavy it is. Our feeling one way or another does not settle matters one way or the other'.[10] This is serious, for it means that our feelings are no guide to inherent value: when you stand above and survey the Grand Canyon, you are not entitled to conclude, merely because of your wonder and amazement and awe, that you are standing above something of inherent value. Something more is required, though Regan has not as yet settled in his own mind what this something more is.

In fact, I myself think that the real difficulty with trying to use our feelings as indicators of inherent value, is simply that no environmentalist possesses an *a priori* guarantee that we shall not have the requisite feelings before things which he does not wish to concede inherent value. I return to this point later.

Mistakes about Inherent Value

Before continuing, I want to comment briefly, and in two quite distinct ways, upon the claim that we can be mistaken in our judgment that something is inherently good.

First, what sort of mistake is in question and where does it come? Regan does not go into the matter, but, in one clear sense, it is hard to see how one can be mistaken about inherent value. Let me use, I hope, a not misleading analogy: you maintain that the criterion of a good film is that it contain plenty of sex and violence, and you go to see the film *Caligula*, in which sex and violence exude from the screen. Now you might be mistaken that *Caligula* contains plenty of sex and violence, though I am at a loss, assuming you are not blind, to understand how this mistake might arise; but if you do see that it contains plenty of sex and violence, then your criterion of a good film guarantees that you are not mistaken in your judgment that *Caligula* is a good film. You simply cannot be mistaken about its goodness, if your criterion is satisfied.

May not your criterion, however, be mistaken? But how mistaken? I can see that one may find it objectionable, indeed, deeply reprehensible, but the only way I can see that it could be mistaken is if we had in the case of films what Regan has not given us in the case of the environment, namely, if we knew in what the goodness of films really consisted and so could see whether our criterion of goodness actually mirrored or captured that goodness. If we do not know in what the goodness of films really consists, we cannot be mistaken in our criterion of goodness; and, in the case of the environment, Regan concedes that he does not know in what the (inherent) goodness of natural objects really consists. So how could we be mistaken in our judgments of inherent goodness about these objects?

Of course, Regan may only be intending to point out that, if we ever did come to settle and agree upon in what the inherent goodness of natural objects consists, mistakes would then be possible; but here, also, I would urge caution. Consider morality: there are competing moral theories, with different accounts of the goodness of man and the rightness of his actions. Is there any reason *a priori* to think that there will not or cannot be competing environmental ethics, with different accounts of the inherent goodness of natural objects? If this occurs, is there really any reason to think that we will be able to forgo with environmental ethics what we have been forced to engage in with moral theories, namely, arguing about and trying to test their adequacy and trying to agree among ourselves upon a test of adequacy? I am not asserting that one ethic or other cannot be mistaken, only that, at least very often, we only see a theory mistaken because we embrace some other for which we think there are better arguments; the mistake involved, if that is the right way of putting it, is of an altogether different order and at an altogether different level from that involved, in Regan's example, in mistaking how heavy something is.

Second, I think another vantage point on the question of deciding about inherent value, and understanding mistakes with respect to it, is very instructive. Admittedly, the case I shall discuss is a special one, but I am not sure that destroys any point it might teach us with respect to deciding about inherent value. The case concerns art forgeries.

Imagine the following: there is a gallery wall in London from which has hung for some years a print labelled 'A Suffolk Landscape by Samuel Palmer'. It is one of the main works in the collection, and those critics who are devotees of inherent value agree that, if any work in the collection has inherent value, this one does. It is portrayed in the gallery's catalogue, without opposition, as one of the significant art objects of our culture. As the result of a series of enquiries about the provenance of another print, suppose it now gradually comes to light that someone named Thomas Keating has been turning out 'Palmers' over the years, and that the gallery has had all these years a Keating, not a Palmer, on its walls: if the print was originally considered to have had inherent value, has it now lost it? If so, what exactly has it lost that it previously had and which conferred inherent value on it? In his paper, Regan speaks of inherent value as a supervenient property,[11] supervenient in this case on other objective properties of the print; but what properties of the print have altered? That object which has been on the wall for these years still has the same lines, the same perspective, the same colours, etc.

As readers may know, I am describing a real case. Thomas Keating was a master forger of Palmer who, I believe, has been unable to recall all the Palmers he has forged; undoubtedly, therefore, there remain Palmers on walls somewhere which are not really Palmers but Keatings, all presently with inherent value, if you think art objects can have this sort of thing, but all quite possibly about to lose it.

What has changed overnight about the print on the wall of the gallery? A rather silly London dealer might say this: 'I am not saying anything mysterious happened to the print. A picture of it today would show the same thing as a picture of it yesterday, and the enjoyment people get from it may be the same as before. It's just that the print is no longer good in itself.' Another dealer, with a more theoretical bent, might bring out the absurdity of this response as follows: 'What my colleague is saying is that, if just this arrangement, just this grouping, just this feeling for his objects, had been executed by Palmer, the print would have had a good of its own; but because this same arrangement, grouping, feeling and the like were the product of Keating's efforts, it has no good of its own.'

I should mention three further matters, the first two of which I believe are still true in Keating's case. First, Keating was not merely a good but a very good forger; without his help, though Palmers everywhere have come under scrutiny, all his forgeries may not be detected. Second, it remains the case, I believe, that an inspection of the print does not in all cases settle the matter. The way Keatings have been uncovered − through checking the provenance of a work, correlating the subject matter with Palmer's diaries and letters, etc. − bespeaks Keating's skill. Third, Keating was not a copyist. That is, Keating's forgeries are not copies of works that already exist by the hand of Palmer; there are, in other words, not two pictures of the same scene. Keating's forgeries are, in the sense intended, original works, works in which he directly attacks the canvas.

As I have indicated, Regan speaks of inherent value as a supervenient property; but if we cannot tell the Keatings from the Palmers, and we think the latter have inherent value, then why do not the former have inherent value?

Finally, suppose the gallery's print turns out to be a Keating, and it is now said that we were mistaken in judging it to have inherent value: exactly what sort of mistake have we made? Does it really make sense to say that yesterday we construed just this X, just this Y to be properties on the basis of which we postulate inherent value, but that today, just this same X, just this same Y, does not constitute such a basis, where the only difference between the two cases is seemingly the identity of the person who, so to speak, put those properties there? How can authorship make this difference? Suppose it were to turn out that the plays of Shakespeare really were written by Francis Bacon: do you think their inherent value, if you think they have such, would be altered in the least? Everything is the same as before, except the identity of the author.

As I say, I am discussing a special case; but it does show a certain range of difficulty with decisions of inherent value, in circumstances where we want to puzzle over the nature of the mistake Regan insists we can always make with respect to them.

A Leopoldian Picture of Inherent Value

So far I have been alluding to problems (a) with actually assigning inherent value to natural objects, (b) with specifying precisely what that value is, (c) with knowing that some natural object actually has that value, (d) with conflicts between values of humans and of objects, and (e) with the inability of our feelings and attitudes to serve as guides to the inherently valuable. These problems must be overcome in developing a theory of value with which to equip an environmental ethic.

It may be thought, however, that many of these problems can, rather than be *overcome*, simply be *avoided*. I want to comment upon one means of trying to avoid them.

The expression 'biotic community' figures quite prominently in the writings of environmentalists influenced by Aldo Leopold, whose claim that 'a thing is right when it tends to preserve the integrity, stability, and beauty of the biotic community' and 'wrong when it tends otherwise'[12] is quoted by them with firm approval. I have strong doubts about this view of rightness, but this is not the place to air them.

I think someone in the tradition of Leopold will see the way Regan and others proceed over inherent value as deeply mistaken. The picture Regan conveys is this: if we can decide about the inherent value of the parts of nature, then we can build up a view as to the inherent value of the whole. If the trees, rocks, and rivers have inherent value, then the whole of which they are part will have inherent value. The picture Leopoldian environmentalists convey, however, is quite the opposite: it is the biotic community which is prior in value, and what value the parts have stems from the inherent value of the whole. It seems quite clear in this sort of picture that the value of the respective parts of the biotic community will mirror exactly their respective contributions to that community as a whole, in terms of its Leopoldian qualities of integrity, stability, and beauty. It seems to follow that not every natural kind must have the same value, since there is no *a priori* reason to think every natural kind needs must make exactly the same contribution to the flourishing of the biotic community; and this in turn leaves open the possibility that some species of animal life makes a greater contribution than some humans, and that some species of plant life a greater contribution than some species of animals.

The picture of determining the value of the whole and then working out the value of its parts is very much at odds with the picture of building up the value of the whole out of the value of its parts; and two environmentalists, each wedded to a different picture, are in deep disagreement over the whole approach to the construction of a value theory, with which to equip an environmental ethic.

I have a good deal of difficulty with the Leopoldian picture, not least in its stipulation of integrity, stability, and beauty as earmarks of the valuable; but I shall leave this matter aside here. What remains, even from the outset, are two, rather obvious but nevertheless important facts that make it difficult to grasp that picture.[13]

First, there is the sheer enormity of the task before us: we earlier had difficulty in approaching questions of inherent value even over a limited range of thing; but the task laid upon us now is to decide upon the inherent value of an entire biotic community, an entire spectrum of nature. Somehow, where we had difficulty in pronouncing over a small expanse, we must now pronounce over a (relatively) vast expanse. I do not myself really see any way to do this. Possibly some cosmic suggestions will help, but on the whole such suggestions are generally unargued for and suspect.

Second, the fact that this community undergoes change also defeats me.

Suppose there is a river and a delta area which it supports, and suppose, further, that human beings form no part of this picture: any change which occurs is not of human doing. Now imagine this relatively self-contained biotic system first at one point and then at a much later point, when change has occurred: how do we decide which state of the system is inherently valuable? How do we decide that one state of the system is better than another? I do not really see what answers can be given to these questions. It is, to some extent, like the natural process by which caterpillars turn into butterflies: if someone asked, 'Which state of the system is better, when it is a caterpillar or when it is a butterfly?', I do not see any sensible way to respond except, perhaps, to repeat that, in time, caterpillars turn into butterflies. Likewise, quite independently of our help, bodies of water stagnate and become impure, with the result that some things thrive and other things die: to be asked which is the better state of the system, when these things thrive and those things die, or when those things thrive and these things die, is to be asked something to which the only sensible response is perhaps to repeat what exactly happened to the river. Again, I am not suggesting that anything here renders the Leopoldian picture untenable; I am merely indicating why I find it difficult to get a grip on that particular picture of inherent value.

I suspect that those who hold this picture of inherent value will be forced to a cosmic suggestion of the form 'whatever is, is better', since something of the sort can seem to enable that picture to deal with change. But the problem then becomes one, obviously, of seeing any reason to think this suggestion true.

Artifacts and Nature

I have said that the real difficulty with trying to use our feelings and attitudes as indicators of inherent value is that we may well have these feelings and attitudes before things to which the theorist may not wish to concede inherent value. I put the matter this way — that the theorist may not wish to concede inherent value — in order to distinguish between, say, the symphonies of Beethoven and Rolls Royces. In their development of a value theory for an environmental ethic, some theorists may be perfectly prepared to see significant artifacts of our culture, such as Beethoven's symphonies, conceded inherent value, but very few moral theorists indeed have been prepared to see automobiles encompassed by their theory of inherent value. At best, if they have value at all, cars have instrumental value. Yet nothing in Regan's paper, and nothing I have said so far, precludes Rolls Royces having inherent value. Indeed, I should have thought that they fit Regan's demands perfectly. For consider: someone who all his life has been condemned to a Ford is, if he acquires a Rolls Royce, very likely, in view of its quality, to have an attitude of admiring respect towards it. He talks of it as environmentalists talk of natural objects: he speaks of his awe, amazement, and wonder at the car and its performance; he raves about its beauty; he tells his friends of its controlled fury, its power and force, its response to the touch, its sleekness; he marvels at the extraordinary harmony and functioning in its parts. And if Regan had not given up his earlier view of inherent value, our car owner would have said his car satisfied that view precisely; for if to have inherent value is for a thing to be good of its kind, then, most definitely, Rolls Royces have inherent value. If, however, they have inherent value, then we have *prima facie* no reason to exclude them from the theory of value being developed for an environmental ethic.

Those distressed to find that their ethic encompasses automobiles require criteria for including natural objects but not cars within the class of things which have inherent value. It is easy to see how some possible attempts to exclude cars — to deny that they are sentient or conscious or possessed of some psychological state or living, for instance — will be prejudicial in the extreme to (many or all) natural objects.

From Value Theory to Ethics

There is embedded in this discussion of the inherent value of artifacts and of attempts to exclude (most or all of) them from our theory of value a possibility which, if realized in a particular way, poses a stern test of an environmental ethic. It is a possibility to do with the relationship between a value theory and a theory of ethics.

The point I want to try to defend is that a theory of inherent value is *per se* unrelated to ethics, so that, even if an environmentalist were to overcome the sets of problems I discussed earlier, he would require something more in his value theory to make it of interest to ethics. My contention is that this something more is not available to us in the case of the environment. In other words, in trying to develop a value theory with which to equip an environmental ethic, we have focused so, in Regan's terms, on postulating inherent value in natural objects that we have overlooked that mere inherent value alone will not make natural objects of ethical concern.

This is a rather ambitious line to take, and I am not altogether certain at the moment that I can argue for it in the way I should like to. I can, however, sketch the views which lie behind it.

I should note at the outset that some readers may want to construe my remarks as accusing environmentalists of committing the Naturalistic Fallacy. Holmes Ralston, in his essay 'Is there an ecological ethic?',[14] has tried to defuse this charge, not altogether satisfactorily to my mind; but in any event I do not here take myself to be making it, certainly, at least, in any direct sense. I am after something a little different, namely, to show that the destruction of inherent value in the world may be of ecological concern but it is not *per se* of moral concern and that to make it of moral concern we should have to find in the environment precisely what, except on cosmic hypotheses, we cannot.

I am not now concerned either with the unsettled nature of environmentalists' value theory or with the postulation of inherent value in objects and the problems which arise as a result, but rather with an assumption upon which all this work in value theory is predicated, namely, if we can postulate inherent value in objects, we can thereby make them of moral concern. The way this is supposed to make them of moral concern is that, if we can say of, for instance, trees that they have inherent value, then we can say that it is *prima facie* wrong to destroy them. What can we make of this assumption?

To begin with, when Leopold speaks of a thing as right or wrong, depending upon whether or not it tends to promote the integrity, stability, and beauty of the biotic community, does he mean the terms 'right' and 'wrong' to be understood morally? If so, then his dictum generates an obvious puzzle. Imagine a tree, in which you postulate inherent value, and imagine further two possibilities with respect to it, one in which lightning destroys it, the other in which your setting fire to it destroys it: I do not see how morality has any purchase in the lightning case. Yet, inherent value has been destroyed; the world, so to speak, is a worse place. Suppose a volcanic eruption destroys an entire forest, an entire, relatively self-contained eco-system: morality has no purchase in that situation either. Yet, the integrity, stability, and beauty of that eco-system have been more or less completely destroyed. And consider a variation on a well-worn example: a racoon destroys the sole remaining member of a particular species of plant. Depending on who you read, an eco-disaster has occurred, but morality still has no purchase on the situation.

What I am pointing to by such examples are two things, that an eco-disaster is neither synonymous with nor a sign of a moral disaster and that, much more importantly, the diminution of inherent value in the world is not *per se* a moral phenomenon.

Consider the tree in which you postulate inherent value: whether the lightning or you destroys it, inherent value in the world is diminished; but whereas morality has no purchase in the lightning case, I certainly can see how it might in yours. But it has purchase, it enters the picture, not through anything further to do with the tree, but through something to do with you. The point is vital, for it makes the diminution of inherent value of moment, morally, neither because of sheer diminution in value nor because of anything else to do with the tree, but because of something to do with you. Thus, even if the tree posseses inherent value, by talking of the diminution in that value you are not as yet talking morals; and the only way you can talk morals is to shift from the lightning to you, your behaviour and, say, the reasons for it.

Again, whether the racoon or you destroys the sole remaining species of plant, an eco-disaster has occurred, but morality has purchase in the situation only if you are the cause. It has purchase, not because of anything further to do with that plant or species; morality has entered the picture because you, and not the racoon, have entered the picture.

The notion of undergoing harm will not effect the transition from value theory to ethics. For consider: if my proud owner of a Rolls Royce leaves his car out in the wet, it may rust, and if it does, its goodness is affected. It is, so to speak, not the car it was, and it makes perfectly good sense to speak of its having undergone harm or, indeed, of its having been harmed. Likewise, if lightning strikes the tree, it is harmed. But morality still has no purchase: the harm suffered by the car and the tree is not of moment, morally.

In the case of the tree, when lightning strikes it, 'being harmed' is just another way of referring to its diminution in value, nothing more. Imagine this case: in earlier years, farmers frequently exhausted the fertility of their soil because they did not know to rotate their crops; the soil, we may perfectly well say, was harmed. But this is only another way of referring to its diminution in fertility; it is not some way of turning that diminution into a moral phenomenon. If, however, you imagine a farmer whose ignorance in the matter was culpable, then that diminution in value, that harm, might become a moral phenomenon; but, then, it would be so through the farmer's culpability, not through anything further to do with the soil.

One way of trying to use the notion of harm to effect a transition from inherent value to ethics is to equate being harmed with being wronged. Notice at once, though, how awkward such an equation proves: if we agree in the lightning case that the tree has been harmed, then we seem condemned to saying it has been wronged by the lightning, in spite of our general reluctance to speak of lightning as capable of wronging anything. In short, what is wanted at best from the equation of being harmed with being wronged is that it apply only with respect to those agents capable of wronging.

A further question arises: if we can ask whether the agent can wrong, we can also ask whether the patient can be wronged. There is a well-known argument to show that natural objects cannot be wronged. I think I accept it, at least under my own interpretation of it; but I also think its proponents often obscure its real import.

The argument runs as follows: if I dump waste into Regent Street, who can be wronged? There seem only three points of view to consider, namely, my own, that of other people, and that of birds and, possibly, the cats and dogs which frequent Regent Street. It does no good to ask me to consider the situation from the point of view of the street, since the street has no point of view on the world. Without a point of view, however, the street cannot mind my dumping waste onto it. So, imagine a river utterly polluted with poisonous chemicals, debris of all sorts, and human excrement: we may presume that some or all people mind, and we may presume that fish and birds and perhaps other animals mind; but we may not presume that the river minds, since it has no point of view on the world. The linkage between minding and being wronged is then drawn in the argument: if something not merely does not but also cannot mind what is done to it, then it cannot be wronged. Notice this is not to say that the thing cannot be harmed; but, as we have seen, being harmed is not identical with being wronged.

Here, too, we can see the attraction of Stone's and other cosmic suggestions, such as panpsychism, postulating spirits in nature, or endowing natural objects with, as it were, personalities. Environmentalists who eschew cosmic suggestions, however, may find themselves unable to get as much of nature past the above argument as they would like. Consider this passage from an essay by Paul Taylor:

> Scientists who have made careful studies of particular plants and animals, whether in the field or in laboratories, have often acquired a knowledge of their subjects as identifiable individuals. Close observation over extended periods of time has led them to an appreciation of the unique 'personalities' of their subjects . . . As one becomes more and more familiar with the organism and its behavior, one becomes fully sensitive to the particular way it is living out its life cycle. One may become fascinated by it and even experience some involvement with its good and bad fortunes (that is, with the occurrence of environmental conditions favorable or unfavorable to the realization of its good). The organism comes to mean something to one as a unique, irreplaceable individual. The final culmination of the process is the achievement of a genuine understanding of its point of view and, with that understanding, an ability to 'take' that point of view.[15]

Taylor speaks of animals and plants together: even if we grant what he says (which I should be loath to do, either about all animals or about most plants), much of nature will not escape the above argument. For example, rivers such as the Colorado and the Mississippi and rock formations such as the Grand Canyon do not escape the argument. Taylor's point at best only concedes a point of view to particular sorts of living things, that is, those with particular sorts of life cycles. A (more elastic) cosmic assumption, of course, could perhaps get round this problem.

I think that proponents of this argument, about whether nature can be wronged, sometimes obscure its real import. This does not consist in its being a device for keeping an environmental ethic at bay, as it seems sometimes to be purveyed; its real import consists in the fact that, even if, say, a tree cannot be wronged, we can still quite consistently allow that it can be harmed.

Consider the example of the tree, which is destroyed by lightning or by you: you are an agent capable of wronging and remain such even if the tree is not a patient capable of being wronged; and even if the tree cannot be wronged it can be harmed. Imagine, then, to take only the most obvious case, some explanation of your setting fire to the tree which is utterly discreditable, and let us assume, in order to avoid certain other difficulties to do with clashes between moral theories on other grounds, we agree as to the discreditableness in question: in that case, we agree you act wrongly, you inflict harm on a discreditable basis. Notice, however, what this implies: you act wrongly in harming the tree even if the tree cannot be wronged. Volcanic ash can also harm the tree even if the tree cannot be wronged, but it, unlike you, cannot act wrongly. Thus, we are not debarred from moral assessment of our actions with respect to the environment, even if we concede that the environment cannot be wronged.

In sum, the environmentalist must effect a transition from value theory to ethics, and I have sketched some of the problems he faces in trying to do so. If he cannot effect the transition, he will have a value theory but not an ethic and, hence, not an environmental ethic. If I am right about the notions of harm and wrong, he will not successfully make the transition by their means; and if I am right in the earlier sections of this chapter, there are problems for his value theory quite independently of this matter of the transition. Yet, none of this involves me in denying either that the environment can be harmed or that we can act wrongly with respect to it.[16]

Notes

1 Frey, *Interests and Rights*, chs 3, 4, and 11.
2 For a taste of this vehemence, see J. Baird Callicott, 'Animal liberation: a triangular affair', *Environmental Ethics*, vol. 2, 1980, pp. 311–38.
3 By a 'genuine' environmental ethic, I refer, of course, to one that is not human and animal centred.
4 'The nature and possibility of an environmental ethic', in Tom Regan's *All That Dwell Therein* (Berkeley and Los Angeles, University of California Press, 1982), p. 203.
5 Ibid., p. 202.
6 C. Stone, *Should Trees Have Standing? Toward Legal Rights for Natural Objects* (New York, Avon Books, 1975), ch. 2. For a discussion of some of the issues surrounding the use of mental states to confer moral standing, see Frey, *Interests and Rights*, ch. 4 and pp. 163–7.
7 Regan no longer holds this view:'The nature and possibility of an environmental ethic', p. 202.
8 Ibid., p. 201.
9 In the eyes of a good many moral and political theorists, such erosion is not allowed to occur. Thus, Dworkin, in *Taking Rights Seriously*, does not envisage the fundamental right to equal concern and respect with which he endows us to be susceptible to erosion through moral transgressions; even a morally corrupt person retains this right.
10 Regan, 'The nature and possibility of an environmental ethic', p. 203.
11 Ibid., p. 199.
12 A. Leopold, 'The land ethic', *A Sand County Almanac* (New York, Oxford University Press, 1949), pp. 201–6.
13 My remarks on these issues have been anticipated by Edward Johnson, and I have redrawn them in the light of his comments. See his 'Animal liberation versus the land ethic', *Environmental Ethics*, vol. 3, 1981, pp. 265–73.

14 Holmes Ralston, 'Is there an ecological ethic?', *Ethics*, vol. 85, 1975, pp. 99 ff.
15 Paul Taylor, 'The ethics of respect for nature', *Environmental Ethics*, vol. 3, 1981, p. 210.
16 I am grateful to Peter Miller for providing me with copies of his papers 'Towards a value theory for an expanded naturalism in environmental ethics' and 'Do animals have interests worthy of our interest?', from which I have benefited.

Part V

15

Killing, Replaceability, and the Amelioration Argument

I turn now to the argument from pain and suffering, which, as I indicated in chapter 6, gains renewed life from the introduction of the distinction between positive and negative vegetarianism, but only at the cost of becoming a hostage to fortune on the issue of effectiveness, with all that that implies for the likelihood of its being the agent of widespread, dietary change.

It may seem odd that I should begin Part V with another chapter on killing, and, in fact, this chapter can be regarded as belonging to my assessment both of the argument from killing and of the argument from pain and suffering. To the extent that it is about the replaceability argument, it belongs to the discussion of killing; to the extent that it is about the amelioration argument, it belongs to the discussion of pain and suffering.

As we saw in chapter 11, Peter Singer, whose *Animal Liberation* did not specifically concern itself with killing animals, has turned to this issue in his paper 'Killing humans and killing animals';[1] and the substance of his remarks there are repeated in his book *Practical Ethics*.[2] I indicated in chapter 11 why Singer's position on killing was unlikely to appeal to non-(act-) utilitarians; here, I want to show that it will alienate all vegetarians except for the most devout (act-) utilitarian ones and that it plays into the hands of the meat-eater. On both counts, it is the replaceability argument that is the source of the problem.

Killing, Side-Effects, and Preferences

Singer has nowhere fully stated the act-utilitarian normative ethic he accepts; it is probably most on view in chapters 4 and 5 of *Practical Ethics*, in his discussion of killing. It is an unusual amalgam.

Most act-utilitarians today distinguish between classical and desire, or preference, utilitarianism, the former with a conception of utility formulated around pleasure/pain, the latter with a conception formulated around the satisfaction of desires or preferences; and most of them make the distinction in order to go on to reject the classical position, often, to free themselves from a mental state view of utility and value and so broaden the scope of their theory. Singer draws this distinction in chapter 1 of *Practical Ethics*; but though he goes on to embrace the preference theory, he does not do so at the expense of the classical position. In chapters 2 and 3, in his discussion of racial, sexual, and species equality, Singer wields a moral principle of the equal consideration of interests, grounded both in the univeralizability of moral judgments and, with respect to interests, in the capacity to feel pain (hence, being able to feel pain is a *sine qua non* condition for possessing interests); and his entire discussion of animal equality is founded upon, and in terms of, their ability to feel pain. In chapters 4 and 5, however, in the discussion of killing people and animals, the desire/preference model is very much to the fore in the case of people but without the pleasure/pain model having been discarded in the case of others.

Accordingly, Singer appears to be both a classical and preference utilitarian. Exactly what this mixture comes to is not clear, not least because it is unclear whether (and how) it is supposed to encompass more than cases of killing; but at least where killing is in question, Singer seems to favour a blend of theories. For he appears to think that such a blend enables him to offer a more convincing account of the wrongness of killing people than classical utilitarians can manage, armed, as they are, only with the argument from side-effects.

Where the rightness of killing some creature is at issue, Singer wears his classical or preference hat, depending upon whether the creature is a person, in his sense of the term. A person for him is a rational, self-conscious creature, where self-consciousness is explained in terms of envisaging oneself with a future and of having desires related to it, including the desire to go on living. So, where the creature is a person, in addition to the argument from side-effects which classical utilitarians deploy in order to make out a case against killing, there are all the person's future-related desires or preferences to be considered as well, including his very strong desire to go on living, all of which will be frustrated if he is killed. Unlike an argument from the effects of killing, therefore, preference utilitarianism provides a direct reason for not killing persons. If, however, the creature in question is not a person, then preference utilitarianism can get no grip on the situation, and Singer is left wearing his classical hat. Only the argument from side-effects applies, and this provides no direct reason for not killing that creature.

Diminution in Pleasure and Replaceability

At this point, however, a problem arises: in the case of killing, e.g., food animals, the presence of side-effects upon other animals or upon us (except for pets) is, as I noted in chapter 11,[3] very questionable; so not even the argument from side-effects seems applicable. Here, Singer claims, as so many other act-utilitarians have often been reduced to claiming even about killing people, where for whatever reason there are no discernible side-effects, that killing food animals reduces the amount of pleasure in the world. If directed at the meat-eater, however, this argument admits of a perfectly straightforward reply: though the killing of food animals does diminish the amount of pleasure (happiness, utility) in the world, this loss is made good by the creation of additional food animals, who lead lives roughly as pleasant as those of the animals consumed. Thus, just as the level of water in a glass falls but is made up again, if, after a drink, the glass is replenished, so, while replacement remains possible, the loss in the amount of pleasure in the world is constantly made good; accordingly, there can be nothing wrong in killig, say, chickens for food.

It is worth stressing that the replaceability argument, in addition to licensing killing animals for food and so meat-eating, also licenses the replacement of human beings. So long as we are careful to create additional human beings, whose lives are roughly commensurate in pleasure to the lives we take, the diminution in pleasure in the world which killing people produces is continually made good. In different terms, another act-utilitarian, Jonathan Glover, in his book *Causing Death and Saving Lives*, clearly envisages the replacement of human beings of a very low quality of life, in his discussion of infanticide.[4] But there is no reason in principle, so far as I can see, why it is germane to the replaceability argument itself what the quality of life or amount of pleasure at issue is, so long as a life of roughly equal quality or pleasure replaces it; and this means that the class of candidates for replacement is not confined to unfortunate children but includes even quite healthy adults.

Obviously, it is to block the replaceability of all of us that the appeal to self-consciousness, to envisaging oneself with a future and of having desires related to it, including the desire to go on living, is made. My very powerful desire to go on living will be thwarted, if I am killed, and the creation of another person neither undoes nor offsets this loss in satisfaction which my death produces. My desire for continued life is not satisfied through my death and your creation; hence, my death inflicts a loss that your creation cannot make good. Thus, if I am killed, even if there are no side-effects to killing me, there are still my future-related desires to be considered, including my very strong desire to go on living, all of which will be frustrated, with consequent loss in satisfaction. In this way, Singer tries to reach the conclusion that, while creatures which lack the desire to go on living may be replaceable, creatures which have this desire are not.

In fact, then, unless food animals can be squeezed into the category of self-conscious creatures, into the category of persons, the killing of animals for food is not ruled out and is not affected by the preference utilitarian hat in Singer's cupboard.

It seems, therefore, that the reasons Singer favours a mixture of preference and classical utilitarianism in cases of killing are, first, to provide a direct reason against killing persons and so improve on the argument from side-effects, second, to forestall the use of the replaceability argument over persons, since there is more than mere side-effects and diminution of pleasure in the world to consider in their cases, and third, possibly to forestall the use of the replaceability argument over some animals, while making certain the pains of all of them are taken into account.

I cannot see that Singer under two hats substantially improves on the classical utilitarian under one; at least, they have to face many of the same problems.

Replaceability of non-persons

Singer's position renders as candidates for replacement all creatures who are not persons (in his sense), and this pretty certainly includes, even if we leave aside animals, babies, the severely mentally-enfeebled, foetuses, and comatose human beings. Accordingly, only possible side-effects of killing stand in the way of replacement in these cases, and Singer is at once exposed, in order to neutralize side-effects, to all the well-canvassed moves the classical theorist has had to contend with (the act takes place in secret, the baby is unwanted, etc.).

Replaceability of persons

There is no suggestion that, because you are self-conscious and prefer to go on living, your preference is sacrosanct and its preponderance cannot be eroded. True, it is there to be considered, where on the classical account it probably would not have been; but this fact does not amount to much, if the preponderance of your preference can be eroded through others coming strongly to prefer your demise. For in this case, a Singer utilitarian, just as a classical one, will think it right to override your perference, in favour of the concatenation of stronger preferences, and, once again, he becomes exposed to all the moves and objections the classical theorist has had to face in this regard.

Again, if one had to choose whether to kill a baby in order to save five persons (in Singer's sense), then, given the baby is not a person, the choice is not even between one person and five. So what could possibly be entered on the baby's side of the balance, given it is replaceable, not merely to offset the weight of five persons future-related desires, including their desires to go on living, but also even to make the choice in one sense a difficult one? To reply that the baby counts for something is to say something that cannot easily be got onto the utilitarian balance: if it is to offset the weight of five persons desires, the baby must get onto the balance either through preference utilitarianism, which it cannot, or through classical utilitarianism, which it can, but which immediately renders it a candidate for replacement, provided possible side-effects are negligible or neutralized. In short, a Singer utilitarian, just as his classical forebears, would kill the baby (or anything else, including a person, in Singer's sense, if it were in the baby's position).

Singer's blend of preference and classical utilitarianism does not admit of incommensurable (types of) preferences or desires. However fervently you desire to go on living, that desire is not incommensurable with other desires, including the desires of other parties; its strength may give it preponderance at first, but in principle, because it is commensurable, it can be overridden. Whether it is or not is purely a contingent affair, and one's life or well-being or whatever is as much at the mercy of contingency with Singer as with the classical utilitarian. I cannot see that Singer can avoid this conclusion, and, so long as he cannot, I do not see how he can effectively still, or improve on the classical utilitarian in stilling, the disquiet so many people feel over act-utilitarian accounts of the wrongness of killing.

Self-consciousness and the future

Finally, Singer's view of self-consciousness, which he takes over from Michael Tooley,[5] strikes me as very odd. To explain self-consciousness in terms of future-related desires, including a desire to go on living, presents a problem. Imagine someone, to whom you are talking, who, for whatever reason, presently does not desire to go go living: he is nevertheless, I should have thought, self-conscious. Or imagine someone who, over time, slowly begins to shed a great many of his future-related desires: it seems most odd to think of him as progressively lapsing from self-consciousness. Or imagine someone, influenced by the Stoics, who has ideas about why, in order to avoid disappointment and discontent, it is necessary to shed desires and expectations with respect to the future: it seems odd to think of him, even as we discuss his ideas with him, progressively ceasing to be self-conscious.

It seems very much a contingent affair whether self-conscious creatures have future-related desires, *especially* some desire to go on living, though equally a contingent affair that the vast, vast preponderance of them do. Put differently, a self-conscious man *can* envisage himself with a future and with desires related to it; but why should we go on to say that he is self-conscious only if he does these things?[6]

Self-Consciousness and Food Animals

As we have seen, Singer's position on replaceability yields the result that, unless food animals are self-conscious, all are candidates for, and so susceptible to, replacement. Obviously, the meat-eater is here very near to sustaining his diet; for if some, many, most, or all food animals lack self-consciousness and so can be replaced, it will not be wrong to kill and eat them. In order to bar the door to the meat-eater, then, Singer must maintain that food animals are self-conscious.

This is not an enviable position to be in; for so few people have ever thought food animals self-conscious that, if this is part of what is involved in getting people to reject the replaceability of such animals, I think the chances of success must be very slim indeed.

Even so, when Singer suggests that, on his position, 'it obviously becomes important to try to decide which animals are self-conscious',[7] the implication is that he thinks some animals *are* self-conscious. He gives no instances in 'Killing humans and killing animals'; in *Practical Ethics*, however, he does. There, he opts for creatures with 'well-developed mental faculties'[8] as possible candidates, and, in this connection, he cites apes, whales, and dolphins, and, with greater reservation, monkeys, dogs, cats, pigs, seals, and bears.

I very much disagree with Singer on this issue of self-consciousness, as readers of chapters 6–8 of *Interests and Rights* will know; and though my arguments there are too technical for present circumstances, I think they place firm barriers in the way of concluding that any non-human animal is self-conscious. Accordingly, my position on replaceability would be that all non-human animals, *a fortiori* all food animals, lack self-consciousness and so, in terms of Singer's argument, are replaceable.

Happily, however, my rather technical arguments on the matter are not necessary here; for, in 'Killing humans and killing animals', Singer is prepared to concede that some important food animals — he appears to instance chickens[9] — are not self-conscious.[10]

This concession in turn draws attention to the obvious fact that, on Singer's list of candidates for self-consciousness (see above), only pigs, among major food animals in Anglo-American society, figure. Presumably, therefore, all major food animals in our society except pigs are not to be included in the class of self-conscious creatures, in which case, of course, in terms of Singer's own argument, they become candidates for replacement.

Plainly, then, on this issue of self-consciousness, Singer does not slam the door on the meat-eater but leaves it slightly ajar; with one foot in the door, however, I think the meat-eater can force it wide open. For consider: if chickens are replaceable, why not turkeys? (I might mention, to give readers some idea of figures, that, of poultry, we are talking about the annual processing, in the United States alone, of more than

5,000,000,000 birds; the figure world-wide greatly exceeds this.) Again, if babies are replaceable, why not lambs and the young of other, major food animals? And what about sheep and cattle, who only exceedingly rarely, if at all, figure on lists of candidates for self-consciousness, presumably because, confining ourselves to Singer's terms, they are not considered to have 'well-developed mental faculties'? All these cases, render Singer's position more difficult, and each time he fails to be convincing about the self-consciousness of a species of food animal, the meat-eater further consolidates his case. And this remains true, I want to emphasize, even if my position on food animals — that none is self-conscious — is wrong, and Singer's — that some are self-conscious — is right, so long as the animals held to escape replaceability include the concessions which Singer is, and, in my examples here, I think, must be prepared to make. With this the case, the meat-eater will be able to work the replaceability argument over a sufficiently large number of animals to preserve his diet more or less intact.

To most vegetarians, however, the actual range of the replaceability argument is, I suspect, neither here nor there. To them, it is not how numerous the kinds of food animals over which the meat-eater can work the argument but the fact that he can work it at all which is of central importance (and greatly to be regretted). And this he can do, even were it to be found that among important food animals only one or a few kinds lacked self-consciousness. True, if the replaceability argument worked only over animals of a few kinds, meat-eaters would be condemned to a monotonous diet, which in turn would doubtless lead to (more) vegetarian meals in the course of the week, by way of a change. But the important point, as most vegetarians will see it, is that the argument would still license killing and eating animals of those kinds.

Clearly, matters cannot be left as they stand: the point about self-consciousness cannot keep the meat-eater at bay, and the point about working the replaceability argument, even for a few kinds of food animals, is going to upset many vegetarians. Given his view that not all food animals are irreplaceable, therefore, how does Singer hope to prevent the meat-eater from cashing in on this fact? In 'Killing humans and killing animals', he has two observations to this end, neither of which I find convincing.[11]

Population Policy

Singer observes that, if it is good to create life, which the replaceability argument may be regarded either as assuming or as at least not denying, 'then presumably it is good for there to be as many people on our planet as it can hold'; and non-meat foods can support more people than meat foods.[12]

I find this observation puzzling. While it rests upon the assumption that people have a greater pleasure-potential than animals, which explains why it is the number of *people* and not animals which is to be radically increased, it seems to ignore that this potential is only actualized in particular time-states of the world. Dramatic increases in the amount of pleasure-potential through massive population growth do not inevitably mean an increase over time in the amount of actual pleasure in the world. This only appears to be the case because one leaves out of the picture every other consideration but increase in pleasure-potential, such as radically reduced housing, living space, health services, privacy, parks and gardens, heating and energy fuels, etc., and radically more numerous social and economic problems. If creating life is good, so too is providing people with adequate housing, health care, freedom from economic worries, etc; and the quality of any particular individual's life will almost certainly begin to diminish through massively increased demands on finite resources. In short, increases in the number of people to the outermost limits will almost inevitably mean ever greater reductions in the actual pleasure of individual persons, as they battle each other for limited resources; and it is by no means clear that there would not be more actual pleasure in the world by forgoing populating it to the limits it can hold.

The much more important point here, however, concerns the kind of population policy a meat-eater is to have. The world can sustain far fewer people than it can hold (Singer's term), and it can support at an enviable quality of life even fewer people than it can sustain. I see no reason why a meat-eater cannot advocate a population policy in which the optimal population growth and size is a function of the limits of resources, *including meat resources*. In this case, one of the indexes of quality of life will be degree of physical and economic access to meat. Thus, far from being good to populate the world to the limits it can hold or sustain, it is on this view wrong to populate the world in a way which outstrips our ability to preserve a quality of life that entails, among other things, a particlar level of access to and consumption of meat. I am not suggesting, of course, that this is the only factor relevant to a population policy, only that level of access to and consumption of meat can be (and, in many countries, is)[13] one of the indexes of quality of life. Such an index in turn can be used as a constraint upon what counts as an acceptable population growth,[14] and a constraint of this sort is much more likely to produce a contracting than an expanding population.

Miserable Lives

Singer's second observation is that, even if the replaceability argument works with animals leading pleasant lives, it does not license eating factory-farmed animals, since these animals 'are so crowded together and restricted in their movements that their lives seem to be more of a burden than a benefit to them'.[15]

This, plainly, is Singer's main hope for preventing the meat-eater from cashing in on the fact that, on the appeal to self-consciousness, nearly all major food animals become candidates for replacement. His point is that the replaceability argument works only over food animals which lead pleasant lives (he says explicitly in *Practical Ethics* that the argument 'cannot justify factory-farming, where animals do not have pleasant lives');[16] accordingly, even though not all food animals are irreplaceable, the meat-eater is barred from taking advantage of this fact.

Before I explain why this attempt to bar the replacement of factory-farmed animals probably fails, I want to draw attention to the effect of this attempt on other vegetarians.

The preservation of meat-eating

I think it obvious that all non-(act-) utilitarian vegetarians will be deeply unhappy with this way of trying to bar the replacement of factory-farmed animals, and for several reasons.

First, one plain implication of Singer's defence here against the meat-eater is that food animals which do lead pleasant lives may be eaten. He thinks this will at best license eating only non-intensively reared animals,[17] such as those one has raised oneself. Even so, we are talking about many millions of animals; vast numbers of people continue to raise their own food animals on farms that are by no means factory farms.

Second, Singer's defence commits him to the view that it is not wrong to kill and eat some animals, and the amount and availability of such meat depends upon the number and size of livestock farms which avoid the abuses of factory farms and which enable animals to lead pleasant lives. It follows that, as such farms increase in number, Singer's argument will license greater killing and eating of animals; and this is true, I want to stress, even if the number of factory farms does not diminish in the least.

Third, vegetarianism is not demanded of us by Singer, if we have access to animals bred and killed under the right conditions. Thus, far from Singer's argument providing him with an outright condemnation of the killing and eating of animals, it actually commits him to sanctioning the killing and eating of some animals. With respect to those animals, the alleged iniquity of eating meat has vanished entirely.

These implications of Singer's attempt to bar the replacement of factory-farmed animals will almost certainly be very worrying indeed to all but a tiny handful of (act-) utilitarian vegetarians. For they reveal that Singer's attempt, far from leaving the meat-eater without a leg to stand on, actually supports him in part of his diet.

The amelioration argument

To the above considerations, one more must be added. It is of the utmost importance, particularly to the assessment of the argument from pain and suffering. It consists in the meat-eater's use of an amelioration argument.

Singer has placed a practical obstacle in the way of meat-eaters having instant recourse to the replaceability argument in order to sustain their diet, namely, that present conditions on factory farms do not produce animals with pleasant lives. Now I think most vegetarians will find a mere practical obstacle in this regard exceedingly worrying; for purely practical difficulties all too frequently admit of purely practical solutions, without, among other things, any corresponding change in moral outlook. Thus, if conditions on factory farms were significantly improved, so that the lives of the animals became increasingly pleasant, the replaceability argument would become more likely to encompass them.

Thus, in the face of Singer's practical obstacle to working the replaceability argument over factory-farmed animals, the meat-eater will take steps to try to bring factory-farmed animals up to replaceable levels. If such practical steps required a reduction in the number of animals bred, then the price of the resultant meat might increase; but the economic cost of producing such meat is not for the moment germane. The point here is that, on Singer's argument, it would be perfectly permissible to eat this factory-farmed meat, whatever its price.

It is true that Singer writes as if he is convinced that factory-farmed animals cannot be brought up to replaceable levels of pleasure; but this is a practical affair (as we shall see later, some steps have already been taken in the direction of amelioration) and cannot be decided *a priori* one way or the other. And this very fact, that no decision is possible *a priori*, will, if anything, increase the unease of most vegetarians with Singer's position on killing and replaceability.

To sum up, we might characterize Singer's position thus: there is no objection to working the replaceability argument over some food animals and only a practical objection to working it over factory-farmed food animals. Such a position, therefore, either presents no objection whatever to killing and eating animals, or a practical one, which meat-eaters will take steps to meet. An objection of principle, to the effect, say, that taking animal life for food is simply impermissible, is precisely what someone committed to a replaceability argument cannot have.

Vegetarians unaware of the utilitarian underpinnings of *Animal Liberation* will probably be shocked, therefore, by Singer's position in 'Killing humans and killing animals' and in *Practical Ethics*. But it is all of a piece, in that it is his utilitarianism which explains why he appears far less the friend of animals over killing and replaceability than he does over pain and suffering.

Failure to Bar Replacement

As I have indicated, I think Singer's attempt to bar the replacement of factory-farmed animals probably fails; I now want to say why, and, in so doing, to make use of the amelioration argument.

What is supposed to prevent the meat-eater from working the replaceability argument over intensively farmed animals is that they do not lead pleasant lives, that 'their lives seem to be more of a burden than a benefit to them'.[18] In reply, there are several points to notice.

First, in terms of Singer's own position, it is not obvious that this type of defence is to the point. Suppose, for example, that we could quantify pleasure on some scale and found out that intensively farmed chickens registered from 3 to 5 out of 100 on this scale: while it might be true to say of lives with scores this low that they were 'more of a burden than a benefit', so long as these chickens were replaced with chickens whose lives were *at least equally as high* on the scale, it would not matter to the morality of killing chickens for food that their scores were so low. To ensure no loss of pleasure in the world, which is what the replaceability argument is about, all that matters is comparability of scores. So it is not obvious why Signer's remark about pleasant lives is to the point.

Second, I can see only two ways of making that remark to the point. One is to suppose, on our scale of pleasure, that intensively farmed animals score 0 (or, if possible, negative scores), so that there is, as it were, no pleasure to be replaced. The other is to suppose that there is some point on the scale − say, 10 − below which counts as having a miserable life and that miserable lives are not replaceable, on the ground that a strong likelihood of a miserable life is a reason for not bringing an animal into existence. But both alternatives, I think, play into the hands of the meat-eater. For, consider: if intensively farmed chickens score 0 (or below 10), and so are not replaceable, then all the meat-eater has to do is to raise the scores of chickens beyond 0 (or 10), and they become candidates for replacement. And all he has to do to raise scores is to ameliorate the conditions under which chickens are raised on factory farms. Again, the fact that fewer chickens might have to be bred, so that their flesh might become more expensive to consumers, is not here germane; for however many chickens are bred, so long as they can be brought to scores above 0 (or 10), they become candidates for replacement. Thus, all the meat-eater has to do to work the replaceability argument over intensively farmed animals is to improve their low scores, and intensive farming does not have to be abolished in order to do this.

Third, the replaceability argument, as we have seen, becomes entangled with a concern with pleasure-potential, and there is a consideration in this regard which is worth mentioning. It may well be the case − it seems likely − not only that animals do not have the same potentialities for pleasure as human beings but also that they differ in this regard even among themselves. This means that there may be considerable difficulty in deciding upon a scale of pleasure which does justice to the pleasure-potential of all species of animals indiscriminately. It also may mean, however, that there is a considerable discrepancy in the levels of pleasure in their lives which members of different species require, in order to be said to be leading lives which are more of a benefit than a burden to them. For example, it may be that dogs, cats, and the other animals on Singer's list of creatures with 'well-developed mental faculties' have a greater pleasure-potential than those food animals not on the list; but this in turn may mean that there is less to do to bring important food animals up to replaceable levels of pleasure, which will be looked at in terms of a species' pleasure-potential. Thus, it may require less to bring chickens, steers, and sheep to a level at which their lives are more a benefit than a burden, than it would dogs and cats.

Fourth, it may be objected that improving the lot of intensively farmed chickens will never bring them up to a replaceable level of pleasure; but I suspect this kind of *a priori* fiat is possible only because one selects some artifically very high level of pleasure as that required to be a candidate for replacement. Of course, nothing prevents one doing this (this is why I say of Singer's attempt to bar replacement that it 'probably' fails), since talk of 'leading pleasant lives' is sufficiently nebulous to admit of this sort of thing. But *why* must a commitment to the replaceability argument entail a commitment to some very high level of pleasure as necessary for replaceability? I can see nothing about the argument that demands such an entailment.

Fifth, so far as the intuition that probability of a miserable life is a reason for not bringing an animal into existence is concerned, the meat-eater has a two-fold reply. On the one hand, he will try to accommodate it by arguing that improved conditions on factory farms will raise the scores, say, of chickens to replaceable levels, so that their lives are no longer more of a burden than a benefit to them. In other words, amelioration of conditions removes the basis for the application of the above intuition to the case at hand. On the other hand, he will try to dispel a mistaken impression. Talk of intensively farmed animals leading lives which 'are a misery to them' inevitably brings to mind those cases of abuse, such as the treatment meted out to veal calves; and it is right that it should do this, since these abuses must be rectified. But it would be wrong to assume that all intensively and commercially farmed animals, of whatever species, lead lives whose score on our scale of pleasure, as it were, comes to 0. For example, steers and sheep are intensively farmed, and though I am aware of some practices in each case which may be painful to the animals in question, it is not true either that these animals lead lives which are, on balance, equally as miserable as those of veal calves or that the same methods of production are used on them as on veal calves.[19] Yet, it may be claimed, even if they are not as miserable as veal calves, they still lead miserable lives. But what is the evidence for this? The fact that steers, sheep, hogs, and, for that matter, dairy cows, all suffer at points in their lives does not show that their lives are, on balance, more a burden than a benefit to them, any more than it shows this in the case of human beings. From what I know of present farming practices with respect to these important food animals, one will not be able to show that they lead lives which never manage to score above 0 on our scale of pleasure. Thus, even though some (species of) intensively farmed animals are profoundly abused, a state of affairs in need of correction, not all (species) are abused (a) to any extent or degree, (b) to the same extent and degree, or (c) to an extent and degree which would enable one to claim that, on balance, all (species) lead lives which 'are a misery to them'.

Sixth, in connection with replaceability and this intuition about miserable lives, it may be worth mentioning again the intuition to which I drew attention in chapter 11. For I think a great many people will find it odd that animals leading pleasant lives are candidates for replacement whereas animals leading miserable lives are not; so to speak, a contented animal, whose life is more a benefit than a burden to it, will appear to them to have more to lose than an animal whose life is more a burden than a benefit. Their natural inclination will be to say that, if any animals are replaceable, miserable ones are. What this enables us in turn to see is a very curious feature of Singer's position, namely, that if it is contented and not miserable animals who are replaceable, then the one sure way of making all important food animals *irreplaceable* is, on Singer's argument, to increase their misery. Not to do so is to leave them or some of them open to the application of the replaceability argument; to do so, on the other hand, is to make their lives more miserable.

Replaceability and Animal Generations

Finally, in conjunction with the requirement that animals lead pleasant lives, in order to work the replaceability argument, Singer remarks that it must be the case that a replacement animal 'would not have existed if the first animal had not been killed'.[20] One may take this to imply that intensively farmed animals could not be known to satisfy this demand, because intensive farming involves so many animals that the past of any individual one is lost from view.

Why must the past of animals in this sense be known, however, so long as the size of a farmer's livestock and poultry holdings is roughly constant? Modern farmers, as farmers of old, work under constraints of money, feed, housing, land availability, and so on, and their animal holdings either remain reasonably constant or diminish, without substantial loosenings in these constraints. (For many farmers, without government or organizational support grants and loans, their holdings would fall drastically, as the price of feed soars, available land diminishes, power and machine expenses increase, the cost of labour rises, and so on.) If, then, a farmer's holdings remained reasonably constant, he would be replacing animals sent to slaughter with animals which would otherwise not have been a part of his holdings at all. Certainly, he is not so foolish and incompetent as not to mesh his breeding and rearing with his slaughtering policies, so as to avoid ending up with vastly more hogs than he can feed, vastly more steers than he can graze, and so on. Accordingly, the important figure is the number of animals the modern farmer of whatever size can support within the operative constraints; for so long as his rearing policy makes up the loss in his holdings incurred through sending animals to slaughter, his holdings will contain animals which would otherwise not have existed except as replacements for slaughtered ones. This arguably suffices, I think, to work the replaceability argument.

I say 'arguably' suffices, because one can still insist that, in large-scale farming, the farmer cannot know that it is precisely animal B which would not have existed except for the slaughter of animal A. What he can know, however, is that animal B and its generation owe their existence to the slaughter of animal A and its generation, since operative constraints demand co-ordination of rearing and slaughtering policies; and this is all he need know, in order rightly to consider animals of B's generation replacements for those of A's generation.

I have tried to show in this chapter why non-(act-) utilitarian vegetarians will be seriously disturbed by the replaceability argument, and why and how that argument can be made to yield considerable ground to the meat-eater, more than enough, I think, to sustain his diet. As I have indicated, I suspect that what to many will be the sinister-looking replaceability argument, is Singer's cross to bear, the price to be paid for loyalty to his act-utilitarian convictions. In this sense, the argument is but further evidence of some of the difficulties act-utilitarians can have in making out a convincing answer to the question of why it is wrong to kill.

Notes

1 Peter Singer, 'Killing humans and killing animals', *Inquiry*, vol. 22, 1979, pp. 145–56.
2 Peter Singer, *Practical Ethics*, Cambridge, Cambridge University Press, 1979.
3 See ch. 11, note 2.
4 Jonathan Glover, *Causing Death and Saving Lives*, Middlesex, Penguin Books, 1975, pp. 158 ff.
5 See Tooley's 'Abortion and infanticide', *Philosophy and Public Affairs*, vol. 2, 1972, pp. 37–65.
6 Merely having the capacity to do these things is not enough, if one wishes to say of babies, who are not regarded as self-conscious, that, though they do not for the moment do these things, they have the capacity to do them.
7 Peter Singer, 'Killing humans and killing animals', p. 153.
8 Peter Singer, *Practical Ethics*, p. 103.
9 Peter Singer, 'Killing humans and killing animals', p. 153. I say that he 'appears' to instance chickens because, while he concedes that some important food animals are not self-conscious, all he says by way of illustration is that 'chickens could be an example' (p. 153).
10 As I remarked in chapter 12, in connection with questions about the value of life, chickens are mass-produced in their billions, rarely achieve any individuality in our eyes, are not noted for their behavioural or intellectual affinities to ourselves, are almost never considered to be self-conscious or persons, and, on the whole, lead us to think that, for most purposes, one is as good as another.
11 I do not consider these observations in their order of presentation.

12 Peter Singer, 'Killing humans and killing animals', p. 149.
13 I have in mind, for example, Eastern European countries such as Poland and Hungary, Latin American countries such as Argentina and Venezuela, and the Soviet Union.
14 Again, it would not be the only constraint.
15 Peter Singer, 'Killing humans and killing animals', p. 149.
16 Peter Singer, *Practical Ethics*, p. 105.
17 Ibid., p. 104.
18 Peter Singer, 'Killing humans and killing animals', p. 149.
19 To appreciate the point, think only of the differences in freedom of movement and (healthy) diet, so far as these animals and veal calves are concerned.
20 Peter Singer, 'Killing humans and killing animals', p. 153.

16

Pain, Amelioration, and a Choice of Tactics

If, in the hands of Singer and his argument from pain and suffering, vegetarianism is one way of giving voice to one's concern for the welfare of food animals, it is not the only way; if it becomes in his hands a tactic for combating the pains of these animals, it is not the only tactic. Why, then, choose or adopt vegetarianism? In the end, this is the crucial question; but before examining Singer's answers to it, I want first to elaborate on the two tactics before us.

Bases of the Argument from Pain and Suffering

A moral vegetarian who finds the source of the moral wrongness of eating meat in the pain and suffering which some intensive methods of farming inflict upon some food animals can, as we have seen, dispense with the arguments from moral rights and killing. This in turn means that he can allow certain things to be the case, yet still press ahead with his argument.

So far as moral rights are concerned, a Singer vegetarian can allow that animals do not possess a moral right to life, that they are not the subjects of moral rights, and that there are no specifically moral rights whatever. His argument nevertheless gets underway if animals can suffer.

So far as killing is concerned, a Singer vegetarian can allow that the wrongness of killing is correlated with the value of the life in question, that the life of the ordinary man is far more valuable than the life of the ordinary animal, and that the whole question of whether it is wrong to take animal life is irrelevant. This does not mean that he approves killing food animals, only that he thinks his case for vegetarianism can be made without getting into the many problems which surround talk of the value of life and without raising questions about the actual value we place upon the lives of different food animals. Thus, the fact that we place an exceedingly low value upon the lives of chickens, though important in the assessment of some cases for not eating them, is irrelevant here.

If the argument from pain and suffering does not require anything about moral rights and the value of animal life to be the case, then what does it require to be the case, in order to get underway? Only three things are necessary.

First, food animals can and do feel pain. I should myself prefer to say that they can have unpleasant sensations, but this is a nicety I should wish to introduce in another context for another purpose; here it may be dispensed with.[1] In fact, I doubt that there are many Cartesians left where animals are concerned. True, remarks occasionally made by this or that scientist seem to betoken a view not unlike that attributed to Descartes; but I suspect that what these scientists in fact believe is not that animals do not feel pain but, as was discussed in connection with vivisection in chapter 12, that the pain inflicted upon them can be justified by the appeal to benefit.[2]

Second, the wrongness of inflicting pain, unlike the wrongness of killing, is not correlated with the value of the life in question. Pain is pain, an evil, the infliction of which must be justified; and it cannot be justified merely by reference to the species which undergoes the pain, since pain is not a species-specific datum. It is as much an evil to one species as to another. Of course, human beings may suffer more and in different ways because of their additional, mostly mental capacities; but this in no way shows that animals do not suffer and cannot on occasion suffer acutely.[3]

Third, some intensive methods of farming used on some kinds of food animals often involve the infliction of considerable pain. In the case of veal calves, for example, the pain and suffering involved appears substantial.

Thus, animals can and do feel pain, which is an evil; and since some intensive methods of rearing them for human consumption inflict a good deal of pain upon them, such methods are to be morally condemned.

The Argument and the Concerned Individual

If the pain food animals undergo and the period over which they undergo it were insignificant, then I suspect many people would not be unduly worried by factory farming, with the result that they might well either see no need for the argument from pain and suffering, or see it as a manifestation of an undue sensitivity. Either way, the chances of the argument serving as the vehicle of widespread dietary change would recede.

The above, however, is certainly not the picture of factory farming which Singer paints, which, whether one considers *Animal Liberation*, *Practical Ethics*, or (with James Mason) *Animal Factories*,[4] is in the blackest terms. As we saw in the last chapter, he thinks, and would have us think, of factory farming in terms of animals who 'are so crowded together and restricted in their movements that their lives seem to be more of a burden than a benefit to them'[5] and who 'do not have pleasant lives'.[6] His view is that these animals lead miserable lives, that, in short, the pain inflicted upon them is substantial and its duration prolonged.

The argument itself points the direction in which the meat-eater will try to move: since what is held to be wrong with the particular farming practices objected to is that they are productive of pain, the meat-eater will, among other things, try to make improvements in and to find alternatives to these practices. It is by no means obvious that such improvements and alternatives are not to be had, so that the only remaining course is to abolish intensive farming. Nothing whatever in, say, *Animal Liberation* rules out such improvements and alternatives; thus, any conclusion to the effect that the only way to mitigate, reduce, or eliminate the pains of food animals is to abolish factory farming is simply not licensed by that book.

If we do think of factory farming as Singer would have us, then, as we saw in chapters 6 and 15, vast numbers of intensively farmed food animals, such as cattle, cows, sheep, a great many hogs, some pigs, elude the argument from pain and suffering. For vast numbers of commercially-farmed animals lead lives which are not, on balance, miserable, nor are those methods of rearing which are held to produce misery in the cases of laying hens and veal calves used on all food animals. Singer concedes the point: he remarks that, for example, 'as long as sheep and cattle graze outdoors . . . arguments directed against factory farming do not imply that we should cease eating meat altogether.'[7]

Two things follow. First, even if the argument from pain and suffering were successful, it would demand only that we abstain from the flesh of those creatures leading miserable lives; and even if we did so, large-scale, technology-intensive, commercial farming would by no means disappear, since there are numerous food animals so farmed who do not lead miserable lives.

Second, the amelioration argument becomes applicable. The more animals that can be brought to lead pleasant lives, the more animals that escape the argument from pain and suffering and so may be eaten. A concerned individual, therefore, can perfectly consistently strive, not for the abolition of factory farming, but for improvements and alternative methods on factory farms, in order that the animals no longer lead, on balance, miserable lives. With this the case, factory farming could continue, consistently with the application of the argument to it.

In short, if the argument demands that we abstain from the flesh of creatures whose lives are a burden to them, then a perfectly consistent response from the concerned individual, besides pointing to the huge numbers of commercially-farmed as well as traditionally-farmed animals which escape the argument, is to do his best to reduce the misery incurred on factory farms. Thus, when Singer has us think of factory farms in terms of the quality of life being lived upon them (and remarks such as 'our society tolerates methods of meat production that confine sentient animals in cramped, unsuitable conditions for the entire duration of their lives'[8] leave little doubt that, at least for those animals covered by his argument, he regards the quality of their lives as very low), the task of the concerned individual is to improve the quality of the lives being lived on those farms. It is just not true, however, that the only way to do this, the only tactic available, is to abolish large-scale, commercial farming.

One can always insist, of course, that the quality of life of the commercially farmed animals in question (remember, vast numbers of such animals are not in question) will never rise high enough; but this sort of issue cannot be decided *a priori*. Precisely how high a quality of life must be reached before animals may be said to be leading pleasant lives is, as we have seen, a contentious and complex issue; but we may at least use as a benchmark the situation at present. As improvements in and alternatives to the particular farming practices objected to arise, we can reasonably regard the pain associated with these practices as diminishing, if the improvements and alternatives are of the sort our concerned individual is seeking.

We have here, then, two parties, the Singer vegetarian and the concerned individual, both of whom are concerned to reduce the pain and suffering involved in factory farming. The Singer vegetarian's way is to adopt vegetarianism; the concerned individual's way is, among other things, to seek improvements in and alternatives to those practices held to be the source of the pain and suffering in question.

Suffering: Miserable Life and Single Experience Views

Singer's remarks on suffering in farming are not always of the sort depicted in the previous section. In both *Animal Liberation* and *Practical Ethics*, he occasionally writes as if any amount of suffering whatever sufficed, in terms of his argument, to condemn some method of rearing animals for food. For instance, he remarks that his 'case against using animals for food is at its strongest when animals are made to lead miserable lives . . .',[9] with the implication that his argument applies even when food animals suffer on a few or even a single occasion. Again, of traditional livestock farming, he maintains that it involves suffering, even if one has on occasion to go to such things as the breaking up of herds in order to find it, and he remarks in *Animal Liberation*, of these and other aspects of traditional farming, that 'it is difficult to imagine how animals could be raised for food without suffering in any of these ways.'[10]

Passages such as these suggest that Singer believes his argument condemns any method of rearing animals for food which causes them any suffering, however transient, however low-level, indeed, which causes them even a single, isolated painful experience. When he speaks of the permissibility of eating only 'the flesh of animals reared and killed without suffering',[11] therefore, he might be taken to mean by 'without suffering', not suffering of an amount and duration short of that required to make a life miserable, but any suffering whatever, so that the permissibility claim extends only to animals who have not had a single painful experience, a single trace of suffering in being bred and killed for food. But if this is what he means, how can he allow, as we have seen that he does, that sheep and cattle (these he cites as examples only, [12] so there may well, even in his eyes, be others) escape his argument? For it seems extremely unlikely that sheep and cattle are reared for food without a single painful experience. So either he is inconsistent to allow these exceptions, because he is operating with something like the single experience view of suffering, or he consistently allows them, but only because he is operating with something like the miserable life view of suffering.

These two views of suffering plainly do not come to the same thing. In order to lead, on balance, a pleasant life, pain, even significant pain, need not be absent from that life; indeed, it can recur on a daily basis, provided it falls short of that quantity over that duration required to tip the balance in the direction of a miserable life. Certainly, isolated, painful experiences or, for that matter, painful interludes, cannot, without further argument, be said to produce a miserable life.

Singer's whole position is affected by this ambiguity, if not inconsistency, over suffering. For instance, one of the most important points he wants to make concerns the possibility of rearing animals painlessly:

> Whatever the theoretical possibilities of rearing animals without suffering may be, the fact is that the meat available from butchers and supermarkets comes from animals who did suffer while being reared. So we must ask ourselves, not: is it *ever* right to eat meat? but: is it right to eat *this* meat?[13]

In *Practical Ethics*, he says that the question is not 'whether animal flesh *could* be produced without suffering, but whether the flesh we are considering buying *was* produced without suffering.'[14] But he has already allowed that vegetarianism is not demanded of us with respect to sheep and beef cattle, precisely because they do not lead miserable lives; so how can he say of all meats that it is a fact 'that the meat available from butchers and supermarkets comes from animals who did suffer while being reared'? Again, there is a question of consistency. The problem can be favourably resolved, of course, if Singer shifts from the miserable life view of suffering to something like the single experience view; for he can be reasonably certain that the meat on display in supermarkets, including that from sheep and beef cattle, has come from animals who have had at least one painful experience, in being reared for food.

Without this shift, Singer has difficulty in discouraging you from buying the meat in question. If you are standing before the meats from sheep and beef cattle in your supermarket, if you have read Singer's book, and if you put to yourself the question of whether the meats before you have come from animals who have suffered in the course of being reared for food, then, on the miserable life view of suffering, you may cite Singer's own works to justify your purchase of the meats. You have every reason to believe that sheep and beef cattle do not lead miserable lives and so escape his argument; you have no reason whatever to believe, of course, that commercially- and traditionally-farmed food animals of any sort have not suffered at least once at human hands.

We have here, then, two views of suffering and, accordingly, two views on the argument from pain and suffering of what counts as a morally unacceptable method of rearing animals for food. On one, a method is unacceptable if it so affects an animal's quality of life as to make it miserable. This is why Singer so often stresses confinement in cramped conditions: this has the effect, which isolated painful experiences or interludes do not, of converting a life from a benefit to a burden. This view of suffering is compatible, however, with farm animals experiencing pain. On the second view, a method of rearing is unacceptable if it produces any pain or suffering whatever, whether or not the animal's general quality of life is affected thereby.

This division over unacceptable methods has several obvious implications here. First, to see one's task as reducing suffering in commercial farming is on one view of suffering, at least in many cases, not really to the point. Since the reduction of suffering is nevertheless compatible with the presence of suffering, only if the method of reduction eliminates all suffering in rearing may reduction, on something like the single experience view, really be to the point. On the miserable life view, however, any reduction in suffering is *prima facie* to the point, since that view is concerned with the quality of life of animals. That is, though it is tempting to think one method of rearing more acceptable than another if it involves considerably less suffering, this is only true on the miserable life view, at least if the method which causes less suffering causes any suffering; for reduction in suffering is very likely to affect animals' quality of life. This is true of any attempt to reduce suffering in farming, whether it succeeds partially or wholly, since, extraordinary circumstances aside, any decrease in suffering represents an increase or a contributory factor to an increase in quality of life.

Second, a meat-eater will not respond to both views of suffering in the same way; in the case of the miserable life view, his response will be much more varied. Broadly speaking, there are the methods of rearing themselves and the animals, and the meat-eater will, for example, seek ever gradual reduction in suffering through, for example, ever better improvements in and alternatives to (very) painful methods and the development of new pain-preventing and pain-killing drugs. He will seek development on these fronts simultaneously. In the case of something like the single experience view, however, since it is unlikely that any improvements in or alternatives to present methods would not involve even a single painful experience, a single trace of suffering, there may seem little point in seeking continuous evolution in rearing methods, beyond, say, those initial measures which substantially improve on the methods under attack. Accordingly, the meat-eater will be forced to rely primarily on pain-preventing and pain-killig drugs, an area in which he will seek continuous technological advances.

There is also the further possibility of genetic engineering to consider, to which both John Rodman[15] and Michael Martin[16] have drawn attention. So far as something like the single experience view is concerned, genetic engineering would have to take the form of the development of food animals which lacked the ability to feel pain. Precisely how feasible that is, I do not know; but given the incredible advances in genetic engineering during the past 30 years, it would be rash to dismiss the idea out of hand. On the miserable life view, however, nothing so dramatic is required; here, the development of animals who felt pain less intensively or who felt it only in some minimal sense or who felt it only above a certain threshold would, especially given evolution in rearing methods and pain-preventing and pain-killing drugs, suffice to ensure the animals did not have miserable lives.

Finally, though the single experience view may strike some readers as reflecting an undue sensitivity, I shall not pursue this claim; rather, I want to draw attention to a rather curious upshot of the view. If the only acceptable method of rearing animals for food is one free of even a single painful experience or trace of suffering, then it is hard to see why the same should not be said of pets. It is extremely unlikely, however, that any method of rearing and keeping pets could be entirely without pain and suffering; so if we must give up farming animals because there are no morally acceptable ways of doing so, then it would appear that we must give up rearing and keeping pets on the same ground. But if the only acceptable method of rearing animals, whether for food or companionship, is one free of all pain and suffering, then it is hard to see why the same should not be said of our own children. It is extremely unlikely, however, that any method of rearing children could be entirely without pain or suffering; so if we must give up farming animals because there are no morally acceptable methods of doing so, then it would appear that we must give up having children on the same ground.

On the other hand, if it is acceptable to rear children by painful methods, why is it unacceptable to rear food animals by painful methods? Nothing is gained by saying that the pain we inflict upon children is in order to benefit them (this, I think, is questionable anyway, a good portion of the time), whereas the pain we inflict upon food animals is in order to benefit ourselves, i.e., in order to eat them; for, so far, it has not been shown that it is wrong to benefit ourselves in this way, that the end of eating meat is immoral. Indeed, it was the infliction of pain that was to have shown this. Nor is anything gained by saying that, in the case of children, we at least seek, or, probably more accurately, ought to seek to rear them by methods as painless as we can devise, since the concerned individual I have been describing is quite prepared to consent to this in the case of animals. Nor will it do to say that the level of pain and suffering in food animals cannot be brought to a level commensurate with their leading pleasant lives; not only is one not entitled to legislate in this way on what is not a conceptual matter but it is also not at all obvious, if the concerned individual pursues evolution in rearing methods, drugs, and genetic engineering, that this claim is true.

It is tempting to say that the suffering of children is necessary whereas that of food animals is unnecessary, but it is not at all clear that this is the case. If there is no method of rearing children which is free of all suffering, and if there is no method of rearing animals for food or as pets which is free of all suffering, then the suffering in each case is necessary. If there were a way to rear children or to turn them into responsible, upright citizens without suffering, then it would be incumbent upon us to adopt it; and if there were a way of turning animals into food without suffering, it would be equally incumbent upon us to take it. Certainly, my concerned individual concurs in this; so, on this score, if the suffering in the one case is necessary, then so is it in the other. If we shift the terms of the argument to a different level, so that suffering is necessary *only if* it is inflicted in order for us to live, then the suffering in both cases is unnecessary. Just as I can live without meat, so I can live without children; they are as superfluous to my existence, to my carrying on living, as cars, houses, rose bushes, and pets. In this sense, then, if the only way to avoid unnecessary suffering in pets and food animals is to give them up entirely and cease breeding them, then it seems that we should give up having children for the same reason. (I return to the issue of unnecessary suffering in chapter 19.)

Now I am not suggesting that one cannot draw any differences among these cases; that would be silly. On something like the single experience view of suffering, however, the criterion of acceptability in rearing methods is pitched so high that we appear barred from rearing any feeling creature, including our own children. Readers may well believe, therefore, that we must cast our sights lower. To do so, however, is to settle for a criterion of acceptability which permits some suffering. Precisely how much will be a matter of dispute; but a strong contender for the criterion, in both man and beast, will be the miserable life view. This in turn makes the varied course advocated by the concerned individual into an option on all fours with Singer's option of vegetarianism.

The Concerned Individual's Tactic as a Response to the Argument

The concerned individual's tactic is a direct response to Singer's argument: it addresses itself precisely to what the argument from pain and suffering objects to in factory farming. Indeed, it arises directly out of the terms of that argument. This fact enables us to appreciate several further points about the two tactics before us.

First, someone who took *Animal Liberation* and Singer's argument seriously might maintain that what Singer has shown is not that it is wrong to eat meat but that it is wrong to rear and kill animals by (very) painful methods; and this same reader might very well go on to conclude, not that we must all become vegetarians, but rather that we must (a) strive to improve conditions on factory farms, to eradicate some of the devices and practices upon them, and to replace these devices and practices with more humane ones, (b) divert resources into the develop-ment of new and relatively painless methods of breeding, feeding, and killing animals, of new pain-preventing and pain-killing drugs, of new types of tranquillizers and sedatives, etc., and (c) seek further appropriate breakthroughs in genetic engineering. After all, as we have seen, if we could be practically certain that the meat before us did not come from an animal bred and/or killed by (very) painful methods, and if we ate the meat, then Singer's argument would provide no ground for complaint against us. Accordingly, why not seek to obtain that practical certainty? The problem would then be how to go about this, and the concerned individual's tactic arises as an option.

Once we see that the concerned individual's tactic arises out of the terms of Singer's argument, we are in a position to appreciate that, even if we take that argument in its own terms and take it seriously, vegetarianism is not the obvious conclusion to draw from it. The course advocated by the concerned individual could equally well be the conclusion drawn. One needs some further reason for picking the one tactic as opposed to the other.

Second, as the meat-eater's option flourishes, Singer's case for vegetarianism is progressively undercut. That case loses its applicability, as the amount and intensity of pain produced on factory farms diminish. In other words, his case for vegetarianism hinges upon the actual state of evolution in rearing methods, drugs, and genetic engineering: each development in these areas which reduces pain in farming undercuts Singer's position still further.

If it is true that pain in farming has been drastically reduced or eliminated, however, why should the erosion of his position bother Singer? Whether or not it bothers Singer, it certainly is going to bother countless other vegetarians. For the concerned individual's tactic envisages the continuation of meat-eating and, with (some) changed methods, intensive farming; and the whole point is that, under the conditions set out, the argument from pain and suffering is compatible with, and places no further barrier in the way of, these things.

Third, the meat-eater's option must be faced by all readers of *Animal Liberation* who feel the force of the argument from pain and suffering; *per se*, there is nothing about Singer's position which enables them to avoid a choice between the two tactics I have described. A concerned reader of *Animal Liberation* may well feel impelled by what he reads there about factory farming to take up the cudgels and seek among people at large for a commitment to evolution in rearing methods, drugs, and genetic engineering. Could he not thereby be said to be following the book's lesson, that what is seriously wrong is not eating meat but raising and killing animals by painful methods? Certainly, this individual, who seeks the elimination of (very) painful devices and practices on factory farms and their replacement with more humane ones, who seeks technological advances on all fronts likely to be relevant to the diminution of pain in farming, and who actively tries to stir people up to commit themselves to these ends, is responding directly to Singer's message.

Accordingly, anyone convinced by Singer's argument, anyone convinced that we must reduce, if not eliminate, pain in farming faces a choice between the concerned individual's tactic and vegetarianism as the way to go about this. Neither tactic is *per se* more favoured than the other.

Attempts to Prejudice the Choice between Tactics

Finally, before turning to Singer's reasons for choosing vegetarianism as one's tactic for combating the pains of food animals, I want to consider two ways in which one might try at the outset to prejudice this choice in tactics between Singer and the concerned individual.

A life proper to their species

One way of trying to compromise the concerned individual's tactic involves a quite specific use of a very broad sense of pain or suffering.[17] It might be suggested, that is, that to deprive animals of the sort of life proper to their species is a form of pain or suffering in some broad sense, even if the means involved in carrying out this deprivation are, as the result of the concerned individual's option flourishing, so far as new rearing methods and new advances in technology are concerned, free of all pain or suffering in the narrow sense. Thus, even if the concerned individual's tactic was entirely successful in its aims, so long as some intensive methods of rearing were held to deprive some food animals of the sort of life proper to their species, it might be suggested that these animals would continue to have pain or suffering inflicted upon them.

Singer's argument from pain and suffering takes these terms, in the light of the above distinction, in the narrow sense; and I myself do not find much value in inflating their extension, in the way the broad sense envisages.

So far as the concerned individual's tactic is concerned, one must not focus upon his concern with technology to the exclusion of his concern with improvements in and alternatives to some present rearing methods.

Take confinement in cruelly narrow spaces, which is by far the most commonly cited reason not only for food animals' miserable lives but also, so it is claimed, for their not leading lives proper to their species: this is a cardinal instance where the concerned individual will seek improvements and alternatives. Already there is some movement in the right direction. For example, in perhaps the most widely cited case of abuse, veal calves, Quantock Veal, which dominates the British veal market, has introduced a new method of rearing these calves.[18] They are not kept alone but in groups of 30; they are not kept in narrow stalls with slatted bottoms but in straw-filled pens in which they can move around freely; they are not kept in darkness but in light; they are not fed an iron-deficient diet but can obtain iron-laced milk from automatic feeders at any time. In this particular case, too, Quantock Veal maintains that this method of rearing veal calves, particularly given the availability of the European Community's dairy surplus, is cheaper than the objectionable method. Plainly, a development of this sort is likely to have a profound, positive effect on the quality of veal calves' lives; as well, it moves to meet the claim that, under present conditions, veal calves are not allowed to lead lives proper to their species.

Or consider the other, major case of abuse commonly cited, laying hens: one development in this area has been the Aviary method. It does not confine hens in cages but allows them to roam freely in poultry sheds, as a result of which they can scratch, flap about, and exercise; they lay in nest boxes or shelves above the ground. So far as I know, de-beaking forms no part of the method. This development is not the end of evolution in rearing laying hens, but it seems a beginning.

I give these two examples as instances of the sorts of developments the concerned individual will favour, but I do not pretend either that they are the end of the process of evolution or that they are representative of recent developments as a whole in intensive farming. Rather, they are but two sorts of developments for which the concerned individual must lobby and work, examples of the kinds of evolution in rearing methods for which he must press.

It may be objected, however, that while the concerned individual is pressing for such developments and for advances in technology, food animals are still suffering. But so they are on the other tactic, vegetarianism.

If you face up to the choice of tactics I have been delineating, and you opt for vegetarianism, you would be wrong to think the suffering of food animals is going to come to a halt. In fact, of course, you are going to be left waiting for a sufficient number of others to make a similar choice, in order to give your act any efficacy whatever on the rearing of food animals.[19] And, clearly, you are in for a long wait: even as the number of vegetarians in the United States has grown, the amount of meat consumed there has reached ever more colossal heights. It was estimated in December, 1979, that meat consumption in the United States would amount to 214.4 pounds per person during 1980.[20] For a more homely example, a single hamburger establishment in Oxford reported in mid-1981 that it had, since it had opened only six or seven years previously, sold more than 5½ million hamburgers. That is a single establishment, in a single, relatively small city, with a host of fast-food and other restaurants. In facing up to the decision before you, you know beyond doubt that, if you decide in favour of vegetarianism, food animals are going to continue to suffer.[21] On this score, you have no real basis for choosing one tactic over the other.

In sum, evolution in rearing methods seems likely to meet the objection that some methods do not permit some food animals to lead lives proper to their species, if only because improvements in and alternatives to these methods can be sought specifically on this basis. And this moves to meet another objection: it might be charged that the concerned individual's tactic is uncharitable to food animals because it only tries to relieve and not abolish their pains; but this is not true. While the concerned individual does want to relieve animal pain, his response to that pain is varied and includes, through his stress on evolution in rearing methods, the search for improvements in and alternatives to precisely those rearing methods held to be the primary source of the pain in question.

I am also unhappy with this first attempt to prejudice the choice between tactics on another count as well. This has to do with the expression 'the sort of life proper to their species'.

The contemporary *penchant* for studying animals in the wild, in order to find out what they are really like, and, therefore, what sort of life is proper to their respective species, cannot be indulged here, since virtually none of our food animals are found in the wild. Beef, ham, pork, chicken, lamb, mutton, and veal all come from animals who are completely our own productions, bred by us in ways we select to ends we desire. Indeed, the gene pools of these creatures of ours have been manipulated by us to a point today where we can in a great many respects produce the type and strain of creature we want,[22] and the amount of research presently going on in this area is enormous. My point is this: it is a mistake to use expressions like 'the sort of life proper to their species' as if this sort of life were itself immune to technological advance; for by manipulating the gene pools of food animals, by varying our drugs and breeding practices, and by having funded research for progressive advances in all these areas, we already breed these animals to a sort of life which to their bred species — there is no other — is proper.

For example, chickens have been bred with weak leg and wing muscles and with shorter necks, both to reduce their mobility and so to help fatten them and to reduce the sheer amount of each chicken which cannot be turned into food. Even a variation in the size of their bones can now be bred into them. In a word, the descendants of these bred chickens have had bred out of them many of the traits which food producers have wanted eliminated, and they are characterized by reduced mobility, a larger appetite, increased lethargy, significantly increased (or decreased) size, etc. We have manipulated them to this end, and we are carrying on research in this area, funded by major food interests, government organizations, international bodies, and universities, at an accelerated pace. Thus, one very recent development has been a featherless chicken, for use in warm climates. In the southern United States, for example, plumed birds succumb to the heat at a sufficient rate to be a significant cost to farmers, and the featherless bird has in part been developed to meet this problem.[23] (Developments to meet specific problems are increasingly commonplace. For example, cows have a slightly longer gestation period than women, which has meant that they can have only one calf a year; farmers have long wanted more. A procedure has now been developed, which involves the use of multiple ovulation hormones, artificial insemination, and the non-surgical implantation of fertilized eggs in other cows, to solve this problem.)

What sort of life is proper to these chickens? One cannot appeal to chickens in the wild or 'non-developed' chickens for an answer, since there are none; chickens are, to repeat, developments or productions of our own, produced in order to satisfy the fast-food chains and the demands of our Sunday lunches and school picnics. But if one asks what sort of life is proper to 'developed' chickens, we get the above answer. Or are we to turn back the clock and say that the sort of life proper to chickens is the sort they enjoyed when, say, they were first introduced into the United States, long before the first of the developmental farms and any thought of mass-producing them arose? Unless we artifically select some time as that time which reveals to us what chickens are really like, to ask 'What is it in the nature of chickens to be like?' is to ask a question the answer to which must be framed in the light of 'developed' chickens and of technological change.

Now the manipulation of animal gene pools to the extent that we have long since affected the very species of animal in question may well be repugnant to many, and I can easily imagine it being condemned as tampering with nature (and, through nature, with our kith and kin) or with God's handiwork. But I do not really see how it can be condemned on the grounds of inflicting pain and suffering, unless the extension of these terms is simply bloated, not merely beyond anything Singer envisages, but beyond any reasonable degree. There does not seem to be much difference, in fact, between the animal and human cases in this regard: much of the genetic research being conducted with respect to human beings, including experiments involving determination of sex and number of children, test-tube breeding, cloning, and eliminating an extra Y chromosome in males, is widely condemned; but no one condemns it on the ground of inflicting pain and suffering.

I think many people see nothing wrong *per se* in tampering with nature or with God's handiwork; indeed, in some sense or other, we have been doing it for ages. Rather what worries them about genetic engineering, in addition to qualms in the United States about massive profits for private companies and individuals, as the result of allowing genetic techniques and products to be patented, is the possibility of frightening results. Thus, the idea behind recombitant DNA methods, i.e., tampering with the genetic make-up of bacteria in order to produce useful products, such as insulin and interferon, seems to them a good one; but the thought that something might go wrong, that bacteria should be created which posed a serious threat to health and life, or which caused diseases in men or animals that we could not control, or which grew resistant to present methods of detection and elimination, is a chilling one, which has provoked demands for rigid licensing of genetic research. As the possibility of frightening results recedes, however, I suspect most people will embrace the benefits of such research. Of course, in the human case, this fear of frightening results is magnified many times. I have in mind nothing so dramatic as the creation of monsters or Frankensteins, merely the creation of beings with abnormalities of some sort. And there are, too, social offshoots to consider as well. For instance, I once read that, particularly in poorer countries, if parents could select the sex of their children, they would choose overwhelmingly to have sons. The effects on society of such a practice, however, were it sustained over a period of time, seem likely to be harmful, for all sorts of obvious reasons.

Valuing suffering but not life

A second way of trying to compromise the concerned individual's tactic is, in a quite specific way, to try to reduce it to absurdity. The concerned individual seeks to relieve, minimize, and eliminate the pains of food animals but continues to eat meat; it is tempting to portray him, therefore, as valuing animal suffering but not valuing animal life, and then, on the basis of this portrayal, to force him to draw the unpalatable conclusion that, since every animal is going to suffer at some time in its life, he ought now to exterminate all animals painlessly.[24]

I do not myself think well of this argument, which I believe Michael Martin has shown how to answer;[25] but, I contend, if it works against anyone, it works against Singer.

The difficulty with the argument, apart from the very obvious fact that the concerned individual is in no way whatever committed to giving animal life a value of zero, is that, in typically simplistic fashion, it makes it appear that minimizing animal suffering is the only factor applicable to the situation. This is obviously false. For example, to destroy all animals now would result in financial collapse of the meat markets, in financial ruin for food producers and those in related and support industries, in massive unemployment in these industries as well as among farmers, in financial loss to rail and road haulage firms, in a substantial loss in television, newspaper, and magazine advertising revenues, with consequent effect upon the media's viability and profitability, and so on. Here, in quite mercenary terms, is one good reason why the concerned individual will not exterminate all animals. It is the effects upon human beings and their interests, financial and otherwise, which are here held to outweigh minimizing animal suffering through total extermination or are held at least to be applicable to the situation. Other factors come to mind with equal facility. To kill all animals now would mean the collapse of all experimentation upon animals for human benefit, would depopulate our zoos, which so many children and adults enjoy visiting, and would deprive countless lonely people of their companions. Here, it is human well-being and enjoyment which are held to outweigh minimizing animal suffering through total extermination, or are held at least to be applicable to the situation.

I must stress again, however, that the concerned individual is not compelled to give animal life *no value whatever*; all he has to do is to give human interests, human well-being, and human enjoyment the same or a higher value than minimizing animal suffering through complete extermination.

I do not, then, think much of this argument. But what is little recognized, is that, if the argument applies to anyone, it applies to Singer. His case for vegetarianism, as we have seen, turns exclusively upon minimizing animal pain and suffering, and not in the least upon the value of animal life, which, for the purposes of his case, he is prepared to allow to be anything you like, including zero. Again, he openly endorses the view that a genuine concern for the pains of animals demands that we become vegetarians, without in the least endorsing a view about the value of animal life demanding that we become vegetarians. Pain alone is the basis of his case, and its diminution, minimization, and elimination is his goal. Surely, if anyone must now envisage the complete extermination of animals, because of a concern with the minimization of their suffering, if anyone is forced to conclude that all animals should now be painlessly eliminated, it is Singer?

I am not concerned here to go into possible ways in which Singer might resist this conclusion, except to emphasize that, if they begin even partially to include or make reference to those already sketched, he will be using human interests, well-being, and enjoyment to justify restraint in slaughtering animals, a surprising result in his case.

Notes

1 My reasons for preferring this nicety, and the context in which I prefer it, are to be found in Frey, *Interests and Rights*, chs 8, 9, and 11.
2 In his paper ' "A brute to the brutes?": Descartes' treatment of animals', (*Philosophy*, vol. 53, 1978, pp. 551–9). John Cottingham argues that Descartes did not hold the view with which he is traditionally credited, viz., that animals are without feeling and so cannot feel pain.
3 If one absolutely insists upon injecting moral rights into the discussion, then the only right required is the right to be free of undeserved pain, which is not a species-specific

right, since pain is not a species-specific datum. Such a right is superfluous to the argument, however, on grounds given in Parts II and III.

4   Peter Singer and James Mason, *Animal Factories*, New York, Crown Publishers Inc., 1980.
5   Peter Singer, 'Killing humans and killing animals', p. 149.
6   Peter Singer, *Practical Ethics*, p. 105.
7   Ibid., p. 56.
8   Ibid., p. 55.
9   Ibid.
10 Peter Singer, *Animal Liberation*, p. 165.
11 Ibid.
12 'These arguments do not take us all the way to a vegetarian diet, since some animals, for instance sheep and beef cattle, still graze freely outdoors' (Peter Singer, *Practical Ethics*, p. 56).
13 Peter Singer, *Animal Liberation*, p. 165 (italics in original).
14 Peter Singer, *Practical Ethics*, pp. 56–7 (italics in original).
15 John Rodman, 'The liberation of nature?', *Inquiry*, vol. 20, 1977, pp. 90 ff, 103 ff, 112 ff.
16 Michael Martin, 'A critique of moral vegetarianism', *Reason Papers No. 3*, Fall 1976, pp. 16, 18, 20.
17 See, e.g., John Benson, 'Duty and the beast', *Philosophy*, vol. 53, 1978, p. 532.
18 See Hugh Clayton, 'Veal farmers aim to erase the stigma of cruelty', *The Times*, 8 May 1980; Ena Kendall, ' "Welfare" for veal calves', *Observer*, 4 May 1980.
19 I return to this point in the next chapter.
20 See Sue Shellenbarger, 'Pork Gains on Beef as Meat Choice in U.S.', *International Herald Tribune*, December 23, 1979.
21 In the next chapter, I take up Singer's recent statement that he envisages (his argument working over) a considerable period of time in bringing a halt to the meat industry. Had this statement appeared in *Animal Liberation* alongside the picture of the effects of becoming vegetarians sketched there, I think readers might have found it at odds with that picture.
22 See Rodman, 'The liberation of nature', pp. 90–1; Martin, 'A critique of moral vegetarianism', pp. 18, 20; Benson, 'Duty and the beast', p. 531.
23 See, for example, 'Plucky US poultry experts breed featherless fowl for better eating', *International Herald Tribune*, 28 December 1979.
24 See A. Linzey, *Animal Rights* (London, SCM Press, 1976), pp. 29 ff; and R. Godlovitch, 'Animals and morals', in S. and R. Godlovitch, J. Harris, (eds), *Animals, Men and Morals* (London, Gollancz, 1971), pp. 167 ff.
25 Michael Martin, 'A critique of moral vegetarianism', pp. 31–2.

17

Alleged Reasons for the Choice of Vegetarianism

Of the two tactics before us for combating the pains of food animals, why choose Singer's? Why choose or adopt vegetarianism, in preference to the course advocated by the concerned individual? As I say, this in the end is the crucial question, and though Singer does not put it to himself in this form, I think what few remarks he makes in chapter 4 of *Animal Liberation*, on the effects of becoming a vegetarian, can be cast in the form of answers to it.

The overall picture Singer gives of the effects of becoming vegetarian I have sketched already and alluded to numerous times; the claims to be considered in this chapter are the foundations upon which that picture rests. In fact, though several of these claims have played a major part in the positive reception accorded *Animal Liberation*, none of them will do for Singer's purpose; and I find it difficult to understand why, in spite of numerous critics,[1] people have fallen in with them. Though Singer has returned to several of these claims in his more recent paper 'Utilitarianism and vegetarianism',[2] his comments there do not succeed in breathing new life into them.

In Part II, we saw that it does not follow from the fact that it is wrong to inflict undeserved pain on animals that it is wrong to eat them; thus, the reason for choosing vegetarianism as one's tactic cannot be because Singer has shown that it is wrong to eat meat. We also saw, however, that the introduction of the distinction between positive and negative vegetarianism gives the argument from pain and suffering new life, as a vehicle for dealing with the pains of food animals. But the problem now is this: vegetarianism is not the only such vehicle, and we need reasons for choosing it over its competitors, in circumstances where we have no apparent reason for thinking it morally preferred to them (or, in any event, to some of them). What, then, are Singer's reasons?

I might remark that I have changed my position here, from what it was when I first began to think about this matter of choosing vegetarianism. I initially accepted Michael Martin's characterization of Singer's central problem as having to get 'from the premiss that meat production causes great suffering in animals to the conclusion that one ought not to eat meat'[3] without the addition of dubious premisses, which Martin denies that Singer can do. I accepted this characterization because it seemed to me essential to Singer's case that he had to show that eating meat was wrong; though I still agree with Martin that Singer can only reach the conclusion that eating meat is wrong through the addition of dubious premisses, I no longer believe, as the reader knows, that an adherent to the argument from pain and suffering has to reach this conclusion. That is the point of my distinction between positive and negative moral vegetarianism: an adherent to the argument does not need to show that eating meat is wrong in order for his argument to constitute a case for negative moral vegetarianism. For example, if the boycott of meat were truly the most effective step I personally could take to lessen the pains of food animals, I would have a reason to boycott meat, without in the least having to think that eating meat was morally forbidden. I might simply like or feel for certain kinds of animals and want to do something about their plight.

The distinction between positive and negative vegetarianism is, then, important: what Singer wants is that we should give up meat, and his argument can constitute a case in support of this end even while failing to show that eating meat is wrong. Thus, while my differences with Martin are slight (I still accept his substantive arguments which have influenced my whole thinking on vegetarianism), they nevertheless materially affect what we require of Singer and his argument. I stress this, because one may allege to have reasons for choosing Singer's tactic over the concerned individual's, even if neither tactic requires some view about the morality of eating meat for its success.

The Claim of Symbolic Gesture

At one point in chapter 4 of *Animal Liberation*, Singer remarks that 'becoming a vegetarian is *not merely* a symbolic gesture';[4] it would seem, therefore, to be at least this much. If one condemns certain farming practices, a gesture with respect to them may be thought to be morally required, and vegetarianism can be seen as that gesture.

Does morality require a gesture of us in this instance? I am not convinced that morality does require gestures of us; but, even if it does, there is no reason whatever to think that the specific gesture it requires of us in this case is giving up meat. For example, if the concerned individual joins various animal welfare organizations and vigorously supports them; if he supports the strengthening of present laws against cruelty and the passage of more stringent ones; if he contributes to animal shelters; if he spreads the word about certain practices on factory farms and lobbies government officials to do something about those practices; if he speaks out on the relevant issues, in order to raise the level of public awareness of them; if he supports research into new and painless breeding, feeding, and killing methods and into other, animal-related technology; if, in short, he is assiduous in showing his concern over some aspects of intensive farming, then I can see no reason to think he is not making gestures appropriate to his concern. Certainly, a good deal of argument would be needed to establish — what in any event seems implausible — that giving up meat is the only appropriate gesture, just as much argument would be needed to show that not participating in the Olympic Games in Moscow in 1980 was the only gesture appropriate to condemnation of the Soviet Union's invasion of Afghanistan.

If we bear in mind that Singer's argument and his book as a whole are addressed to individuals, each of whom faces a choice about what to eat, then the sort of symbolic gestures involved here are personal ones. A great many personal gestures are essentially private: two women I know periodically have days of fast, in order to show solidarity with, and indignation at, the plight of the starving poor; a friend in Oxford displays several pictures of aborted foetuses in his flat, as 'a show of sympathy' with the right-to-life movement; and a well-known philosopher, I am told, wears a particular hat in a show of unity with freedom fighters in the country in which the hat was made. But some personal gestures can take a more public form: in July, 1979, British newspapers reported that a woman who camped outside a London department store for nine days, in order to be able to purchase a £750 mink jacket reduced to £79.50, duly obtained the jacket, took it outside, threw it into a rubbish bin, poured gasoline over it, and set it alight, in protest against the fur trade.

With personal gestures of these sorts, it is simply not to the point that others follow one's lead, that, in this sense, one's action or omission prove effective; for it remains a gesture on one's part whatever its degree of effectiveness. Thus, any thought that the woman who burned the mink jacket might better have spent the nine days queueing up to obtain it, or might better have used the money spent on it (perhaps by giving it to one of the organizations seeking to pressure governments and companies over trade in furs) is not to the point; for her act in no way ceases on her part to be a gesture, however many options are available to her and whatever their relative effectiveness in bringing pressure to bear on the fur trade. Again, the philosopher who wears his freedom-fighter hat knows full well that his doing so is not going to bring freedom to the country in question; nevertheless, even if not a single other individual is brought closer to the cause by his wearing it, his wearing the hat remains a gesture on his part.

That personal gestures can remain such whatever their effect on others in fact means that there is very little restriction on what can be a gesture on one's part. Even wholly ineffective acts or omissions can count.

Thus, if morality does require a gesture of us in respect of our opposition to aspects of intensive farming, then the fact is that the concerned individual makes such gestures; and, because of the point about effectiveness, it appears that he could make them, if he wished, in a multitude of other ways, none of which involved giving up meat. I stress, however, that the concerned individual *wants* his tactic for combating the pains of food animals to be effective (indeed, it was devised with this in mind) and thereby successful in coming to grips with those pains; I am here only pointing out that his and any tactic, including Singer's, can fail on these counts, yet remain a gesture with respect to his opposition to aspects of intensive farming.

The Claim of Political-Economic Power

Singer claims that the agribusiness lobby is 'overwhelming',[5] that, in effect, it is so powerful that nothing short of vegetarianism will work to reduce suffering on factory farms.

Certainly, especially in the United States, there are powerful lobbies, and the agribusiness lobby is one of these, not least because of the millions of jobs it represents in the food and allied industries. But it is not true that these lobbies are invincible, though it may be good tactics, in order to rally support, to portray them as such.

Manufacturers have long opposed attempts to deal with the problems of water and air pollution and of smog; the automotive industry has strenuously opposed all sorts of innovations with respect to safety, road performance, and pollution; the tobacco industry has vehemently fought restrictions on advertising, health warnings on cigarette packets, and a taxing policy which might reduce sales; the coal industry has fought a good deal of safety and environmental legislation; the baby food industry has long opposed attempts to control its advertising, marketing, and milk substitutes in the Third World; and the food and drug industry as a whole has strenuously opposed laws which force disclosure of a product's contents, restrict the type and quantity of additives and preservatives, and govern the packaging of goods. Yet, all these things are coming or have come to pass, not easily or quickly or as fully as many would like perhaps, but nevertheless with some effect.

As in the case of pollution laws and other environmental legislation, there is powerful opposition to change. This opposition in the case of the environment, for example, has been especially forceful at a time of economic recession in the car and related industries, and at a time of doubt and worry over petroleum supplies, when relaxation of pollution laws with respect to coal and release of government lands for further exploration for oil, coal, minerals, etc., as well as for timber are widely advocated; but change has occurred, and it would be wrong to pretend otherwise. And though it is doubtless true that by no means everyone is satisfied with either the degree or rate of change, it is also true that in some areas, particularly in connection with the environment, significant change has occurred fairly rapidly. It occurred over the environment, however, only after public awareness of environmental issues had been raised considerably, and it is not accidental that part of the concerned individual's tactic is similarly to raise the level of public awareness over certain features of modern farming.

Singer's claim here reminds me of an anti-war rally I attended at a university in the United States during the Vietnam war. The main speaker opposed the war on moral grounds and later, in private, speculated about the necessity of armed violence, including an attack on industrial plants, banks, and university laboratories, in order to force a halt to America's involvement in the war. I could see no reason to think that moral opposition to the war called for such acts, nor do I now think that what burnings and bombings were perpetrated proved more effective in bringing about American disengagement than other actions by concerned individuals, including serious, sustained political work within 'the system' and prolonged lobbying of both people and Congress.

But, the speaker went on, the military-industrial complex possesses the most powerful lobby in America, and it can and will defeat any measure introduced and carried forth through the political process, can and will defeat any measure other than a violent one, which even this lobby is powerless to prevent. In fact, American disengagement was achieved without the destruction of its schools and fire stations, and the military-industrial complex was at least for the moment brought to heel. So far as I can see, as the level of public awareness and debate rose and the number of concerned individuals increased, and as these individuals entered the political arena in different capacities and pressed their views locally and nationally, a sufficiently large and vocal minority of concerned individuals made continued American engagement increasingly, politically impossible. Likewise, in the case of some farming practices, I can see no basis whatever, though it does rally his troops, for Singer's treating the agribusiness lobby as invincible.

And this is what he does: to build the case for his tactic, the opposition to farming improvements is made out to consist of giants, who cannot be moved in the least. Nor is Singer reluctant to saw off the limb on which he is sitting: he pronounces not merely about the past but about the future. These giants with whom we have to contend will never be moved but will always defeat us, no matter what; of intensive farming, he reveals that 'the usual forms of protest and political action will never bring about a major reform.'[6] To pronounce like this; to make it appear that here, unlike all other areas of Anglo-American society, is the one where significant reform 'will never' occur through social/political action; why should anyone believe such a pronouncement? Why, especially, should they believe it, when concerned individuals have battled and do battle other, equally rich and powerful lobbies with varying degrees of success and when they have grappled with the agribusiness lobby in the past, also with equally varying degress of success? (For example, readers might like to research the changes in regulations governing commercial slaughtering since, say, 1850, in the United States and Britain.) Why are the giants in this lobby so much more 'giant-like' than those in other lobbies?

No one pretends, of course, that there will not be often substantial opposition to some proposed reform in farming. In 1979, one of the largest poultry companies in the United States, Federal Company, processed 5 million broilers a week in its plants,[7] while in fiscal year 1980, Iowa Beef Processors, the largest beef processor in the United States, had revenues of $4.6 billion;[8] and companies this large, *not least* because of their effects in all sorts of ways on the lives of human beings, are bound to have economic and thereby political power, which it would be rash to underestimate. But so, too, have had the car, tobacco, coal, steel, and drug companies, not to mention those comprising the military-industrial complex, and concerned individuals have battled these with varying degrees of success for years. Why pretend the opposition is invincible, when it is evident that powerful business interests, including those in the food industry itself, have been, and are being, made to give ground?

Possibly some people on the political left may be unhappy with the idea of the concerned individual having, as part of his tactic, pressure for change through concerted social/political action, at least if the socio-economic system in question is that which prevails in the United States, the apostle of capitalism. But then their unhappiness is with capitalism; it is not because they have prior knowledge that any effort at significant reform in farming through concerted social/political action is, unlike almost every other sphere of activity in the United States, doomed to failure from the outset.

The agribusiness lobby, like any other, is not invincible; it can be defeated, as it well realizes, which is why it increasingly defends itself and attacks its opponents. If it opposes the measures I mentioned earlier, and others like them, the concerned individual will press for its defeat through implementation of these measures. Certainly, though his opponents may find it convenient to paint him otherwise, he is not in collusion with this lobby; he thinks reforms in farming are necessary, and he actively pursues his tactic for achieving them. In time, I think the meat industry and all those even peripherally connected with it will come round to regarding the concerned individual's tactic rather more favourably; for it does represent the middle way between allowing certain (very) painful practices to carry on unchecked, which no concerned individual can support, and virtually eliminating livestock and poultry farming altogether, which it is difficult to believe those in the meat trade can welcome.

Utilitarianism and Vegetarianism: Some Reflections on Practicalities

Anyone interested in substantive questions in ethics faces the very considerable difficulty of apprehending, sifting, and thinking clearly about all the many practicalities which bear upon particular issues. This is particularly true of the act-utilitarian, who is required by his theory to have some view on what will or at least is likely to maximize utility in the situations under consideration.

All too often, however, both act-utilitarians and their critics fail to consider the practicalities of situations. For example, critics not infrequently resort to unusual and bizarre examples and then rig them so that act-utilitarians find themselves committed to the performance of some hideous act; this commitment is then treated as a reason for rejecting act-utilitarianism. Act-utilitarians themselves, however, often forgo the hard work in considering and thinking through practicalities; instead, they resort to saying or implying or supposing what will maximize utility, without ever actually showing anything of the sort. Nor are they helped much by suppositions in this regard, since what is in the end under consideration, at least if they are going to put their theory into practice, are actual situations, in which they must decide what to do.

In *Animal Liberation*, it is Singer's view that the utility involved in eliminating intensive farming and relieving the pains of food animals outweighs the disutility involved. In other words, he believes that if we all turned to vegetarianism, the terrible consequences which would ensue, both as the result of the world-wide collapse of the meat industry in all its forms, ranging from the unemployment of millions of people in the industry itself, including farmers, to the unemployment of millions of people in the numerous industries which support, service, and depend upon it, and in the widespread effect this collapse would have not only upon individual workers and their families but also upon market forces generally, are more than outweighed by the good consequences which would ensue as the result of eliminating (intensive methods of farming and) the pains of food animals. There is absolutely nothing whatever in Singer's book to show that this is the case, however, and it is by no means apparent that it is. Nor am I prepared simply to concede that it is, in view of what seem, upon even cursory reflection, some rather obvious ramifications of the collapse of the meat industry.

Strangely enough, Singer has not generally been challenged on this claim of utility. The only person to press the matter is Tom Regan, in his paper 'Utilitarianism, vegetarianism, and animal rights'.[9] Between Regan and myself, however, there are profound disagreements, which I am sure our challenges in part reflect; for whereas Regan queries Singer's claim as part of his general campaign to find room for the notion of rights in the discussion of vegetarianism and to base substantive claims about our treatment of food animals upon rights, I am not at all inclined in that direction. Nor does an assessment of Singer's claim of utility here, or, indeed, of the other facets of his argument from pain and suffering require a commitment to some truth about moral rights.

(I first began to ponder Singer's claim of utility because, in *Animal Liberation*, it is presented in conjunction with the argument from pain and suffering, about which I have doubts; I did not begin to ponder it because I reject the entire utilitarian underpinnings of Singer's normative views. My predisposition towards utilitarianism gives me a great deal in common with Singer; and it is this predisposition which, despite our contrasting arguments and very different conclusions, is liable to make Singer and I appear to critics such as Regan as, essentially, members of the same camp. There is truth in this,[10] a fact which will doubtless puzzle non-philosophical readers and so should be ignored by them.)

What are some of the practical considerations that must be taken into account, in judging the correctness of Singer's claim of utility? I shall enumerate just a few of them, but enough to exhibit their extent and variety; they are in no particular order, whether of severity or anything else, and the groupings are merely for convenience.

(1) The collapse of the meat industry would have terrible effects on livestock and poultry farmers and on the middlemen who deal in these animals, together, of course, with their families. Slaughterers would lose their jobs, as would all those connected with slaughter-houses. Government meat inspectors, large numbers of those in animal-related government departments, such as agriculture, meat and meat-related economic and political lobbyists, and many of those in government and private research institutes, including institutes devoted to research into animal diseases, would doubtless be dispensed with as well.

(2) All those in the food industry generally whose products, services, and jobs depend upon the meat industry, from those involved in the manufacture of steak and barbecue sauce to those who actually market the products themselves, would be hit. Thus, butcher shops and meat markets would be disastrously affected, and grocery stores would suffer large losses, especially in the short term. The canning industry would be hit hard: canned meat would disappear, and the number of cans required would plummet, with consequent effect upon profits and jobs; for meat and meat by-products and derivatives form a significant part of the can market, especially when one includes pet foods. Those in the cured and smoked meat industry would be affected, and this includes everyone all along the line, from those who actually do the curing and/or smoking to retailers. Thus, the delicatessen trade, deprived of all meats whatever, would find itself in trouble, and a wonderful part of New York and other cities throughout the world would virtually disappear, with a loss of livelihoods and, on many people's part, much pleasure.

(3) It is most unlikely that, with the collapse of the meat industry and, therefore, of a major portion of the food industry as a whole, the dairy industry would escape unscathed. The meat packing industry, of course, would disappear completely. The box, container, and crate industries would be affected at once, as would all those many and varied businesses

which provide and/or service the equipment used in all parts of the meat trade, such as the automated equipment used on modern livestock and poultry farms and in abattoirs. Animal feed manufacturers and all those involved in the industry would find it nearly impossible to carry on; indeed, they would lose out entirely, unless money were available to convert their businesses into something else. Rail and road haulage firms, including the trucking industry generally, since little or no meat, meat by-products, or meat derivatives would be available, would have to shed labour and probably plant. The refrigeration industry would be dramatically affected, not only through the loss of meat industry business, including the substantial business with rail and road haulage firms, but also through the loss of sales in deep freezers, etc., to private families.

(4)   Three major industries in the United States over the last 30 years, and now, increasingly, throughout the world, would be affected, First, the fast food industry, a multi-billion dollar affair, would collapse entirely, with untold losses in jobs, revenues, taxes, and investment capital. In large part, it is this industry which has made the hot dog and the hamburger the symbol of America throughout the world, and one has only to stand of a lunch time in front of a MacDonald's in London or Paris to appreciate the impact the fast food industry has had in Europe. Imitators throughout Western Europe have arisen to make millions. Second, the pet food industry, with annual revenues now in the billions of dollars, would be seriously affected, as meat and meat derivatives, together with fish and fish meal, have come increasingly to figure in its products. Third, the drug/pharmaceutical empire would suffer; for it is estimated, of antibiotics alone, that almost half of those entering the market today are for use in animals. Again, in all these cases, losses in taxes and investment capital would be serious.

(5)   Universities would have to shed labour, as departments of veterinary science and other animal-related departments, particularly those involved in research into food and food-animal disease, came under pressure. Many technical colleges would be affected, where aspects of animal farming and farm management are studied. The United States boasts a large number of agricultural colleges, where teaching of animal husbandry and agricultural economics and research of all sorts, especially into breeding, are reasons for their existence, and these would have either to close or to be radically scaled-down. Either alternative would in turn affect the local, usually rural, communities in which these schools are located, through loss of money flowing into the local economy, loss in social, cultural, and sporting activities, etc.

(6)The publishing business would suffer. Many firms specialize in books related to all facets of animal farming, including textbooks on animal husbandry, animal diseases, agricultural economics, breeding techniques, etc., for the above schools, and this is a substantial business in the United States and not an insignificant one in Britain. These firms would suffer serious reverses, certainly in the short term. The publishers of cookery books would be affected, as would all those in the cookery book industry, including the cooks themselves, some of whom have reached millions through television. The publishers of technical/scientific periodicals on animal husbandry, etc., would be immediately affected, as would all those involved in the production of those more popular farming magazines directed at the farmer himself. And there are as well those magazines devoted to farm-related services, such as those on equipment and maintenance and those which amount virtually to financial papers on prices, markets, and the like. Some, such as *Farmers Weekly* in Britain, cover all this ground. Finally, there are some specialized journals, such as *Pig* and *Poultry World*, devoted more or less to a single type of animal farming, and these would go into decline, if not die. How much all these losses could ' be made good by the production of more books on vegetarianism, of television programmes on vegetarian cooking, and the like is not very clear.

(7)　The advertising industry would be seriously affected, as would the revenues of those publications and newspapers that carried meat and meat-related advertisements. Radio and television revenues would be hurt (the media are not government-owned in the United States), through the demise of advertising from the meat and related industries. Also affected will be those adults and children who either watch programmes sponsored by these industries or suffer from the decline in revenues through having their favourite programme affected, and the range of programmes they can watch reduced. Consumer information programmes and publications will be affected, as meat markets, bargains, information, etc., will more or less cease to exist.

(8)　Social life will be seriously affected. The restaurant business and all those connected with the catering industry would suffer loss, probably catastrophically in the short term. Teenagers would be deprived of carousing at the local hamburger establishment, but adults would be affected as well; for it is hard to believe that all the restaurants of New York, London, Paris, and Alice Springs, with only non-meat dishes on offer, however varied, could stay in business. So there probably will be fewer places to go to. Moreover, what places there are will be, in essentials (grains, vegetables, etc.), alike. Perhaps we shall continue to frequent restaurants as often as we do now, for the evening out, for celebrations and festivals, for the entertainment of guests and friends, for the special treat, etc. It is not, however, clear that would be so. For, at least in part, it is precisely the food that attracts us to them. Gone forever will be *petto di pollo alla crema, scaloppine zingara, saltimbocca alla romana, coda vaccinara, carré d'agneau paloise, tournedos Rossini, filet de boeuf au poivre à la façon du Moulin, lapin bonne femme, dinde à la creme, médaillons de veau biscayenne, entrecôte bourguignonne, mutton tikka, chicken tandoori, rogan gosht, sheftalia, moussaka,* and *Peking duck.* Perhaps the great pleasure we take in these dishes will be made good by a vegetarian diet, but at least intially I think their loss is going to affect our social life. With the demise of the outdoor barbecue and the grilling of steaks, surburban life in the United States will be affected, and with the loss of steak and kidney pie, hot pot, and Scotch eggs, working-class Britons will be affected. From aeroplanes to armies, baseball to banquets, common room to Christmas dinners, meat permeates our lives and our relations with others to an extraordinary degree, and its social role can neither be ignored nor, I suspect, readily supplanted by something else. To appreciate this, think only of the many roles the sandwich plays in our lives and then of the role meat plays in the sandwich.

(9)   The leather and leather goods industries will collapse, with massive losses; or, if a few skins remain available, the cost of leather products will exceed the purse of all but the very wealthy. The various uses we make of leather — in clothes, shoes, belts, purses, cars, furniture, etc. — are obvious upon reflection, so that the losses to be suffered here will fall throughout a substantial and diverse part of manufacturing industry. And they will be severe, despite recent inroads by manufacturers of synthetic fibres and leather substitutes, which the present boom in the soft leather industry has partially (but only partially) offset. Affected as well, of course, will be all the many retailers of leather goods and their employees.

(10)   One must not overlook uses we make of food animals other than eating them and tanning their hides. Consider only one other: the wool industry, and, through it, the clothing industry generally, are likely to suffer, if the number of lambs and sheep diminish substantially; and, depending upon how severely numbers are affected, woollens will either disappear or increase, perhaps greatly, in price. The latter would offset whatever advantage the wool industry has gained as a result of the oil crisis of the last few years, whereby the cost of producing synthetic fibres has risen in order to reflect increases in energy costs.[11] Nor is the clothing market a small one: even if menswear, as is typical in recessions, is suffering acutely at present, the vastly greater, absolutely gigantic womenswear market, as is also typical in recessions, is as vibrant as ever; and wool plays a prominent role in womenswear. (Of course, it is a truism in investment circles that women spend heavily on clothing whatever the state of the economy, so one cannot pretend that, in the long term, the demise of wool is not, in sheer economic terms, likely to be made good; all those in and connected with the wool industry will have suffered, but the clothing industry overall will doubtless have seen the economic loss stemmed.)

(11)   Whole economies, and at various levels, would be affected. First, just as some small communities in Virginia depend vitally upon tobacco, so some depend vitally upon livestock and poultry, especially hams and turkeys. (I include here meat processors, whose plants often make a substantial contribution to the local economy.) Smithfield hams and Rockingham turkeys are famous names in the United States, and parts of Virginia depend upon trade in them. Often, in these local communities, little alternative work is available; certainly, within them, substantial sums of money would be required to put into the local economy what is currently put into it through the trade in meat. Second, wider communities will be affected. For example, in the United States, the economy of the state of South Dakota is founded not only upon wheat but also upon dairy farms, hogs, and cattle. It is difficult to imagine quite what would ensue — or what its citizens would do — if a major portion of that state's economy lay in ruins. What is true of South Dakota is true of other states, a great many of which depend economically upon farming animals for meat. Third, some countries, such as Argentina, Poland, Australia, and New Zealand, as well as the United States and the European Economic Community as a whole, have a massive stake in the meat trade, and dislocation in a national economy is, plainly, a very serious matter. Certainly, it is something all governments strive mightily to avoid, so that actually to bring about such dislocation deliberately, through seeking the collapse of the meat industry, is likely to require prolonged argument indeed at the national level. After all, the collective life of a country is bound to be affected by dislocation in its economy. (The collapse of prices, let alone the disappearance of whole trades and markets, shows this: if the collapse of sugar prices can severely disrupt Jamaican economic (and, thereby, social and political) life, and if the collapse of tin prices can severely disrupt Ecuadorian life, there is no reason to think the complete disappearance of the sugar and tin markets would not have at least equally severe effects. If a good many cartels come into existence initially because of prices, some can, once in existence, seek to regulate the market by price in order to ensue demand. Thus, OPEC members express varying degrees of concern over oil prices *vis-à-vis* the cost to industrialized countries of encouraging the use and development of alternative fuels, and the phenomenon of price regulating (by ensuring) demand rather than demand regulating price may yet be in store for consumer countries.)

(12)   Some countries depend upon meat, less as producers than as consumers, though consumers with a difference; thus, France, the bastion of *haute cuisine*, and Italy, would see one of their glories disappear. What is virtually an art form would have been lost, or nearly lost. Moreover, with every restaurant serving vegetarian meals, it is difficult to believe that the tourist business would not suffer. After all, France is not the United States or Britain, and Paris is not Alice Springs; a great many people, both individually and in groups, visit France, including some of its lesser cities,

such as Lyon, with food in mind. And with the tourist business affected, much would follow in its wake, such as a drop in hotel business, in the use of taxis, in the sale of postcards and goods, and so on. Moreover, with meat in all its forms (virtually) gone, what of the wine industry, another of the glories, and lucrative exports, of France and Italy? In the absence of meat, it is hard to believe that the wonderful red wines of these countries would not be affected, even if we assumed that the sales of white wines remained stable, which seems optimistic. And what of the great cheese industries of France and Italy?

13)   I shall not go into the extensive use made of food animals in religious rites and festivities in general, though this is an area in which I think a good many readers would be in for a surprise.

(14)   Finally, there is the general financial picture to consider. First, loss of tax revenues from all those businesses and industries even indirectly associated with the meat trade will affect local, state, and national budgets and programmes and will almost certainly affect export markets and the financing of imports from other industrialized countries and the Third World. Second, loss of revenues and of earnings by a great many people will increase the need for costly subsidies and social programmes, which in turn seem likely to feed inflationary pressures. Third, the loss of investment capital and of plant; the loss of income, with consequent effect on mortgages, loans, and credit of all kinds; the disruption in community, regional, and national economies; the demise of savings from individuals who would otherwise bank them; all these and a great many other factors are likely in the United States to place some banks, savings and loan institutions (which are already under great pressure, as a result the rise of money market funds), and loan companies in trouble. This in turn affects confidence, which, when lost, can spell disaster for banks and for financial policy generally. Fourth, loss in confidence will be exacerbated as whole businesses and industries fail or are threatened with going under, and, given that we are talking about countless billions of dollars, this loss in confidence will be difficult to make good. Certainly, banks with outstanding loans to meat and meat-related businesses and with a loan policy, whatever the prime or lending rate, which reflects the extensiveness of the importance of meat and meat-related business throughout the economy will have a storm to weather. Fifth, financial storms of the sort in question are bound to affect the stock market, including the futures markets; for it is foolish to suppose that the collapse of a substantial portion of the food and dependent industries will not affect business confidence generally. A massive loss of confidence is likely to be reflected by panic in the market. Sixth, growth in the economy is likely to cease, as whole areas come under intense pressure and confidence is so low as to deter investment; besides, a great many people will be out of work and out of hope, as whole industries disappear or contract. I could go on, but the

general sorts of consequences likely to attend the wholesale demise of the meat and meat-related industries are not difficult to envisage.

The above, then, are some — by no means all — of the sorts of practical considerations relevant to the assessment of Singer's claim of utility. Myself, I suspect that merely those listed, if thoroughly gone into, would cast serious doubt upon that claim; but not even to bother with them, not even to touch the practicalities surrounding it gives that claim, a claim of utility, an air of fantasy, of make-believe.

The Claim of Progressive Collapse

In his paper 'Utilitarianism and vegetarianism', Singer adopts the line, which was by no means apparent in *Animal Liberation*, that the argument from pain and suffering envisages not so much the relatively immediate collapse of the meat industry as its eventual collapse over some extended, unspecified period.[12] Perhaps some readers will think this makes all the difference *vis-à-vis* Singer's claim of utility, in order to avoid harmful consequences of the sorts depicted above; but, again, the practical considerations need to be looked at carefully. And some further practical considerations intrude with respect to this new claim of progressive collapse. I shall mention only some, since I hope that the sorts of considerations relevant are now apparent and that readers can go on to supply others themselves.

(1) Singer may have difficulty with his supporters. The message purveyed in *Animal Liberation* is that the argument from pain and suffering has direct and immediate effect on factory farming and so on the meat industry, and whenever I have discussed that argument with others it is this prospect of having an effect, of now making a difference which has most often been cited as perhaps its cardinal feature. Thus it is far from clear to me that Singer's argument would have had the impact it has if it had had appended to it the rider that the meat industry will nevertheless not disappear in our lifetimes. The more adherents to the argument who fall by the wayside, however, the less likely it is that the future will see the demise of the meat industry.

(2) In a society such as ours, if a Singer vegetarian adheres to the idea that change in diet must come through voluntary means, then it seems likely that the demise of the meat industry must indeed be a distant accomplishment at best. For with voluntary means, the Singer vegetarian must constantly face the prospect of either failing each year to convert more people than come into the market as meat-eaters or failing sufficiently to convert enough people to have other than a transitory and negligible effect on the meat industry. Should this happen, as presently it

does, the temptation for the Singer vegetarian to consider non-voluntary means of securing his goal will be considerable. Just as many of those who object to painful scientific experiments involving animals want to see this use of animals stopped now and not a hundred years from now, so, I suspect, most vegetarians want to see the meat trade eliminated at once or in the immediate future. Here, as elsewhere, no doubt, it is difficult to keep people loyal to a cause when its triumph, if it does triumph, is so far in the future as constantly to appear elusive. And the triumph is delayed, at least in part, by the Singer vegetarian having to wait for enough people voluntarily to come round to his views. Just as the Animal Liberation Front in Britain has begun to resort to non-voluntary means in the face of what its members see as inaction on the part of others about the use of animals in (painful) scientific experiments, so I can readily imagine a similar Front arising with respect to vegetarianism, when the triumph of that cause is, on the argument of one of its major proponents, seen as distant *at best*. Just how productive, and counter-productive, violence will prove will need to be assessed rather carefully.

(3)　In trying to envisage and gauge the progressive decline of the meat industry, why should Singer be allowed optimum assumptions, as opposed to assumptions which reflect present economic realities? For example, unemployment in Britain is greater than it has ever been, and unemployment throughout the EEC is very high indeed; when, then, do we start to throw more people out of work, through an assault on the meat, and, therefore, meat-related industries? Yet, every year we hesitate that industry becomes more entrenched, its tentacles reach further throughout the economy, and more meat-eaters come into the market.

　　Argentina's external debts are in excess of $40 billion, and it is utterly dependent upon external rescheduling of loans, refinancing by international banks and agencies, and direct governmental assistance. Just when is the moment for us to begin, if not actively to seek, then at least to envisage the collapse of one of its major exports, a further rise in its levels of unemployment, etc.?

　　Poland's debt to the West alone is now in excess of £25 billion, and, unlike, say, Argentina, its economic infrastructure is in disarray. Its export of meat, particularly hams, sausages, and cooked meats, has been one of its significant, hard currency earners, which has enabled it to purchase consumer goods from the West and to assist its citizens in reaching a tolerable standard of living. Just how long are we to wait, before urging the Poles to begin to give up these sources of hard currency? How do we gauge the moment to commence the attack on New Zealand's economy and its export of lamb? When is the time that we go to hog farmers in South Dakota, in that cold, rather barren, windswept state, and tell them that they must in increasing numbers look elsewhere for something that the soil and climate can support and that at the same time can provide them a living?

When our corner florist goes out of business, we can usually, depending upon the level of unemployment, comfort ourselves that he will find alternative work; but can we really comfort ourselves with similar thoughts, when whole communities, regions, and countries are increasingly hit through the decline in meat and meat-related businesses? For what are these would-be alternatives? And even if we can dream up such alternatives, will they actually come to pass and, more importantly, come to pass on the scale required to solve the problem?

(4) Are the hog farmers of South Dakota simply to turn to producing grains? Even assuming this is possible, which it is not, over much of that barren state, if a great many animal farmers turn to grains, then, according to Singer's own guidelines, prices will plummet; but if prices fall, can these farmers, who presently make a living (farming hogs), continue to do so? The plain fact is that in order to make a living from growing grains one needs considerably more land under cultivation than one needs for raising hogs; this is often overlooked, in the rush to condemn animal farming and to encourage farmers to desist. So what is a hog farmer to do, without the acres to make the grain business a profitable one and without the money to buy the acres?

(5) Job retraining programmes have never been a prominent part of the British landscape (in most countries, such programmes do not exist), and in recent years, as both major political parties have tried to control public expenditure, they have largely been shunted aside. While such programmes can at least be found in the United States, they have never been conspicuously well-funded or successful; to a great extent, moreover, they have been directed towards minorities. But the amount of job retaining Signer must envisage, however, is simply colossal, even if we confine our attention to the United States; for, in principle, every single person who depends either directly or indirectly upon the meat industry for a livelihood is potentially a candidate for retraining. The funds, facilities, etc., required are going to be staggering, and it is not clear either what less well-off communities, regions, and countries are going to do to overcome these obstacles, assuming we can induce them to start up such programmes, or what well-off communities, regions, and countries are going to do to overcome them, in difficult economic conditions.

(6) Job retraining is useless, unless there are jobs for retrained people to fill; so what are the industries Singer imagines springing up to absorb these people? Unemployment in Britain and the United States is at the levels of the Great Depression, and were these new industries springing up in abundant supply, we might already expect to see a diminution, not an increase, in the number of unemployed. Presumably, therefore, what we are to assume is this: over a period of time, the meat industry and all those businesses and industries connected with it are going to disappear or

suffer grievous losses; but the economic/industrial situation will be so markedly different from what it is today that the virtual catastrophe which would otherwise ensue will be averted. I can see absolutely no reason whatever for conceding this optimistic assumption, especially in the absence of any evidence; and I cannot conceive any government, now or in future, beginning a partial or wholesale assault on meat and meat-related industries, in the hope that, in time, though at the moment it is not clear when or how, the loss in jobs, revenues, taxes, capital, exports, etc., will be made good.

Of course, it may always be argued that, given a long enough period, Singer's claim of utility may turn out to be correct; but would any government, however optimistic, act on such a basis? Besides, to take a very long time span would require from Singer even more, not no, evidence in support of his claim, would demand of him an even more extensive, not no, examination of practicalities and of economic, social, and political circumstances.

(7)   Finally, we must not lose sight of sums, which indicate part of the enormity of Singer's task. As we have seen, in fiscal year 1980, Iowa Beef Processors, a single company (not, of course, a single plant), had revenues of $4.6 billion, and this is no small figure. So what is it that Signer thinks will put into the economy what the disappearance of Iowa Beef takes out? With or without a lengthy time span, we are talking about a *degree* of economic activity, which trickles down through the economy and so is good for the economy overall, that it will be difficult to make good; and this is the activity of a single (admittedly, large), meat-related company. If, therefore, we come across a utilitarian making some claim about the utility of the demise of Iowa Beef, we shall certainly want to be clear as to how exactly he proposes to make good the loss sustained by the economy, and business activity overall.

Thus, in the absence of any careful sifting of practical considerations, I can see no reason for accepting, and good reason for treating sceptically, the claim that, if we all turned to vegetarianism, the good consequences involved in eliminating the pains of food animals would more than outweigh the bad consequences involved in the immediate or progressive collapse of the meat industry. Any final rejection of this claim, however, must await a thorough examination of the practicalities involved, of which I have surveyed only some.

The Claim of Practicality/Effectiveness

In chapter 4 of *Animal Liberation*, Singer puts forward a very bold claim indeed on behalf of vegetarianism:

Becoming a vegetarian is not merely a symbolic gesture. Nor is it an attempt to isolate oneself from the ugly realities of the world, to keep oneself pure and so without responsibility for the cruelty and carnage all around. Becoming a vegetarian is the most practical and effective step one can take towards ending both the killing of non-human animals and the infliction of suffering upon them.[13]

Though this claim of practicality and effectiveness is a factual one, Singer presents no data to show that it is true, nor am I prepared to concede that it is. Indeed, it is deeply implausible.

First, however, I should note that, if the concerned individual supports the measures set out in this and the last chapter, and more, then it is hard to see why he should think that his tactic will obviously be less effective in reducing food animal suffering than giving up ham sandwiches and fried chicken.

Of course, part of this individual's tactic calls for social/political action, and, as I have already remarked, it is common today to dismiss demonstrations, hard and serious lobbying, and sustained work through the political system as ineffective because of counter-pressure by powerful, vested-interest groups. But I believe this kind of activity has borne fruit in the United States, in the face of enormously powerful opposition, in the civil rights legislation of the 1960s, culminating in the Voting Rights Act of 1965, in the end to American involvement in Vietnam, and in many other instances, and I see no reason to dismiss in advance its effectiveness in coming to grips with some present farming practices.

Indeed, in Britain, in July 1981, a House of Commons Select Committee on Agriculture found against many of the abuses in factory farming, and called for sweeping reforms, including the abolition of battery cages for hens after five years, the abolition of individual stalls with concrete floors and no straw bedding for pregnant sows, the abolition of purely liquid feed for veal calves, and the increased use of a British method for rearing these calves (described in chapter 16), which dispenses with the crate system in favour of roofed yards, where animals can roam freely.[14] The House of Commons as a whole has yet to decide on this report, and it may well be in the end that it is diluted; but, even so, there is no doubt that it represents a significant advance in combating the abuses of factory farming. It owes nothing, however, to some tidal wave of vegetarianism sweeping Britain, to some nearly universal refusal to eat meat; there has been no such phenomenon. The plain fact is that, at least in this instance and to this extent, animal welfarists and other concerned individuals have succeeded in precisely the way that the tactic of the concerned individual encourages and envisages.

Who can say, if the concerned individual and others like him are successful in raising public awareness of needed reforms in farming and bringing about action in support of these reforms, that each of them would obviously have been more effective or have acted more effectively by their not eating ham sandwiches and fried chicken?[15]

And this is the point: Singer would actually have us believe that the most effective step each of us individually can take to lessen food animal suffering is to give up ham and chicken. But this *obviously* will not do; for my individual act of giving up ham sandwiches and fried chicken will make no impression whatever, either on the way pigs and chickens are treated, or on the number of pigs and chickens reared for food. As I noted earlier, a single poultry company in the United States processed five million broilers *a week* in 1979, and it is quite fantastic to suppose that my individual act of giving up fried chicken could affect, for this single company, let alone the poultry industry nation- and world-wide, either this number or the conditions in which these birds are raised. Plainly, for my act to have any effect whatever, it must form part of an extensive and sustained series of similar acts.

Nor do I agree that giving up meat is obviously the most practical step one can take to deal with the farming practices in question. If my house is on fire, I put water on it; it is not obviously more practical for me to advocate a ban on the sale of matches. In the case of factory farms, if I want to do something immediately practical in respect of the cruelly narrow spaces in which veal calves have been raised, I press hard for the necessary legislation and the search for substitutes (much in the way the Commons Select Committee has, as we have seen, advised). I do not obviously do something more practical by deciding one night in my study to give up veal cutlets, ham sandwiches, and fried chicken, especially if the overwhelmingly vast majority of people continue to eat meat, a prospect I simply must accept as a practical certainty. (The result of more stringent legislation on confinement in rearing may mean that fewer food animals can be raised; but it may not. Allowing animals considerably more room in which to move about may not mean that numbers will plummet; it depends upon the particular method envisaged, the amount of space available, and the type of animal in question. In the case of veal calves, for example, the alternative to the crate system which was put before the Commons Select Committee did not lead to sharply reduced numbers of calves being farmed.)

Again, if I object to the number of hens kept in a battery cage and want to do something immediately practical about it, how could I think that I was doing so by giving up the two fried eggs I have for breakfast three days a week? And is my forgoing these eggs really doing something immediately practical to stop the de-beaking of laying hens?

Do I really take the most practical step I can to stop the spread of (overcrowded) rather small feed lots for beef cattle by giving up hamburgers? Can I really pretend in all honesty that my giving up hamburgers is going to do anything at all about those feed lots? And if I have doubts that stunning prior to slaughter is being carried out as rigorously and thoroughly as is necessary always to prevent beef cattle being conscious at the moment of slaughter, can I really pretend that my no longer eating steak is going to do anything about this, let alone that it is the most practical and effective step I could take to rectify matters?

(Curiously, Singer's position would appear to call always and inevitably for a single course of action, whatever the particular complaint against intensive farming. If I want hogs to have straw bedding, then, presumably, I must on Singer's view give up eating them; I am not to rectify matters by seeking to ensure that they have straw bedding.)

Ultimately, of course, Singer's position here comes to this, that the most practical and effective means of reducing suffering on factory farms is to eliminate factory farms (and, depending upon how far the charge of cruel practices is carried, traditional livestock and poultry farms as well). Now it is perfectly true that one way of, say, eliminating and preventing the abuse of child labour in factories is to abolish all factories; but it is also true that there is a middle way between allowing such an abuse to persist unchecked and abolishing all factories, a way which many nations have adopted. Likewise, there is a middle way between allowing certain farming practices to persist unchecked and eliminating all animal farms; it is the way of the concerned individual, who attacks the issue of these practices head-on through the measures I have indicated (and who, accordingly, is not obviously open to complaints against animal farming which turn upon his being insensitive to cruelty).

The Claim of Knowledge

After the practicality/effectiveness claim, we come to Singer's equally bold claim of knowledge. He claims that each person can 'know' that his individual act of becoming a vegetarian will 'contribute to a reduction in the suffering and slaughter of animals, whether or not he lives to see his efforts spark off a mass boycott of meat and an end to cruelty in farming.'[16] In this, he contends, the boycott of meat is different from most other boycotts: 'the person who boycotts South African produce in order to bring down apartheid achieves nothing unless the boycott succeeds in forcing white South Africans to modify their policies.'[17] On what does this purported knowledge of contributing to a reduction in suffering rest? Singer's answer is that, 'although we cannot identify any individual animals whom we have benefited by becoming a vegetarian, we can assume that our diet has some impact on the number of animals raised in factory farms and slaughtered for food.'[18] In short, Singer's knowledge claim here rests upon the assumption that each individual's act of becoming a vegetarian directly affects the number of animals raised on factory farms, and only if this assumption is correct is his knowledge claim viable.

Michael Martin is obviously right to regard this claim as dubious; indeed, it is, I think, little short of astonishing. To see just how astonishing, simply consider: while it is true that the number of vegetarians in the United States has increased substantially since 1950, until, today, there are millions of them, it is also true that, as a recent television documentary reported, the amount of poultry bred on American farms since 1950 has increased in stupendous proportions (5,000,000,000 birds are processed annually), until today, American poultry and poultry by-products not only are a common foodstuff throughout the United States but also are exported abroad in such quantities as to have bestowed upon the poultry industry vast fortunes many times over. In other words, though the number of vegetarians has increased significantly, the number of chickens and turkeys has not decreased but increased, to a degree so colossal that a single company processes five million broilers a week, that a single restaurant chain, Kentucky Fried Chicken, requires countless millions of chickens monthly, that a single nation, the United States, processes more than five billion birds each year. How could any individual who has become a vegetarian in the last 30 years possibly think his act contributed to a decrease in the number of chickens (and turkeys) bred on factory farms? Nor is it the case, obviously, that any single one of these acts of becoming a vegetarian has contributed to a diminution in the demand for poultry. On the contrary, every person who has become a vegetarian in the last 30 years has done so in a period which has seen the greatest increase in the demand for chicken (and turkey) since records have been kept. And this is only poultry, not livestock generally.

There are some additional factors that should be noted with respect to Singer's claim of knowledge.

(1) The implausibility of the knowledge claim has repercussions for the practicality/effectiveness claim. For what are we to think of the practicality and effectiveness, so far as animal suffering is concerned, of a specific individual's act of becoming a vegetarian during the last 30 years? More importantly, what is that individual himself to think? He gave up meat in order to reduce animal suffering; he now finds, however, that vastly more animals are being factory farmed. In the United States, for example, he finds that the consumption of meat has risen to more than 200 pounds per person per year, that a single fast-food chain McDonald's, has sold more than forty billion hamburgers in a relatively short period (and it is but one of many such chains), that the sales of ground beef generally have reached astronomical heights,[19] that the import of lower-grade beef under a quota law now exceeds 1 billion pounds annually, with more than 250 million pounds of that supplied by Australia,[20] that meat production (in these figures in the United States, 'meat' does not encompass poultry and fish) for the first ten months of 1981 totalled an unbelievable 32,000,000,000 pounds,[21] and so on. Might it not now occur to him, if he really is concerned to take practical and effective action to reduce animal suffering, that he would do better in these circumstances to deal directly with the specific abuses on factory farms?

(2) It might be maintained, of course, that each act of becoming a

vegetarian at least does not contribute to an increase in the demand for poultry and so in this way might be held to affect the number of birds bred and thereby the amount of suffering inflicted. This line of argument, however, gets nowhere. The basic suggestion which underlies it, viz., that each person's act of becoming a vegetarian directly affects the demand for poultry, and so spares some birds the agony of being bred into a cruel life, is implausible. It is most unlikely that one's own individual act of forgoing chicken in one's diet has reduced by even a fraction the number of chickens bred, not only because the diets of other people more than make up for one's own, but also because a single act of giving up chicken, special circumstances apart, simply has no effect upon market forces. If I give up eating apples, I am most unlikely to reduce by even one apple the number grown this year, and I can see no reason to think there is a difference in market forces here between chickens and apples. Of course, it may well be that, if everyone in Ohio, New York, Pennsylvania, and California were to give up eating apples, the market would be affected (in the absence, that is, of offsetting factors, several of which I mention below); but Singer's present claim is that each of us can know that our own individual act of giving up chicken directly affects the market, whether or not we live to see our act reflected in the acts of other people.

(3)   We must not be misled into thinking that by not increasing suffering through one's own act one decreases suffering on factory farms. True, one may not oneself contribute to an increase; but every individual who has become a vegetarian since 1950 knows, as a well-informed person, that even as he has been embracing vegetarianism the total amount of suffering being inflicted on, say, poultry farms has been increasing by huge proportions. There is no way that an individual's not increasing suffering can amount to a reduction in total suffering, when demand for poultry is soaring.

But has one not kept oneself pure? Readers will recall, however, that it is Singer's view that vegetarianism is not 'an attempt to isolate oneself from the ugly realities of the world, to keep oneself pure and so without responsibility for the cruelty and carnage all around.' It is not purity but a reduction in animal suffering that Singer is after and that his tactic of vegetarianism is supposed to secure. But his tactic comes unstuck: in a situation where demand for poultry is soaring (or, for that matter, relatively constant) even as the number of vegetarians is increasing, it is very difficult indeed to see how becoming a vegetarian is the most practical and effective step one can take to reduce suffering, since total suffering is increasing, and I know it is increasing, whatever my individual decision about eating chicken. In these circumstances, I would seem, once again, to stand a better chance of reducing suffering on poultry farms by dealing directly with the practices and devices which inflict that suffering, in the way depicted by the concerned individual.

(4)   We must not be misled into thinking, in some simplistic fashion, that, by not eating chicken, we at least do not increase the number of chickens bred. For this suggests that poultry farmers will simply keep on increasing the size of their holdings if even one more person eats chicken than is presently doing so, and here also, special circumstances apart, it is quite implausible to assume that any single act can affect the market in this way. In other words, if everyone who is at present a vegetarian were to begin to eat chicken, the market would doubtless be affected; but if only one present-day vegetarian were to begin to eat chicken, it is unlikely in the extreme that his act would affect the market in the slightest.

(5)   A simplistic view of market forces such as the above − that if even one more person eats chicken than is presently doing so poultry farmers will increase their holdings − overlooks a host of additional factors which any realistic view must take into account. For example, the cost of feed, machinery, labour, electricity, housing supplies, and transportation may deter farmers breeding additional chickens, if one more person takes to eating chicken; the use of support prices, credits, and surpluses to regulate holdings is common throughout advanced nations, and these can work in favour of keeping up production as well as in favour of preventing a loss in production; local cartels, such as the European Economic Commission, which buys up beef at support prices in order to keep market prices firm, increasingly attempt to regulate production as well as demand (through prices); and the use of induced shortages, of not producing or breeding up to demand in order to force a higher price for what is produced or bred, is an everyday market phenomenon, as useful to the poultry as to the coffee industry. A host of other factors, such as government regulations, the tax situation of individual farmers, the availability of long-term loans, interest rates, the state of the various meats' futures markets, general economic confidence, overall energy costs, and the firmness of markets, would have to be taken into account as well, and this the simplistic view of market forces set out above signally fails to do.

(6)   Having mentioned surpluses and support prices, I should perhaps warn against a mistake. This is to assume that, if support prices are in existence, a farmer will go increasing the size of his holdings, in order to increase his income; thus, it might be held, the existence of support prices assists Singer's case. I have already indicated some of the constraints on farmers increasing their holdings; but even if there were no constraints whatever, Singer must attack, not support, support prices.

Anyone familiar with the EEC's Common Agricultural Policy will know that, in the absence of control over production, surpluses are inevitable,[22] if support prices work inflexibly. A Singer vegetarian is, in political terms, going to have to attack the use of support prices for meat in the most serious and sustained way, even if it means grievous financial losses and doom for numerous farmers and others. (Here, too, is another factor to be weighed in assessing Singer's claim of utility.) For if support prices produce a state of surplus, then no individual could think his act of becoming a vegetarian was going to have any effect at all on animal suffering. Support prices would insulate the farmer from any adverse effect of that person's act, even assuming it had one. But the whole point of Singer's case for vegetarianism is to affect the farmer's profits and, through these, the number of food animals bred. Accordingly, he must do everything he can to remove any barriers in the way of the farmer's feeling the effects of the vegetarian's giving up meat.

The situation, then, is this: if support prices obtain (which, if unregulated, means a surplus), farmers are exceedingly unlikely to feel the effects, assuming there are some, of one more person becoming a vegetarian; if support prices do not obtain (or do not work inflexibly, or in the absence of controls over production), then there are the relatively straightforward reasons I gave earlier why it is exceedingly unlikely that one more person's eating chicken will increase the size of farmers' holdings.

The Appeal to Thresholds

In his post-*Animal Liberation* paper, 'Utilitarianism and vegetarianism', Singer claims that, even if 'the loss of one consumer from the millions who buy animal flesh makes so small a difference that it is impossible to say that it affects the number of animals reared and killed', there, nevertheless, 'must be some point at which the number of vegetarians makes a difference to the size of the poultry industry.' He goes on:

> There must be a series of thresholds, hidden by the market system of distribution, which determine how many factory farms will be in existence. In this case one more person becoming a vegetarian will make no difference at all, unless that individual, added to the others who are already vegetarians, reduces demand below the threshold level at which a new factory farm would have started up (or an existing one would have remained in production, if the industry is declining).[23]

Clearly, the claims of effectiveness and knowledge are here relinquished; what Singer is now saying of your individual act of becoming a vegetarian is that you have no reason whatever to believe (or to claim to know) that it will affect in the slightest the number of chickens bred and killed, let alone that it will affect that number directly and immediately. Unless, Singer now maintains, your act occurs at the threshold, where one more act of that kind tips the balance against a new or presently existing factory farm. This new addition, however, is of scant use to you and your decision about whether to become a vegetarian. For the fact of the matter is that you do not know what the threshold in question is, do not know whether your act of giving up meat is at the threshold, do not know whether your act approaches but does not exceed the threshold, do not know at the time of deciding how many others are contemplating giving up meat, and do not know how many additional meat-eaters are at the very time you are thinking of leaving the meat market about to come into it and so about to cancel out altogether your departure from it. The situation, then, is this: your act of giving up meat will, under this threshold condition, only have an effect on the meat market if it occurs at the threshold, and you lack all knowledge in the above respects; plainly, therefore, if your act does occur at the threshold, and so does have an effect on the market, it is purely by chance. As for probabilities, they are strongly against such a chance; the overwhelming likelihood is that your act will, as we have seen, fail to make any impression whatever on the market.

Not only do you lack knowledge of thresholds in the above respects, but it is also far from clear how you are to acquire that knowledge. For exactly how are you supposed to find out whether a sufficient number of others are, at the time you are contemplating giving up meat, also about to decide to do so? Notice, as Signer concedes, that unless they do so decide, your act will have no effect. Notice also, however, in confronting this question that you do not know how many a 'sufficient number of others' is. How, then, are you supposed to position yourself in order to obtain the requisite pieces of information?

I have written a good deal about the above sorts of problems and thresholds elsewhere.[24] But there is one further point I should mention here, since so much discussion of thresholds, as in the passage from Singer above, ignores it. This is the fact that the threshold is not always a point, such that one more act of the kind in question is sufficient to cross the threshold, but sometimes a range, such that a series of acts of the kind in question is necessary to exceed the threshold. Thus, it is most implausible to suppose that a single further act of walking on the grass will damage the lawn irreparably; a series of acts of walking on the grass, a series of such acts at the threshold, seems required for this. It seems much more plausible to assume something of the sort in the case of factory farming, namely, that it is not a single additional act of becoming a vegetarian at the threshold that will exceed it and so tip the balance against a new or presently existing factory farm, but a series of such acts at the threshold that is required to exceed it. If this is so, then even an act of becoming a vegetarian at the threshold will, unless it forms part of a series of similar acts at the threshold, have no effect on factory farming. How you are supposed to position yourself to find out that your act is not merely part of a series of similar acts but also part of a series of similar acts at the threshold is not explained.

Thus, at its most basic, the problem with the appeal to thresholds is our ignorance about them, in the ways I have indicated, and our seeming inability to position ourselves to undo this ignorance. Singer, in short, has abandoned the claims of practicality/effectiveness and of knowledge but without obtaining much, if anything, in return.

The Concession

Singer concludes his paper 'Utilitarianism and vegetarianism' with the following passage:

> Finally, becoming a vegetarian is a way of attesting to the depth and sincerity of one's belief in the wrongness of what we are doing to animals. Perhaps in a society of sophisticated philosophers there would be no need to attest to one's sincerity in this way, *because sophisticated philosophers would understand that one can sincerely oppose the exploitation of animals in factory farms while continuing to buy and enjoy the product of these very farms.* But to most of the members of our society this would mean, as it seemed to Oliver Goldsmith's fictitious Chinese traveller, a 'strange contrariety of conduct'.[25]

This passage, indeed, the article from which it is taken, was in part written with my remarks in this chapter in mind (Singer saw an earlier version of them), and I take the present passage to concede the case of the concerned individual I have described.

Why, however, is Singer's concession couched in terms of sophisticated philosophers? For what is so very strange about the concerned individual's tactic? He objects to certain practices and abuses on factory farms and takes steps to deal with them, without any reason whatever for thinking his tactic will be any less efficacious (indeed, quite the contrary) than Singer's. Moreover, since abuses are to be dealt with, yet our meat diet retained, I should have thought an act-utilitarian such as Singer would see this twin solution, in view of the claim of utility that could be made on its behalf, as an acceptable (or, at least, a promising) one.

As for a 'strange contrariety in conduct', it is by no means apparent to me that ordinary people are quite so unsophisticated as all that. For consider: a man who strongly disapproves of a law which he thinks arbitrarily discriminates against him, who obeys that law, but who takes every legal step he can, through lobbying, demonstrating, and trying to exert pressure on both public and legislators, to have that law changed, would seem to exhibit Singer's 'strange contrariety of conduct'. But this sort of thing is as familiar as can be, and part of the very stuff and substance of social/political life. To disapprove of that law and take no steps whatever to do something about it would be as open to objection as would disapproving of certain factory farming practices and taking no steps to deal with them; but what is so strange about dealing with them in the way of the above character and the concerned individual?

To speak of a 'strange contrariety in conduct' implies at least in part that one is not behaving as one might be expected to, given, say, one's opposition to certain practices; but why should my opposition to de-beaking lead one to expect me to abstain from chicken more than it should lead one to expect me to seek legislation banning de-beaking, alternatives that do not require it, and so on?

In the case of factory farming, there would be a 'strange contrariety in conduct' only if (a) one disapproved of, say, de-beaking chickens but took no steps to do anything about it and (b) vegetarianism were the only way of doing anything about it. But (a) is not true of the concerned individual, and (b) is not true at all; and the falsity of (a) and (b), once it is brought to the attention of ordinary people, should enable them not merely to appreciate, but also to feel comfortable with, the concerned individual's position.

Notes

1   See Michael Martin, 'A critique of moral vegetarianism', and Martin's 'Vegetarianism, the right to life and fellow creature-hood', *Animal Regulation Studies*, vol. 2, 1979–80, pp. 205–14; Tom Regan, 'Utilitarianism, vegetarianism, and animal rights', *Philosophy and Public Affairs*, vol. 9, 1980, pp. 304–24; Philip Devine, 'The moral basis of vegetarianism', *Philosophy*, vol. 53, 1978, pp. 481–505; and Peter Wenz, 'Act-utilitarianism and animal liberation', *The Personalist*, vol. 60, 1979, 423–8. There is, of course, a good deal of other critical material that could be cited.

2   Peter Singer, 'Utilitarianism and vegetarianism', *Philosophy and Public Affairs*, vol. 9, 1980, pp. 325–37, especially pages 334–7.

3   Michael Martin, 'Vegetarianism, the right to life and fellow creature-hood', p. 205. This passage is intended by Martin as a summation of his (earlier) case against Singer in 'A critique of moral vegetarianism'.

4   Peter Singer, *Animal Liberation*, p. 165 (my italics).

5   Ibid., p. 166.

6   Ibid.

7   See 'American farming survey', *The Economist*, 5 Jan. 1980, p. 10.

8   See 'Occidental to acquire Iowa beef', *International Herald Tribune*, 2 June 1981.

9   Tom Regan, 'Utilitarianism, vegetarianism, and animal rights'.

10 This is not to say that Singer and I hold precisely the same theory; in this regard, see my discussion of his theory, as manifested in his discussion of killing, in chapter 15. But I have not yet spelled out in detail (there are just more or less unrelated, published papers), precisely what my utilitarianism is; so it is perhaps unfair to Singer to allude to further differences between us.

11 See John Huxley, 'Oil price uncertainty gives wool a boost', *The Times*, 3 Oct. 1980.

12 Peter Singer, 'Utilitarianism and vegetarianism', p. 334.

13 Peter Singer, *Animal Liberation*, pp. 165–6.

14 See *Animal Welfare in Poultry, Pig and Veal Calf Production: Commons Paper 406 − I*, First Report, Vol. 1 (London, HMSO, 1981). See also Hugh Clayton, 'Select committee votes for ban on battery hen cages', *The Times*, 24 July 1981; and his 'Britain to press EEC for urgent reforms', *The Times*, 27 July 1981.

15 See Michael Martin, 'A critique of moral vegetarianism', p. 28.

16 Peter Singer, *Animal Liberation*, p. 169.

17 Ibid.

18 Ibid., p. 168.

19 See Robert Lindsey, 'Nation's love of beef cools', *New York Times*, 24 Oct. 1981. This article makes clear that sales of chicken, pork, and fish have increased at the expense of beef, as the result of price increases.

20 See 'Horse meat from down under?', *Huntington Herald-Dispatch*, 13 Aug. 1981.
21 See 'Meat output off in October', *New York Times*, 28 Nov. 1981.
22 They are also costly. In addition to the money the EEC Commission pays to buy up goods at support levels, there are the sizeable costs involved in transporting, storing, and preserving whatever is in question. The 'butter mountain' sat upon by the United States costs more than a million dollars a day to house and preserve.
23 Peter Singer, 'Utilitarianism and vegetarianism', p. 335.
24 See, e.g., Frey, 'On causal consequences', *Canadian Journal of Philosophy*, vol. IV, 1974, pp. 365–79; Frey, 'Judgments of causal importance in the social sciences', *Philosophy of the Social Sciences*, vol. 6, 1976, pp. 245–8; Frey, 'Can act-utilitarianism be put into practice?', *Journal of Value Inquiry*, vol. XI, 1977, pp. 49–58; Frey, 'Causal responsibility and contributory causation', *Philosophy and Phenomenological Research*, vol. XXXIX, 1978, pp. 106–19.
25 Peter Singer, 'Utilitarianism and vegetarianism', p. 337 (my italics).

18

Sincerity and Consistency

The last chapter concluded with Singer's concession to the concerned individual. It may be thought by some of Singer's allies, however, that he has either conceded too much or let the concerned individual off too lightly, though precisely what charge they will themselves want to bring against the concerned individual may vary among themselves. I shall look at what I think would be two such charges, those of insincerity and inconsistency. My replies, as the charges themselves, are linked; they focus on the link between what the concerned individual says and what he does.

An Overview

If readers look again at Singer's paper 'Utilitarianism and vegetarianism', they will, I think, be surprised at how well the concerned individual fares there. This, of course, will be worrying for Singer's moral vegetarian allies; for if the concerned individual cannot otherwise be disposed of, then the success of his tactic will be seen as coming at their expense. If his tactic really does reduce and eliminate factory farming abuses without recourse to vegetarianism, then the case for negative moral vegetarianism, based upon Singer's argument from pain and suffering, will have been undercut.

Accordingly, I suspect that some of Singer's allies will be very sensitive to the fact that he lets the concerned individual off relatively lightly. That is, I do not think they will consider the observation that ordinary people will take the concerned individual to exhibit a 'strange contrariety of conduct' to constitute a charge powerful enough to sustain the view that, even if the concerned individual's tactic will clean up factory farming, we cannot adopt it. It is, they will feel, just not sufficiently damning to observe of someone that he exhibits a 'strange contrariety of conduct', especially when one goes on to add that sophisticated people or philosophers will know that there is nothing so very strange involved after all. Hence, the charges of insincerity and inconsistency.

Singer sees vegetarianism as an attempt to do something effective about the plight of food animals; the concerned individual's point is that we can do something effective about the plight of food animals without becoming vegetarians. Put this way, the concerned individual's point is obvious; after all, as I remarked earlier, it is not because vegetarianism has swept Britain that a Parliamentary Committee has come out against several commercial farming abuses and in favour of alternatives or that an increasing number of non-vegetarians have come to press for improved treatment of food animals. So it is perfectly clear — what is doubtless true in the cases of many of my readers — that there are meat-eaters who are concerned to reduce and eliminate commercial farming abuses. It is equally clear, moreover, that they will go about this task in exactly the way they go about such tasks in the other affairs of life, namely, by seeking and implementing reforms and so in time effecting the desired changes. Complete elimination of abuses will be gradual: in the report of the Parliamentary Committee referred to above and discussed in the last chapter, a period of several years is envisaged for phasing out certain methods of animal rearing, during which, of course, farmers (and the meat industry as a whole) can seek for and/or adapt to new alternatives.

I stress the gradual elimination of abuses, because in this is to be found the ground of the charges of insincerity and inconsistency. If one disapproves of something, and if one continues to have something to do with it while awaiting reforms in it, then one allegedly is exposed to the charges of insincerity and/or inconsistency. Obviously, those who charge the concerned individual with insincerity and/or inconsistency must similarly charge anyone who seeks reform in anything, unless complete reform in whatever is instantaneously achieved. For so long as some but not all of the desired reforms are in place, all such persons continue to have something to do with that of which they disapprove, and so allegedly lay themselves open to the charges of insincerity and/or inconsistency.

If the above picture of the ground of the charges of insincerity and/or inconsistency were correct, reform from within would be impossible. If you are an Anglican priest and favour the admission of women to the priesthood, and if the vote at the General Synod goes against your camp, then you must yourself resign from the priesthood; for remaining a priest and trying to work for the admission of women from within, by, among other things, arguing the matter with your fellow clerics, allegedly constitutes approving of what you say you disapprove, and so exposes you to claims of insincerity and/or inconsistency. (The fact that the resignation of all such priests would almost certainly delay still further the admission of women to the priesthood is unfortunate but, I am sure proponents of the present view would say, not directly germane to the issues of insincerity and inconsistency.)

What has gone wrong here is that the charges of insincerity and inconsistency have become global and without regard to particularities of cases. Thus, all Anglican priests everywhere are insincere and/or inconsistent, whatever the particularities of their cases, if they disapprove of restricting the priesthood to men, yet carry on in it. The fact that a priest may be in favour of change, may have worked for change, may have been in the forefront of the lobby for change, and may have helped to bring about other changes in the church with respect to the position of women is to no avail; he is insincere and/or inconsistent. This is absurd: not to struggle at all is one thing, but to struggle and only partially succeed and to continue to struggle is quite another, and it seems quite misguided to lump both things together under some blanket condemnation.

Absurdity arises because blanket condemnations lose sight of differences; but there is a mistake involved as well. This is to ignore a person's beliefs and attitudes and to refuse to consider a full array of a person's actions with respect to whatever is in question, in trying to answer questions about his sincerity and consistency. The result is either that we cannot give informed answers to these questions, or that we have no reason for picking upon one thing as opposed to another as indicative of a person's sincerity and consistency. If you came across a priest who had fought long and hard for the ordination of women, who deeply regretted that the vote had gone against his camp, and who resolved to work even harder to effect changes in the priesthood, it would be presumptious to dismiss him as insincere because he remained a priest. For why should his not resigning the priesthood be a better indication of his sincerity than his long, hard, but only partially successful struggle to improve the lot of women in the Church? We have no reason to think that it is; whereas, if we do go beyond some blanket condemnation to examine his beliefs and attitudes about the role of women in the Church, and if we do look at a full array of actions with respect to improving the position of women in it, then the weight of the evidence should enable us to decide whether his not resigning the priesthood really is an indication of his sincerity in the matter.

It is true, of course, that the Church will not be fully reformed overnight, and so long as the position of women in it is not what our priest thinks is morally required, he must continue to work to see the deficiency repaired. Should he change his moral views in the matter, then he could rest content with the priesthood as it is; but so long as his moral views remain as they are, he must seek reform or change. To do nothing would expose him to the very charges of insincerity and/or inconsistency from which his present activity shield him.

(Working from within an organization like the priesthood that is not all one would like it to be, is not at all the same thing as working from within an organization that is utterly corrupt, morally. Can one exploit Jews while working for the removal of the Nazi regime? All of us would hope that anyone contemplating this would realize that working for the removal of the Nazi regime is not the only thing to be weighed and assessed in the situation; the nature of the regime, the actual prospect of effectively changing it, and the deliberate, massive destruction of innocent human life obviously are extremely important parts of the picture. Even so, the matter is not open and shut. I believe Israel has honoured Oskar Schindler, who, as I understand it, co-operated with the Nazis by successfully running factories for them, which made use of Jewish slave labour, but who all the while was working to save and was instrumental in saving hundreds of Jewish lives.

On the larger question, of when moral deficiency passes into moral corruptness, I am unsure. Some examples seem to me clearly one or clearly the other; but how great the moral deficiency can be before an organization becomes morally corrupt I am uncertain.)

The above discussion raises the issues on which I now want to elaborate. Since these issues are some of the most difficult and far-reaching in all of ethics, it is not possible that I should do full justice to them in the space allowed me. I shall explain why I think the concerned individual is neither insincere nor inconsistent; but I concede from the outset that my account of the issues raised is but one of many that might be given.

The Charge of Insincerity or Hypocrisy

Singer allows, to recall, that 'sophisticated philosophers . . . understand that one can sincerely oppose the exploitation of animals in factory farms while continuing to buy and enjoy the product of these very farms'; some of Singer's allies, however, may want to charge the concerned individual with being insincere or a hypocrite.

Relation to a fuller context

The difficulty with the charge of insincerity is to see how it is applicable to the concerned individual. For his case is like so many others with which we are all familiar but which very few of us indeed paint in the colours of insincerity.

For example, suppose you are sent to interview President Kaunda of Zambia: you find him strongly opposed to South African apartheid, and you also find that under his leadership the Zambian Government denounces apartheid publicly, votes against it regularly in international bodies, seeks outside pressure to help oppose it, tries to assist those in other black African areas, such as South-West Africa, who want to be free of it, and takes what steps it can to deprive it of any and all respectability. You also discover, however, that from the inception of President Kaunda's leadership, Zambia has traded with South Africa, not in some trivial or insignificant way, but in reasonably substantial terms. Is President Kaunda insincere or a hypocrite with respect to his disapproval or condemnation of apartheid?

Now the point, obviously, is not that few of us think that he is; it is rather that, in order to determine whether President Kaunda is insincere over apartheid, we must look at the matter (a) in the context of all his actions with respect to it and (b) in the context of his beliefs and attitudes about it. As for (a), one typically sees him coming down hard against apartheid and South Africa; as for (b), when you press him in the interview on his beliefs about apartheid, you find that he regards it as an abomination or outrage against which all decent men must struggle, and his attitudes, grounded in his beliefs, are very negative with respect to it.

One simply cannot find out whether President Kaunda is insincere or not except by examining these fuller contexts, and when one does the weight of evidence is very much in the direction of his sincerity. To sever his consent to trade with South Africa from these contexts and then to charge him with insincerity over his condemnation of apartheid is, without any justification, to treat his consent to trade as a more accurate reflection of his sincerity than the weight of all his other actions with respect to apartheid. But what licenses this? One might maintain that in *this* case, unlike others, one can simply read off whether or not he is sincere from the particular action; but any such simple thesis as this clearly will not do. I shall return to this later.

The concerned individual is insincere or a hypocrite only by a similar process, namely, by trying to sever his eating meat from all of his actions with respect to certain intensive farming practices, from his open opposition to those practices, and from his beliefs about and attitudes towards them. Consider a particular case: you are sent to interview a concerned individual who opposes confining pregnant sows in tiny slatted stalls. You find during the interview that he does not disguise the fact that he eats ham;[1] you also find, however, that he implements fully the concerned individual's tactic and so tries to restrict and eliminate the practice in question, by, among other things, persistently drawing the abuse to people's attention, lobbying against it, and actively seeking the necessary improvements, alternatives, and legislation by which progress-ively to eliminate it. When you probe his beliefs, you find that he regards the practice in question as a serious abuse and that his attitudes, grounded in his beliefs, are very negative with respect to it.

One cannot find out whether the concerned individual is sincere except by examining these fuller contexts, and when one does look at the full range of his actions with respect to the abuse in question, when one does examine his beliefs and attitudes, the weight of evidence is overwhelmingly in favour of his sincerity. He is a hypocrite or insincere over his condemnation of the abuse only when these fuller contexts and his beliefs and attitudes are ignored; and the only justification for ignoring them that seems to make any sense is that one somehow knows his eating ham is a more accurate reflection of his sincerity than the weight of all the other evidence. But what makes this the case? Why is his insincerity here so much more transparent than his sincerity in the other instances in which he acts over the abuse? Why is eating ham in the privileged position of being the one, true indication? And how does one come to know this to be the case? Most especially, can we really just ignore the weight of evidence, for what looks very like special pleading over eating ham as the one, true guide to the concerned individual's sincerity?

(Why is the concerned individual not a vegetarian? It must be remembered that he has already shown that there is no reason whatever to think that his becoming a vegetarian would alter in the slightest the treatment of pregnant sows; indeed, as we have seen, he has every reason to think his own tactic, including its strong component of social/political action, will be more effective in coming to grips with the problem.)

Becoming an expression of sincerity

One question that needs to be asked is how one's doing or not doing something gets to be an expression of one's sincerity over a particular matter.

In his memoir of Arthur Prior, Anthony Kenny relates that Prior resolved, because of his opposition to the Vietnam war, not to visit the United States while that war lasted.[2] But how would a visit to that country show that Prior's opposition to the war was insincere? Indeed, how does his refusal to visit that country show that his opposition to the war was sincere? What, in short, does visiting or not visiting the United States have to do with sincerity in opposing the Vietnam war? So far as I can see, the answer is, *per se*, nothing whatever. Yet, a connection can be supplied, not through something further to do with the act or omission, but through something to do with the agent.

The connection most definitely is not supplied by the notion of effectiveness: Prior did not think his refusal to visit the United States would have any effect upon the war or upon the United States Government, but he was sincere in his opposition to that war. Your act of becoming a vegetarian has no effect upon factory farming, but you can be sincere in your vegetarianism.

So what does supply the connection? How does the matter of visiting or not visiting the United States get linked to one's opposition to the Vietnam war and in such a way as to manifest one's sincere opposition to that war? Whatever the complete answer, a part of it clearly seems to be that Prior himself makes the connection, by in part intending, allowing, and making it known that his not visiting the United States may be taken to serve as an index of his *bona fides* over opposition to the war. So to speak, he connects visiting or not visiting the United States with opposition to the war, by making not visiting an index of his *bona fides*; not visiting the United States is thus made a manifestation of his sincere opposition to the war when, *per se*, it has nothing to do with opposition to the war. But, and this is the important point, Prior could have made something else altogether serve as the index of his sincere opposition to the war; for

example, there is nothing whatever to have prevented his refusing to buy
American products, including American books, from serving in the same
capacity.

Just as there are different ways of expressing one's opposition to the
war, so there are different ways of expressing one's opposition to certain
factory farming practices. What makes the one you select an expresion or
manifestation of your sincerity in the matter is that you stand behind your
action or omission, in the sense that you intend, allow, and (if you choose)
make it known that that act or omission may be taken to serve as an index
of your *bona fide* opposition to those farming practices. *You* connect that act
or omission with opposition to those practices; but you could have made
some other act or omission serve as the index of your *bona fide* opposition
to them. There is not a single way only of expressing sincere opposition,
not a single way only of being sincere with respect to opposition to those
practices, so that any and all persons are sincere with respect to them only
if they perform exactly the same act. Two people can behave differently
with respect to them, and both be sincere.

Sincerity is a feature of people, not of actions, and if it is used of actions
at all, it is only because (a) we probe behind an array of actions to the
person who performs them, (b) we try to assess his beliefs and attitudes
and the relationship he sees himself standing in, *vis-à-vis* his *bona fides*, to
the actions in question, and (c), depending upon what we find as the
result of (a) and (b), we are able, over the full array of actions, to regard
them as manifestations of the beliefs and attitudes uncovered. Deliberately
to truncate this process and then to ask after a person's sincerity is to
deprive us of the means of constructing an informed answer.

Sincerity and action

Is it clear, however, that we need to construct an informed answer? Does
not one's eating ham *just show* that one's condemnation of the treatment of
pregnant sows is insincere?

Suppose you are sent to interview one of Singer's allies: does his not
eating ham *just show* that he sincerely opposes certain treatment of sows?
But how could it do this? How could not eating ham show he was sincere
unless you took his not eating it accurately to reflect, and so as a
manifestation of, his beliefs about and attitudes towards that treatment?
So, just as with the concerned individual, you look at the full array of his
actions with respect to factory farming, in order to get at his beliefs and
attitudes and at how he sees himself standing *vis-à-vis* his *bona fides* over
farming abuses in general and the treatment of pregnant sows in
particular, to not eating ham. For you are no fool: you are perfectly aware
that there are all sorts of explanations for this person's not eating ham that
are consistent with his not caring in the slightest about the treatment of
pregnant sows.

You treat this ally of Singer exactly as you do the concerned individual, and, in the way indicated, you do your best to uncover whether his not eating ham is an earmark of his *bona fide* opposition to a particular treatment of pregnant sows. It may or may not be, and the unfortunate truth is that part of what it is to experience life is to discover that what we took to be sincerity was in fact dissemblance. In general, to discover dissemblance, one needs more, not less, behaviour to examine, and this is another reason why it is important to look at a full array of actions with respect to factory farming abuses, by both Singer's ally and the concerned individual. But the result of examining any such array of their actions and trying to get at their beliefs and attitudes will almost certainly be that the overwhelming weight of evidence is in favour of the sincerity of both parties.

Playing us along

It is not always an easy matter to find out whether someone is sincere (indeed, that is my point), and any discussion of the matter has to leave room for the notion of playing us along.

It is sometimes held that we can best tell what a man's moral principles are not by what he says but by what he does, and, though it is obvious why this is thought, it simply will not do unless we add, among other things, that the man is sincere. Because it is difficult sometimes to determine whether someone is sincere, people can play us along, and there is no better way of doing this than by behaving in such a way as to facilitate false inferences about one's beliefs and attitudes, and about how one sees oneself as standing with respect to some proposed act or omission.

It would be silly to treat what one says as the guarantor of sincerity, since, in terms of one's *bona fides*, one can hide behind words; but it would be equally silly to think that we can, in some uncomplicated fashion, simply read off sincerity from actions, since it is just as easy to hide behind deeds. By both words and deeds, we can be played along, and any attempt to determine a person's sincerity must in the end take account of this fact. Our working assumption, that we can rely upon what a person says and does to reveal his *bona fides*, is a useful one, but all of us can attest that it is often no more than this. So, the temptation is to want more, to want behaviour to be not merely evidence for but a guarantor of sincerity; but if this means, as it would seem on one interpretation, that one can read off a person's sincerity simply from what he does or does not do, then one leaves insufficient room for the notion of playing us along.

Of course, the proper retort to all this is that, if you bothered to argue with one of Singer's moral vegetarian allies long enough, you would, so to speak, get beyond or past his not eating ham and appreciate that he was sincere in his opposition to a particular treatment of pregnant sows. That, however, is precisely what I maintain of the concerned individual, that if you probe his position and tactic, appreciate the different aspects of that tactic, and go into how he puts it into operation, then you will get beyond or past his eating ham, and appreciate that he is sincere in his opposition to confining pregnant sows in tiny slatted stalls. (Remember, he has no reason whatever to think that his abstaining from ham would alter in the slightest that particular treatment of pregnant sows, or that abstinence would prove more effective than or as effective as the active implementation of his own tactic in combating that abuse. Remember, also, that, though both tactics take time to achieve results, the concerned individual has reason for thinking his will take less time.)

The pretended cost

There is one other point I should perhaps append to this discussion of playing us along. It concerns playing us along in a slightly different way from that envisaged above.

Prior refused to visit the United States during the Vietnam war, and it was an earmark of his *bona fide* opposition to that war. Suppose, however, you were to discover that he never had any intention of visiting that country, that he strongly disliked travelling and especially disliked travelling by sea or air: does his refusal to visit the United States cease to be an earmark of his *bona fide* opposition to the Vietnam war? Again, Singer's ally refuses to eat ham, and it is an earmark of his *bona fide* opposition to a particular treatment of pregnant sows. Suppose, however, you were to discover that, even when he was a meat-eater he never ate ham, that he detested the taste of it and took considerable steps to avoid it: does his refusal to eat ham cease to be an earmark of his *bona fide* opposition to the treatment of pregnant sows?

In both cases, I am inclined to think the parties *can* remain sincere. They are pretending or playing us along about a cost for being sincere which they do not have to bear, but it does not follow that they are, therefore, pretending or playing us along about their *bona fide* opposition to the war in the one case or to the treatment of pregnant sows in the other. Of course, if you discovered someone pretending about the costs of sincerity you would want to look more closely to be sure that they were not pretending about sincerity itself, but a closer look *might* satisfy you that they were not.

I appreciate, however, that everyone may not be of this opinion, and I have little difficulty in imagining someone taking a firmer line. One such firmer line, however, produces a very curious result in the vegetarian's case.

When Kenny relates of Prior that he resolved not to visit the United States during the Vietnam war, he goes on to say that Prior's refusal was at some cost, since it involved turning down very attractive, academic offers. Prior's sincere opposition to the war cost him something, and this seems but a reflection of the view that a refusal to do something that does not cost one anything is perhaps not as reliable a guide to sincerity as a refusal which does. But this view produces a curious result in the vegetarian's case; for what does his vegetarianism cost him? One can imagine all sorts of peripheral answers, such as that it costs him the ease and convenience which a meat diet allows, the saving in time that shopping in a single supermarket allows, the wonderful culinary delights of French and Italian cooking, and so on. I call these peripheral answers because, were it to turn out that the vegetarian detested the taste of meat and had never, since childhood, wanted the culinary delights enjoyed by his friends, then the above costs are not really going to be seen by him as costs of his vegetarianism. One has not cost oneself (for instance) time by not doing what one never had any intention of doing; and vegetarianism has not cost one the delights of French and Italian cooking if one never would have tasted those delights in the first place.

In short, on this argument from cost, we are rapidly moving towards the view that the vegetarian must either like the taste of meat or want to eat it, or both, in order for his refusal to eat it to cost him something and so to be an earmark of his sincerity. And this is a curious result for a vegetarian; for it seems almost as though it requires him first to teach himself to love meat in order then for his refusal to eat it to exact a cost from him, and it would be an odd academy for vegetarians indeed whose introductory courses consisted in French and Italian meals.

Of course, all this assumes the view that a refusal to do something that does not exact a cost is not a reliable guide to sincerity (or not as reliable as a refusal which does exact a cost), and, though I myself am not convinced that sincerity must cost one, it is, I suspect, a rather common view. Whatever its truth, it is clear that the concerned individual can meet it, since, if readers will recall the different aspects of his tactic, its implementation is likely to require, in addition to money, a considerable amount of time and effort. This is obvious, even if one ignores everything else and concentrates only on his efforts at social/political action, at moving through the political process to capitalize on the desire for reform and through the legislative process to force and to implement reform, and at writing for the public about the problems and his position on them.

The Charge of Inconsistency

I think some of Singer's allies may want to say this, that even if the concerned individual is sincere, he is inconsistent. If he condemns cruelty yet accepts the benefits of some cruel farming practices, i.e., eats the relevant meats, then this shows that he in fact approves of cruelty, which, of course, is inconsistent with his condemnation of it.

Once again, however, it is hard to see how the charge is applicable to the concerned individual, and, in part, at least, the answer in this case resembles the answer to the question of insincerity. Perhaps a single example, developed from one given by Michael Martin,[3] can suffice to illustrate the point.

Approval and Action

President Brezhnev and his colleagues in the Kremlin condemn capitalism, among other reasons, because it in their eyes inevitably exploits workers; yet, the Soviet Union and its East European allies buy the products of capitalism whenever they can, borrow from (and repay) capitalist banks on a large scale, seek massive financial credits from capitalist governments, and so on. (The total indebtedness of COMECON countries to the West now exceeds $70 billion and is growing, even while some of the countries involved, such as Poland and Rumania, are forced by economic difficulties to re-schedule their present loans.) Is President Brezhnev inconsistent in trading with the West?

Actual approval

I do not think President Brezhnev is inconsistent, because trading with the West does not show that he in fact approves of capitalism. At every opportunity, he condemns what he sees as capitalist exploitation; he continually seeks to exploit capitalism's weaknesses on behalf of communism; and he perpetually denounces its harmful effects on workers, such as enforced poverty, unemployment, inflation, and the development of anti-social, acquisitive practices. He does these things in private as well as in public: every report of private conversations with him shows him opposed to capitalism. In short, the overwhelming weight of evidence points to the fact that President Brezhnev does not actually approve of capitalism.

In order to find out whether President Brezhnev does approve, we must at least examine his beliefs and attitudes about capitalism; and it is in order to discover these that we look at a broad array of his words and actions with respect to it. When we do this, we find the overwhelming weight of evidence in favour of his strongly believing capitalism an abomination, and of his having very negative attitudes towards it. To take trade with the West to show his approval of capitalism, and, therefore, an inconsistency with his condemnation of it, ignores entirely this fuller context and so the weight of evidence about his beliefs and attitudes with respect to capitalism.

Likewise, to take the concerned individual's eating meat to show approval of cruelty to animals and, therefore, an inconsistency with his condemnation of it, ignores entirely his beliefs and attitudes with respect to cruelty, which a consideration of a full array of his actions would bring to light. If one does examine his actual beliefs and attitudes, if one does find him in private and in public coming down against cruelty, and if one does observe him rigorously putting into practice those measures which comprise his tactic for combating cruelty, a tactic, to recall, that he has every reason to believe stands a good chance of success, then the overwhelming weight of the evidence is certainly in favour of the view that he does not actually approve of cruelty.

Tacit approval

One might insist that, though President Brezhnev may not actually approve of capitalism, nevertheless, by trading with the West, he tacitly approves of it. Similarly, though the concerned individual may not actually approve of cruelty to animals, nevertheless, by eating meat, he tacitly approves of it. In each case, therefore, the charge of inconsistency is sustained.

I have several problems with this line of argument.[4]

First, I have no very clear idea of what 'tacit approval' in the present context is. I agree that there are ways of approving without using the words 'I approve' (e.g., you ask me whether I approve and I nod), but silently approving is still actually approving. What is meant by 'tacit approval' in the present context is not silently and so actually approving — as I have already shown, the weight of evidence is very much against the view that the concerned individual actually approves of cruelty — but rather approving but not actually approving, and I am not sure what that amounts to. If someone were to say that tacit approval of cruelty was just like actual approval of cruelty only not actual, I do not think I would know what he was talking about.

Second, even assuming that we can make sense of 'tacit approval', there is the problem of the accusation's extent. It is by no means confined to the present two cases: bank with Barclays, and you tacitly condone the suppression of blacks in South Africa; eat an Israeli orange, and you tacitly approve of the dispossession of the Palestinians; attend a concert by the Leningrad Philharmonic Orchestra, and you tacitly condone the suppression of Jews in the Soviet Union; and buy a shirt made in Taiwan, and you tacitly condone the separation of Taiwan from mainland China. It would appear, in fact, that the accusation knows no bounds, that it can be made against one whenever and however one acts: buy a shirt from Taiwan, and you tacitly approve of capitalism; buy a shirt from mainland China, and you tacitly approve of communism; and do not buy a shirt from any Chinaman anywhere, and you tacitly approve of the impoverishment of Chinese shirtmakers around the world. One simply cannot be on the side of the angels with an accusation as cosmic in its application as this one, and its very extent destroys its force.

Third, it is not at all clear why the present accusation cannot be forestalled by an explicit statement denying as approved whatever it is that will be claimed to be tacitly approved. For example, imagine an Irishman living and working in Britain, who utterly disapproves of Britain's occupation of the six northern counties of Ireland but who proposes to visit the north in order to see his family and friends: why can he not say 'I propose to visit the north of Ireland, but I wish it to be understood that I in no way intend my action to be taken as signifying approval on my part of Britain's occupation of Ireland'? Again, imagine a teacher handing back a student's essay, who in response to the student's query about whether he lost marks for spelling mistakes says: 'No, you did not lose marks for spelling mistakes, but I want it to be understood that that in no way signifies that I condone poor spelling'. In these cases, the two parties are making it clear that they do not approve what some claim might allege they tacitly approve; so, provided their sincerity is not in doubt (and, if it is, we revert to the first part of this chapter), what force has the claim against them? Plainly, the concerned individual could make a statement of the sort in question and so make absolutely clear that he in no way wishes or intends his eating ham to be taken as indicating approval on his part of the practice of confining pregnant sows in tiny slatted stalls. Provided he is sincere, it is difficult to see what force a claim of tacit approval has against him.

Conventionally understood approval

One might perhaps say of a piece of behaviour, that behaving like that can be understood as approving. Thus, just as it might be said that trading with the West can be understood as approving of capitalism, so it might be said that eating meat can be understood as approving of cruelty to animals. This approach, however, does not succeed either.

To what is one appealing when one says that doing such-and-such can be understood as approving? Typically, the appeal is to a convention. In meetings of the Faculty of Arts at Liverpool, when the Chairman of Faculty asks 'May I sign the minutes of the last meeting?', a convention has arisen over the years that silence counts as giving one's approval. Sometimes people will say 'Agreed', but sometimes they say nothing, and, after a suitable pause, the Chairman signs the minutes. Members of Faculty have come to understand remaining silent in those circumstances as approving the minutes. But it in no way is conventionally understood that listening to Wagner is approving of the Holocaust, or buying a shirt made in Taiwan is approving of conflict with mainland China, or eating ham is approving of tiny slatted stalls for pregnant sows. One cannot appeal to conventional understanding where none exists.

One must be careful to note that what is a matter of convention in one place may not be in another. In another university, remaining silent over the minutes of the last faculty meeting may not be conventionally understood as approving them. In Britain and the United States, listening to Wagner is not conventionally understood as approving of the Holocaust, but it is just possible that, in Israel, where Wagner is not performed in public, such an understanding exists.

Accordingly, there may be places where eating meat is conventionally understood as approving cruelty to animals, but there is no such convention in Anglo-American society. This is not to deny, of course, that there may be groups within Anglo-American society among whom has grown up a set of conventions which includes one which permits eating meat to be conventionally understood as approving cruelty; but this convention so far is at best a feature of those groups only.

We can, of course, distinguish between something's being conventionally understood as approval and something's being a conventional means of expressing approval. But eating meat is not a conventional means of expressing approval of cruelty to animals either, any more than buying a shirt from Taiwan is a conventional means of expressing approval of capitalism, or listening to the Leningrad Philharmonic is a conventional way of expressing approval of the repression of Jews.

Lastly, we must, I think, resist the temptation simply to turn behaving into approving, merely in order to get round the above points. For it seems implausible to maintain that attending a concert by the Leningrad Philharmonic just is approving of the repression of Jews, or listening to Wagner just is approving of the Holocaust. The connection is too tight; it does not even allow for mistake or accident, for the uninformed who have never heard of Soviet repression, or the Holocaust, for the person who emphatically dissociates himself from these things. Too tight a connection between action and approval distorts people's conduct, by turning it into something it is not. Possibly there is a person somewhere who attends concerts by the Leningrad Philharmonic in order to show his approval of repression of Jews; but to turn every such concert-goer into an anti-semite, by simply turning attendance into approval of repression of Jews, is too strong a distortion to be plausible.

Secret approval

One could, I suppose, maintain that the concerned individual secretly approves of abusing pregnant sows; but there is no licence for such a view. When you probe his beliefs, attitudes, and sincerity, and obtain the results I have sketched, there can be little doubt on the evidence about what he does or does not approve. True, I cannot conclusively refute the view that he could still secretly approve of cruelty, but only appeal to the weight of evidence; and if all concerned individuals are consummate actors, in private as well as public, then perhaps they could fool all of the people all of the time. But this claim of secret approval is really mere idle though malicious speculation, on a par with the claim that, irrespective of what we know of his beliefs, attitudes, and sincerity, Charles de Gaulle could still have secretly approved of France becoming a client state of the United States.

I do not believe, then, that the concerned individual is to be caught out approving what he says he disapproves, that his eating meat shows he approves of cruelty and so is inconsistent with his condemnation of it.

I said, however, that the answer to the charge of inconsistency only in part resembled the answer to the charge of insincerity; I come now to that remaining portion of the answer.

The Demands of Consistency

Though a good many people in ethics speak of the demands of consistency, it is far from clear what these demands amount to. Not only is there widespread disagreement in the matter, but there is also no generally received way of settling such disagreements.

In fact, what consistency demands depends upon what view of consistency one embraces, and different views yield different demands. If the concerned individual, the Anglican priest, and others are to be inconsistent, one must hold a view of consistency that bars them doing what they do, even if (a) they are actively seeking reform and (b) their tactics or behaviour actually will achieve reform. It is plain, I think, that this restricts the view in question to one of very great severity. Let me explain.

One may hold a view of consistency such that, if one disapproves of X, then one must take action with respect to X. The concerned individual can meet this view, since he does take action with respect to commercial farming abuses.

One may hold a view of consistency such that, if one disapproves of X, then one must take effective action with respect to X. The concerned individual can meet this view, since, with the full implementation of his tactic for combating commercial farming abuses, he does take effective action with respect to them, action the effects of which compare favourably with the effects of one's becoming a vegetarian.

Now it is obvious that these two views of the demands of consistency are not sufficiently severe to get at the concerned individual; they do not restrict the only consistent form of behaviour to vegetarianism and so render inconsistent the concerned individual's behaviour. This restriction might be attempted.

One may hold a view of consistency such that, if one disapproves of X, then one must take some specified action with respect to X. (If it does not follow that the specific action in question has to be the most effective or at least an effective action with respect to X, then this view may be in trouble with adherents to the earlier views, who are likely to be numerous; but this possibility is of no concern here.) With the specific action thesis, it might be thought that, depending upon what the specified action is in the case of factory farming, the concerned individual is caught out.

Quite independently of the problem of how we are supposed to know from occasion to occasion what the specific action is that consistency demands of us, the specific action thesis is implausible, and for a reason particularly important to our concerns here. Consider this example: as a result of the Soviet invasion of Afghanistan, President Carter advocated a boycott of the Moscow Olympics in 1980. Now suppose he were to have maintained that a boycott of the Games was the only step another leader could take and remain consistent in his disapproval of the invasion: such a claim seems scarcely plausible. For two people can oppose something, yet in all consistency take different steps to do something about it. Thus, while Britain did not formally boycott the Games, Mrs Thatcher's Government, in addition to denouncing the invasion, refused in international bodies to conduct business as usual with the Soviets and imposed on them an array of economic and political sanctions. It is hard to see why Mrs Thatcher is inconsistent, when there seem many possibilities of action open to her by which to register her disapproval of what happened in Afghanistan.

Similarly, it is altogether too artificial to say that a man who disapproves of Soviet repression of Jews and boycotts concerts by Russian orchestras is consistent, whereas a man who disapproves of repression, attends such concerts, but lobbies the US Congress to increase the pressure on the Soviets to grant more exit visas is inconsistent. When there are various possibilities of action, there is *per se* no reason to think one more privileged than another, so far as consistency is concerned.

In the case of factory farming, therefore, why should the same not be true? Two people can disapprove of certain abuses, yet in all consistency take different steps to do something about them; and different possibilities of action are possible.

In the light of this result, it seems reasonably clear that what is required, if the concerned individual is to be inconsistent, is a view of consistency sufficiently severe to choke off all possibilities of action except vegetarianism, or at least to choke off all meat-eating possibilities of action. Then, whatever the concerned individual does, so long as he does not embrace vegetarianism or at least remains to any degree a meat-eater, he is inconsistent.

It is not difficult to think up two such severe, though not equally severe, views.

(1) One may hold a view of consistency such that, if one disapproves of X, then one must not aid, support, or help to maintain X.

(2) One may hold a view of consistency such that, if one disapproves of X, then one must have nothing to do with X.

As we shall see, adherents to (2) will find (1) objectionable, as will the concerned individual; and (2) is in any event, it will be urged, the more severe view. It does, moreover, it will be further argued, catch out the concerned individual: if one disapproves of cruel farming methods, and food animals are raised by such methods, then consistency demands having nothing to do with (i.e., avoiding) the flesh of these animals. As readers will know from my example of the Anglican priest, however, (2) is objectionable, in that it is too strict; it renders impossible any internal movement for reform unless reform is instantaneously achieved, and it fails to mark differences that we wish to mark.

Two Views of Strictness in Demands

Consider again the case of the Irishman, who lives and works in Britain and who thoroughly disapproves of the British occupation of the six northern counties of Ireland: what can he do and remain consistent in his opposition to the occupation? Can he buy a British car, in order to get to work? Can he in fact take a job? Can he pay British taxes, if only to avoid going to jail and so impairing his family's welfare? Can he send his children to British schools? Can he visit the six counties, in order to see family and friends and to experience conditions of life there? If he is a long-standing member of the British Army, can he serve in the six counties, provided he makes it clear that he is firmly opposed to the occupation?

Because the demands of consistency depend upon what view of consistency one adopts, and because there is no received or accepted view, answers to the question of what the Irishman can consistently do run the full spectrum of responses. Thus, some say he may do all of the above things, provided he makes it unmistakably clear in some way, including public affirmation of an explicit statement or oath to this effect, that he opposes the occupation; others say he may do some but not all of the above things, depending upon whether what he does aids the occupation; and still others say he may do none of the above things, since all of them require him to have commerce with Britain and things British, the sources of Ireland's unhappiness (as he sees it), about which he feels strongly.

Let us refer to these three views of consistency as the liberal, strict, and severe views: it seems obvious that it is only the strict and severe views that might impinge negatively on the concerned individual, so I shall not bother further with the liberal view.

The strict view

Adherents of the severe view are certain to attack the strict view; to them, it, just as the liberal view, falls short of the mark. They will argue that, depending upon how broadly one construes such expressions as 'aids', 'supports', and 'helps to maintain', the strict view collapses into the severe one.

For example, if our Irishman buys a British car, his money helps to swell the profits of the firm involved, which in turn increases the firm's liability for taxation; and a part of British tax revenues goes to support the occupation, both civil and military, of the six counties. So, in buying the car, he can be construed as aiding the occupation. Of course, there are different ways of aiding the occupation, and sending his children to a British school aids it, e.g., by helping to confer respectability upon the British. By conducting business as usual with them, at least in some of the affairs of life, our Irishman helps to play down the tyranny of occupation by making the British appear as otherwise decent fellows, which is useful to them in portraying the occupation in a less immoral and more humane light. In other words, bolstering their general respectability helps the British to portray themselves in Ireland as forces of light battling forces of evil, when the central evil, as our Irishman and his Irish friends see it, is the continued occupation of his country.

So far as I can see, depending upon how broadly one construes 'aids', 'supports', or 'helps to maintain', any dealings with the British whatever can be construed as assisting the occupation, and one must not focus so upon acts of commission that one forgets acts of omission. After all, failure to demonstrate against the occupation might well be construed as giving moral support or encouragement to the British powers that be, in their desire and efforts to continue the occupation, and among the different ways of assisting the occupation, giving it moral support, whether through acts of commission or omission, must be among the broadest, in view of the countless ways of behaving and not behaving that can be construed as showing such support.

I believe that in practice it will be difficult for adherents of the strict view to resist the pressure to move them towards the severe view. The severe view will be held up as the pure view of consistency, of which the strict view is a corruption: if one disapproves of X, then consistency demands having nothing whatever to do with X. Though one may insist that there are different ways and different degrees of aiding the occupation, any particular way and any particular degree is still a way and a degree of aiding the occupation. And this is the point: if what one objects to is aiding, supporting, or helping to maintain the occupation, then one is completely at the mercy of it being shown that what one is doing, or not doing, does just that; and unless one adopts some arbitrary cut-off point to ways or degrees of assistance, such that below that point does not count as assisting the occupation, then assisting the occupation is not going to be a very difficult charge to sustain.

In the Irishman's case, then, adherents of the strict view are being pushed in the direction of a complete break with Britain and, to the greatest extent they can achieve in their lives, with things British. Anything less will be characterized either as temporizing and the adoption of half-measures, or as failure to recognize the myriad ways in which, and degrees to which, one can 'aid', 'support', or 'help to maintain' the occupation. True, many of these ways, in order to be ways of assisting the occupation, assume a broad interpretation of these expressions; but it is altogether too artificial, it will be claimed, to select some narrow interpretation of them and then to look in the face the obvious effect of some act or omission upon the occupation.

For example, an important factor in maintaining the occupation is the morale of the British Army and people, and adherents to the severe view will point to countless ways the Irishman can do his bit to affect their morale. Thus, should he retain his British friends, it is easy to see why he might be held to have failed to strike a blow against British morale and so against a crucial factor underpinning the occupation. Publicly and ostentatiously giving up those friends, it will be urged, aids the cause, as does ostentatiously refusing to shake hands with British people, or having one's small children, if one lives in Northern Ireland, first accept sweets from British soldiers and then, still before the soldiers, throw them away. Conversely, it will be said, the kind but unthinking housewife who gives exhausted British soldiers a cup of tea also affects Army morale, but in an undesirable way; for she in part helps to restore what those committed to getting the British out of Ireland are trying to undermine.

The above explains why adherents to the severe view resist the direct/indirect and active/passive distinctions. It seems too artificial to say that consistency bars directly aiding the occupation, when (a) it is not clear how the appropriate distinction is to be drawn, (b) indirectly aiding the occupation is still aiding the occupation, and (c), depending upon what counts as indirect aid, some act of indirectly aiding the occupation can have a greater effect on the occupation than some act of directly aiding it. A newspaper editor of one of the British dailies can have a considerably greater effect on the occupation than many individual British soldiers; for he can go a long way towards keeping people's resolve to continue the occupation at a pitch it might not otherwise retain. What is true of the direct/indirect distinction is true of the active/passive distinction: it is too artificial to say that consistency bars actively aiding the occupation when (a) it is not clear how precisely the appropriate distinction is to be drawn, (b) passively aiding the occupation is still aiding the occupation and (c), depending upon what counts as passive aid, some act of passively aiding the occupation can have a greater effect on the occupation than some act of actively aiding it. Your passively acquiescing, without a struggle for votes, in the election of a Member of Parliament who is a particularly strong and vocal defender of the occupation may well be more important to the continuation of the occupation than your own public stance in favour of it. As for our Irishman, his passively aquiescing in the election of that MP could well be more important to the continuation of the occupation than the small sums of money he is able to give towards its defeat. Indeed, in one clear sense, failure to act can expose the Irishman to a charge of passive support over a wide range of cases. Should he work in a car plant and fail to disrupt production, for example, he could be construed as passively supporting the occupation; for the greater the productivity of the plant, the better off the British economy is likely to be, which in turn means more money for the civil and military occupation of the six counties.

In short, though one may begin with a narrow interpretation of 'aids', 'supports', and 'helps to maintain', all the pressure is going to be in the direction of expanding their scope until one ends up with what are in fact broad interpretations. With these, however, if one is to avoid aiding the occupation, whether in this or that way to this or that degree, directly or indirectly, actively or passively, a complete severance with Britain and things British seems required. Anything less will be said, in some way or other to some degree or other, to aid, support, or help to maintain the very occupation one says one opposes.

The difficulty for the strict view of consistency, then, is to keep it from collapsing into the severe view. One could, as I have said, resort to the device of a cut-off point, below which aiding, supporting, or helping to maintain the occupation is acceptable. One would then have to defend such a device and, in particular, justify drawing the cut-off point at one place rather than another.

Now it should be obvious how this difficulty creates room for the concerned individual. The whole point behind the employment of a cut-off device is to ensure that not just any degree of aiding the occupation counts; in other words, a cut-off device is one way of giving substance to the thought that, to be guilty of aiding the occupation, one must be assisting it in some significant or at least non-animal fashion. But we have already seen that an individual's becoming a vegetarian or remaining a meat-eater has no significant impact on the market and, through it, on the treatment of food animals. My decision to become a vegetarian or to remain a meat-eater will not alter in the slightest the factory farming abuses to which I object, and it is simply a mistake to suggest otherwise. The point, then, is clear: to keep away from the severe view of consistency, adherents of the strict view place at risk their case against the concerned individual; to retain their case against the concerned individual, they place at risk their position *vis-à-vis* the severe view. (I am assuming in all this, of course, that adherents of the strict view can defend the employment of a cut-off device and can justify drawing the cut-off point where they do.)

A shift to the severe view, therefore, becomes tempting. For, at a stroke, it renders superfluous the concerned individual's manoeuvrings here, since it bars any appeal to the manner or degree of aid or support. It is not that, now, any degree of aid and support, including aid and support of an imperceptible order, renders one inconsistent; it is rather that questions about aid and support are irrelevant to the issue of inconsistency. All that matters is whether one has anything to do with, i.e., eats, animals raised by methods of which one disapproves.

The severe view

I want to suggest that the severe view is not a view of consistency at all but rather an appeal to some particular conception of the good man and of what he is capable.

I think that the overwhelming majority of us will consider that we can remain consistent without going to the lengths of the severe view. There are three points involved here.

First, the severe view constantly demands an extreme response: morally disapprove of any aspect of British domestic or foreign policy, for example, and this view will shortly have you out of work, out of friends, and living on some remote island. Again, if we cannot, except artifically, separate what we disapprove from the people responsible for it, then isolation seems forced upon us. If we disapprove of Soviet repression of Jews, then, presumably, we must cease all dealings with the Soviets, since any dealings at any level on any matter can be interpreted as having something to do with those of whom we disapprove. If we morally disapprove of our community's decision to forgo solar energy in favour of coal, then we may well have to move; for if that decision were unanimous and so supported by everyone except ourselves, then we would seem compelled either to move or to avoid our neighbours. Accordingly, social interaction is going to be possible for us only if we morally approve of every policy, decision, rule, person, and whatever, that makes up the social circumstances in which we find ourselves, and this is simply too extreme to be true of most of us. Finally, gradations within our disapproval get lost. If we approve of our library committee's purchasing policy in all particulars except one, and if we morally disapprove of that particular, say, a ban on the purchase of sexually explicit writers, then must we not give up using the library? For its continued use, *in the knowledge* of the committee's ban, can certainly be portrayed as having something to do with censorship. If this is so, if even gradations get lost, then it is far from clear that we are going to be able to go about our ordinary business.

Second, the view that consistency demands that we have nothing whatever to do with that of which we disapprove amounts to quitting the arena without a struggle, and it is difficult to see that such a response is invariably, without exception, demanded of us. Even if such a response were appropriate in special circumstances, say, of the Nazi Germany sort, where the entire, surrounding milieu was utterly corrupt, morally, why should it be thought appropriate in other circumstances? In these, provided we do battle, can we not remain in the arena and be perfectly consistent in so doing?

Suppose my university fails to adopt an affirmative action programme for blacks, about which I have rather strong moral views: I *could* resign, there is no question of that; but the severe view would seem to demand that I resign, since, in reality, there is scarcely any way I could remain a functioning member of the university and not have something to do with its admissions policy. In fact, in some sense, this is true of virtually all university policies, so if I disagree with any single one of them, then, presumably, resignation cannot be far off.

I tried to get my way over affirmative action and failed. I could resign; but I could also redouble my efforts, expand the circle I argue the matter with, and seek in other ways to persuade my colleagues. So long as I am in this position, I must, it would seem, have something to do with the present admissions policy; but I am working hard to change and improve matters.

It is known by my colleagues where I stand, that I am not happy with matters at present, that, morally, I want change. And I am working to achieve it, not in some sham or utterly fictitious way, but in a way that will eventually, I believe, bring a halt to the present policy and the introduction of an affirmative action policy.

The same phenomenon can occur in larger affairs, though perhaps not in such a pure form. If one morally disapproves of some of Mrs Thatcher's social, economic, and political policies, one could go elsewhere; but one could also, as many do, work hard to oppose those policies and to see that individuals opposed to them are elected to Parliament. To the extent that one lives in a Britain governed by Mrs Thatcher's policies, or to the extent that those policies have become law and one obeys the law, one has something to do with policies of which one disapproves. But one makes it known where one stands, that, morally, one feels strongly that certain policies must be changed; and one works to change them.

I think that for most of us, these cases, and the earlier case of the priest, describe individuals who are perfectly consistent, even though these individuals remain in the arena and continue to do battle. What is vital to their consistency, *if* they so remain, is that they work for change or reform; otherwise, they will, given their moral disapproval of what is in question, be inconsistent. What is crucial to determining their consistency, in other words, is not *that* they remain in the arena but *how* they remain. Thus, to lump together those who struggle with those who do not, as the severe view does, seems misguided.

It is integral to this picture, of course, that reform be possible, and, where factory farming in our society is concerned, it certainly is. On the one hand, unlike Nazi Germany, the social/political system is not so corrupt that meaningful change is either beyond us or impossible; on the other, and the reader will now see the full force of the rebuttal of Singer's defeatist remarks in the last chapter about the power of the agribusiness lobby, the vested interest groups can be, and are being, defeated. In short, reform is possible and abuses can be eliminated, and these are the ends for which the concerned individual works. So long as he actively and seriously pursues them, he remains consistent; should he stop pursuing them, but not cease morally to disapprove of abuses, he becomes inconsistent.

Third, am I not saying, however, that provided one is working for reform, one may do anything, however horrible? No, what I am saying is that, provided one is working for reform with respect to that of which one disapproves, it is not by a charge of inconsistency that one is to be caught out, if, of course, one is to be caught out at all. That is, if what one is doing or allowing is objectionable at all, it is not on grounds of inconsistency. The point is important, and failure to observe it, which is what I think the severe view does, confuses issues of consistency with claims about moral taint and purity. To ask whether what I do is consistent with what I say I disapprove of, is not at all the same thing as to ask whether a good man could do what I do: I fight for reform in the admissions policy from within the university, but it *does not follow* that a good man could continue as part of the university. Consistency is not the, or the only relevant, factor to answering the question of what a good man could bring himself to do, and merely to be consistent in what one does does not in itself place one beyond moral reproach.

Is it *consistency*, then, which demands that we have nothing to do with that of which we disapprove? I do not think so; I think rather it is some worry about moral taint or purity which becomes confused with the issue of consistency and which makes it appear that we must adopt extreme measures in order to remain consistent, when in fact it is some view about taint or purity which requires those measures.

The Good Man

Is the concerned individual, then, even if sincere and consistent, morally tainted? Can he be a good man? This is a broad question, and my discussion here is necessarily limited in scope.

First, the extreme view, as a view of the good man, renders everyone who has anything to do with that which they disapprove a bad man, renders everyone who works for reform from within, a bad man, no matter what, including the general character of that from within which they are working; and this is simply too extreme for most us. Indeed, in circumstances where more than one value is present, the extreme view runs up against the barriers that all absolutist positions do. The literature on utilitarianism (and other forms of consequentialist reasoning) is filled with examples of just this sort, where unless a lie is told a life is lost, or unless a promise is broken a deep injustice is perpetrated; and the good man from the point of view of utilitarianism is certainly not debarred from lying or breaking promises. Where more than one value is present, as we saw in chapter 12, trade-offs become possible, and the concerned individual is in circumstances where more than one value, animal pain, is present.

Second, the charge of moral taint assumes and issues from some conception of the good man and of what he is capable, and the problem is that there are different conceptions. Different pictures of the good man can yield different answers to the question of what he can bring himself to do. Could he lie to save a life? Some say no, others yes, and their answers are perfectly in accordance with, and in part define, their pictures of the good man; but their pictures are different. In one, certain acts by their very nature are forbidden the good man, whereas in the other, the same acts, depending upon their circumstances and consequences, are not.

Third, at a level in ethics this deep, we not so much argue a position as sketch a picture, a picture of the character and life of the good man in the moral order, and I suspect all we can do in the end is to probe and reflect upon each individual picture, and to embrace that one that we find most comfortable and with whose implications we feel best able to live. In the end, when every twist and turn of individual cases has been explored, it is difficult to see what else we can do. Certainly, it is optimistic to a degree to think that there are arguments in the offing which once and for all refute all rival conceptions of the good man to our own, which once and for all erase every picture except our favourite, when the history of ethics teaches us, now thinking in the most general terms, that two competing pictures of the good man, in one of which he reasons consequentially, in the other of which he does not, have been and remain both at war and widely endorsed. Again, no decision between them can be reached by resort to the usual generalizations: it is of no help to be told that the good man is a man of principle or duty unless one is also told what his principles or duties are, how he decides what his principles or duties are, and what these principles or duties amount to in practice; and in trying to answer these questions, of course, we again run up against our competing pictures and the controversies which they generate. Clearly, then, we must face the possibility that there may not be a single answer to the question of what the good man is capable.

Fourth, Singer is an act-utilitarian, and act-utilitarians, in circumstances where more than one value is present, are capable of trade-offs. What makes trade-offs possible for them is, as for so many of us, that they regard values as commensurable. Their opponents, then, must be maintaining that there are at least some incommensurable values. Exactly what the claim of incommensurable values amounts to is difficult to say; the best discussion I know, by James Griffin,[5] concludes that considerably more is required even to make such a claim clear, let alone plausible. But the point I want to stress is that Singer does not make such a claim, whatever it might amount to; he cannot get at the concerned individual by maintaining that pain, and, therefore, animal pain, is an incommensurable value. Indeed, he steadfastly affirms that he is a vegetarian because he is a utilitarian, and the utilitarian argument that he wields, which I criticised in chapter 17, shows beyond a doubt that pain, and, therefore, animal pain, is for him a commensurable value.

Fifth, suppose, then, that conceptions of the good man divide over the commensurability issue: if one plumps for the incommensurability thesis, then one must state clearly what such a thesis amounts to, must develop a case for its plausibility, and must then show that pain is among the incommensurable values. This last is not unimportant, obviously, and the fact that a vast number of people treat human pain as commensurable (just think of the relevant cases of euthanasia and of problems involving pain in medical ethics generally) is hardly likely to indicate that they think animal pain is not. If, however, pain is a commensurable value, then it is far from clear how the concerned individual is supposed to be a bad man, since the myriad values that form part of the circumstances in which he finds himself — the reader will recall those I brought forward in chapter 16 in connection with claims about valuing suffering but not valuing life, and in chapter 17 in connection with Singer's utilitarian argument — are weighed by him. He is doing precisely what those who hold that values are commensurable would have him do; he is weighing and balancing and seeking trade-offs in circumstances where more than one value is present. One might argue, of course, that he is doing this badly or not taking everything he should into account or failing to do this or that, and all this might be true of some particular concerned individual; but the crucial point, that trade-offs are possible where more than one value is present, will have been conceded.

In short, if the good man is capable of trade-offs in values, why cannot the concerned individual be a good man? He does not value in the least cruelty in farming, and actively seeks its reduction and elimination; but he also does not go to the other extreme and hold that the pains of animals, any more than the pains of humans, are incommensurable.

All of the above is compressed and sketchy and would have to be filled out considerably and with great care to be fully satisfactory, but it does outline one of several possible defences of the concerned individual as a good man.

What I want to emphasize is the position *vis-à-vis* Singer. Should my criticism of Singer's utilitarian argument in chapter 17 succeed, should, that is, the negative effects of the collapse of the meat industry, etc., outweigh the positive effects so far as the pains of food animals are concerned, then Singer will be left with a utilitarian argument, with suitable qualifications over cruelty, for the continuation of factory farming. And what that argument will consist in will be the extremely complex business of weighing and balancing and seeking trade-offs between human benefits and animal harms. He thinks, of course, that his argument works and that the saving in animal harms exceeds the gains in human benefits; and, though the concerned individual disputes this, the crucial point is that there is no difference at all in approach between Singer and the concerned individual. Put differently, Singer *is* the concerned individual, if the facts which the utilitarian argument is about run as suggested in chapter 17; and how the facts run is, obviously, an empirical matter and not at all a matter of one's conception of the good man.

Notes

1 I take it as obvious that the concerned individual is an open, not a secret, meat-eater.
2 Anthony Kenny, 'Arthur Norman Prior, 1914–1969', *Proceedings of the British Academy*, vol. LVI, 1976, p. 346.
3 Michael Martin, 'A critique of moral vegetarianism', p. 30.
4 The discussion which follows, in this and the next section, has been influenced by A. D. Woozley's discussion of tacit consent; see his *Law and Obedience* (London, Duckworth, 1979), ch. 5. See also Michael Martin, 'A critique of moral vegetarianism', p. 29.
5 James Griffin, 'Are there incommensurable values?', *Philosophy and Public Affairs*, vol. 7, 1977, pp. 39–59.

19

Needless Suffering

Finally, I want to append a few words on the charge of needless or gratuitous or unnecessary suffering. This is the charge that, even if the concerned individual were successful in cleaning up factory farming and so in ensuring that none of the types of animals that previously were in question now led lives that were a misery to them, any suffering which the animals *did* undergo would be needless and, therefore, wrong.

The Factual Side to The Charge

I think the charge contains within itself a view of what makes suffering needless, but others, apparently unconvinced of this, have searched beyond the charge for such a view, and have thereby, at least often, I think, been led to misconstrue the charge. For reasons of space, I shall confine myself to a single example, namely, an exchange between Donald VanDeVeer and Tom Regan.

In his article 'Animal suffering', VanDeVeer correctly points out that, in the absence of some criterion of what is to count as needless or gratuitous suffering, the charge of inflicting such suffering will not do the work its proponents think it does.[1] He apparently thinks the nature of this criterion is in doubt, however, for he canvasses several possible candidates but is unhappy with them all.

Regan replies to VanDeVeer in his article 'On the right not to be made to suffer gratuitously'.[2] Briefly, Regan distinguishes two types of needless suffering: factually needless suffering is 'suffering that is unnecessary if this or that end or purpose is to be accomplished', whereas morally needless suffering is 'suffering that is unnecessary because it is caused by immoral practices'.[3] The point of this distinction is that, even if a practice were to cause only that amount of suffering necessary to achieve the practice's goal, it could still, if the goal or practice were immoral, involve morally needless suffering. Accordingly, in order to determine whether a piece of suffering *is* morally needless, we require 'some general moral principle(s) by reference to which the morality of the goals or purposes of practices and thus the morality of the practices themselves can be assessed.'[4] Regan repeats the point in his article 'Cruelty, kindness, and unnecessary suffering':

> . . . One does not establish that the amount of suffering caused or allowed is necessary, in the moral sense, by establishing that it is necessary, in the factual sense. To establish the necessity, in the moral sense, of the amount of suffering caused or allowed, one must provide a moral justification of the goal in pursuit of which the suffering is caused or allowed . . .[5]

For Regan, then, morality enters into the very determination of whether a piece of suffering is (morally) needless.

I think this way of looking at needless suffering misconstrues the charge under discussion by mislocating where morality enters the picture. According to Regan, in order to tell whether a piece of suffering is morally needless we have to determine whether the practice which causes it is immoral; but the point of the charge of needless suffering is, I think, that the practice is immoral because it causes that suffering. Needless suffering makes the practice wrong. For example, animals are farmed in order that we may eat them; but whereas Regan seems to imply that we have first to assess the morality of eating meat in order then to be able to determine whether a piece of suffering devoted to that end is morally needless, the point behind the charge of needless suffering is that eating meat is wrong because it involves that suffering. That suffering makes it wrong.

The problem is Regan's distinction; that is, according to my understanding of the charge of needless suffering, the determination of the morality of goals, purposes, and practices has nothing whatever to do with the determination of whether a piece of suffering is needless. Needless suffering is a wholly factual matter, though not a fact quite like that encapsulated in Regan's definition of factually needless suffering; the fact which matters is whether the suffering is avoidable. Needless suffering is not suffering inflicted by immoral practices but avoidable suffering; it may or may not turn out that the infliction of avoidable suffering is immoral, but the moral/immoral distinction is used not to determine whether a piece of suffering is avoidable but to determine whether a piece of avoidable suffering is justified. These are completely different affairs.

We do not first assess the morality of eating meat in order then to be able to determine whether a piece of suffering devoted to that end is needless; if we accept the charge of needless suffering, we try factually to determine whether the suffering of food animals is avoidable. If it is, then we add to this fact the claim that the infliction of avoidable suffering is wrong to yield the conclusion that eating meat is wrong.

Thus, on this interpretation, the charge of needless suffering, as applied to the concerned individual, encompasses two quite different judgements, one factual, one moral. The factual judgement is the judgement that eating meat causes avoidable suffering; the moral judgement is the judgement that the infliction of that suffering is wrong or unjustified. I want to focus upon the moral judgement, but a word on the factual judgement is necessary.

In chapter 17, in connection with Singer's utilitarian argument for vegetarianism, I drew attention to some of the many ways meat permeates out lives and to some of the many individuals, communities, and countries which vitally depend upon meat for their livelihoods. The question arises of whether those factual concerns do not directly affect the purely factual question of whether eating meat causes avoidable suffering. It is hard to see how they are not relevant, since, if I completely destroy one whole side to the economy of South Dakota by eliminating the farming of dairy cows, hogs, and cattle, I am going to affect rather dramatically the lives of the citizens of that state. (There is, *pace* Regan, nothing immoral in pointing to the individual and collective consequences upon people of the collapse of the meat industry in all its forms.) I am not here taking a stand on whether these factual concerns more than counterbalance the fact that we can live without meat; I am only reminding readers that they certainly appear relevant to deciding the factual question of avoidable suffering and that they pull in an opposite direction on this question to the fact that we can live without meat.

The Moral Side to the Charge

The factual judgement of avoidability is to my mind, then, not entirely clear-cut; but it is the moral judgement of wrongness that is the stumbling block. In nearly all discussions of whether eating meat causes avoidable harm, there appears to be a leap from avoidable harm to moral wrongness, and we could not get a value from a fact in quite that way. In fact, however, there is a suppressed assumption or moral judgement in these discussions, to the effect that the infliction of avoidable harm is wrong. It is this suppressed judgement which enables us to get from the fact that a practice causes avoidable harm to the moral conclusion that that practice is wrong or morally objectionable, so this judgement is as crucial to the charge of needless suffering as the factual determination of avoidability.

The problem is this: any simple judgement of the form 'the infliction of avoidable harm is wrong' will not do, and the sort of complication in the judgement necessary to take account of the specific objection the concerned individual brings against the simple form affects the force of the judgement.

Though Stephen Clark makes a good deal of some such simple judgement on avoidable harm in *The Moral Status of Animals*,[6] I know very few people who would accept anything like the bald form of the judgement Clark wields. The reason is obvious: there are countless instances where a great many people think it right to inflict avoidable harm. I do not have space to explore the differences in rationale behind different types of cases, so I shall come at once to focus here, as I did over vivisection, on the appeal to benefit. There are all sorts of cases where we inflict avoidable harm and, as we saw in connection with vivisection, use the appeal to benefit as justification.

We punish children and so inflict avoidable harm upon them; but we use the appeal to benefit to justify the infliction of this harm. We argue that we are teaching them how to behave or making them better persons or helping them to develop into responsible citizens. A GP administers an emetic to a patient and so inflicts avoidable harm; but we justify what he does by the appeal to benefit. We argue that he is assisting his patient to health or at least assisting him in overcoming some complaint. In these cases, we use some benefit or range of benefit to justify some piece or range of avoidable harm, and what we are doing when we do this is treating avoidable harm as a value, to be sure, but a value which can be weighed and set off against an increase or range of increase in a concatenation of other values. In a word, the appeal to benefit manifests our regard of avoidable harm as a value, certainly, but as a commensurable value.

Though it may be tempting to seize upon the cases of the child, and the GP, and argue that the appeal to benefit can only justify the infliction of avoidable harm if the benefit accrues to the person or creature who undergoes the harm, we have already seen, in the case of vivisection, that the appeal is used in cases where the people or creatures who undergo the harm are not the people or creatures who receive the benefit. But we do not have to rely upon the example of vivisection to make the point, since the phenomenon is all about us. In Britain, for instance, single people pay taxes for a series of state programmes from which, because they are unmarried and without children, they cannot benefit; lower middle-class people pay taxes for programmes which, because their income is above a particular level, though still not very great, they cannot benefit; and so on. In the United States, welfare programmes other than Social Security most typically benefit people who have not contributed to the funding of those programmes. Again, conscription in Britain during the Second World War was widely justified by the appeal to benefit, but those who enjoyed the benefit of a free country were not those who, in numerous instances, lost their lives. Or we could turn to almost any instance involving the distribution of scarce medical resources, where the people who benefit only do so at the cost of those who are harmed (say, in the distribution of kidney dialysis machines), where the determination of who benefits is made upon the productive relations in which one stands to other people and society as a whole, and where, generally, people with a productive input to society, such as housewives, are chosen in preference to those who represent sheer consumption, such as tramps.

The simple judgement that it is wrong to inflict avoidable harm, therefore, will not do, and one — but only one — reason why has to do with the appeal to benefit. The judgement, accordingly, must be complicated, in order to take account of the appeal, which, as I have said, reflects the commensurability of values, and the only plausible way to do this, I think, is to have the judgement actually reflect the commensurability of values. It would then look something like this: 'it is wrong to cause avoidable harm when the increase in benefit as a result of the harm is not of a range or order to offset the harm.' Put this way, however, two obvious points arise. First, it is far from clear, as we have seen already in the case of Singer's utilitarian argument for vegetarianism, that eating meat causes more harm than it produces benefits. Second, if the concerned individual's tactic is successful in the way envisaged by the charge of needless suffering at the beginning of this chapter, so that abuses are rectified and the animals lead lives that are not a misery to them, it becomes very far from clear indeed that eating meat causes more harm than it produces benefits. In short, the shift away from the simple to the complicated judgement injects the commensurability of values into the argument, and the moment this is done *it becomes not a moral but a factual matter* whether the benefits produced by the infliction of avoidable harm are exceeded by the harm caused.

A good illustration of this shift can be found in a piece by Dale Jamieson.[7] In reconstructing Stephen Clark's central argument in *The Moral Status of Animals,* Jamieson lists its major premiss as 'to be the cause of avoidable ill is wrong'; he at once produces a counterexample of a medical variety to this premiss and then reformulates it as 'to be the cause of avoidable net ill is wrong.' He produces counterexamples to this reformulation but observes that these are remote from situations involving relations between humans and animals; and he concludes his discussion of this reformulation with the claim that he has 'no doubt that some true principle could be formulated by adding a list of exceptions' to it.[8] But what reason is there to suppose that such a principle will work against the concerned individual? The damage has already been done; for a premiss of the form 'to be the cause of avoidable net ill is wrong' reflects the commensurability of values, something which Jamieson seems to imply when he says of this premiss that it captures the idea that 'to be the cause of more ill than good is never right' but that 'to be the cause of ill may be right if more good than ill results.'[9] The damage has been done, because whether or not eating meat causes more ill than good is an entirely factual matter and so perfectly susceptible to the measures which constitute the concerned individual's tactic for improving the quality of life of those factory farmed animals whose lives are a misery to them. In other words, the effectiveness of the concerned individual's tactic gives him excellent reason to think he does not produce more harm than benefit, more ill than good. Again, a premiss of the form 'to be the cause of avoidable net ill is wrong' emphasizes *the fact* of whether more good than ill is produced. The amelioration argument is tailor-made to deal with this fact, however, and the amelioration argument is but an attempt by the concerned individual to improve the quality of life of those food animals in question. A suppressed premiss of this form, then, seems amenable to the concerned individual's position.

But can the appeal to benefit simply justify anything? One might attempt to block the appeal on the ground of cruelty, by arguing that the appeal cannot be used to underwrite cruel rearing methods. But this overlooks the concerned individual's tactic: his tactic is precisely devised to minimize and eliminate abuses in farming, and its employment is directed with that end in mind. Its effectiveness means, therefore, that one cannot block the appeal to benefit on the ground of cruelty, since precisely what its effectiveness consists in is the reduction and elimination of cruelty and other abuses in farming. To envisage its success is simply to envisage its effectiveness, and this in turn is to envisage an absence of cruel farming methods.

To sum up, if the charge of needless suffering turns upon a suppressed premiss of the form 'to be the cause of avoidable ill is wrong', then, because this premiss is implausible, the charge effectively loses its sting. If, however, the charge turns upon a suppressed premiss of the form 'to be the cause of avoidable net ill is wrong', then the premiss reflects the commensurability of values and so envisages, depending upon how the facts turn out, that the infliction of avoidable ill is right. It is not even at present clear that eating meat causes more ill than it produces good; but the effectiveness of the concerned individual's tactic, which the charge envisages, provides even less reason to think that eating meat produces more ill than good, and so even less reason to think the concerned individual is open to the charge of inflicting avoidable net ill.

Of course, it might be said that everything here would look different if the concerned individual were a deontologist; but he is not, and neither, I stress, is Peter Singer. There is nothing in the concerned individual's position that is foreign to Singer's utilitarianism, yet he remains a meat-eater, concerned, consistent, sincere, and moral. And this means that his position, as a response to Singer, undercuts negative moral vegetarianism by rendering it unnecessary.

Notes

1 Donald VanDeVeer, 'Animal suffering', *Canadian Journal of Philosophy*, vol. X, 1980, pp. 463–71.
2 Tom Regan, 'On the right not to be made to suffer gratuitously', *Canadian Journal of Philosophy*, vol. X, 1980, pp. 473–8.
3 Ibid., p. 474.
4 Ibid., p. 475.
5 Tom Regan, 'Cruelty, kindness, and unnecessary suffering', *Philosophy*, vol. 53, 1980, p. 539.
6 Stephen Clark, *The Moral Status of Animals*, Oxford, Clarendon Press, 1977, e.g., ch. 3.
7 Dale Jamieson, review of Stephen Clark's *The Moral Status of Animals*, *Noûs*, vol. XV, 1981, pp. 230–4.
8 Ibid., pp. 231–2.
9 Ibid., p. 231.

Index

This index focuses essentially, though not exclusively, upon themes and ideas that feature in the text. Further references to individuals and to individual works may be found in the notes at the ends of chapters.

absolutism, moral, and conception of status of vegetarianism 32–3
act-utilitarianism *see also* utilitarianism
  consequentialism and place of rights in 86–8, 89, 90
  Hare and 90–5
  killing and 100–1
  moral rights and 73–4, 83–6
  practicalities of vegetarianism 196
  split-level approach 90–4
  value of life 103
acting and refraining 130–1
aesthetic grounds as basis of non-moral vegetarianism 7–8
aid, bringing, cf. avoiding injury 133–5
amelioration argument 167–8, 247
  pain and 174ff.
Anarchy, State and Utopia (Nozick) 68
Animal Factories (Singer and Mason) 175
Animal Liberation (Singer) 21, 44, 49, 159, 168, 175, 176, 177, 182, 183, 190, 191, 196, 203, 206
Animal Liberation Front 204
animal life *see also* life, value of
  value of 108–10
  vivisection and value of 111–16

animal welfare 23–4
  argument from killing 27, 28–9, 30
  argument from moral rights 27, 28, 30
  argument from pain and suffering 20–3, 27, 28–9, 30
  and moral vegetarianism 17
Anscombe, G. E. M. 132
approval
  and action 228–31
  actual 228
  conventionally understood 230–1
  secret 231
  tacit 229–30
argument
  as basis of practice 3–5
  critical thinking and assessment of 5
artifacts, inherent value of 150–1
Austin, John 61
avoidability and needless suffering 245–6

benefit, appeal to
  avoidable harm and 246–7
  vivisection and 111–16, 246
Benson, John 189n
Bentham, Jeremy 61, 119
  hostility to moral rights 83, 84

'biospiritual ethic' 105
'biotic community' 149–50
boycott of meat, as tactic 38, 39, 191, 209
Brezhnev, Leonid 228–9
Burke, Edmund 3, 4

Causing Death and Saving Lives (Glover) 72, 102n, 161
change, opposition to 193
chicken
    increase in demand for 210
    life proper to species 210
    value of life 109, 172n
children *see also* infanticide
    argument from pain and suffering 180–1
    avoidable harm 246
choice, conscious 6
Clark, Stephen 21, 23, 49, 245, 247
coercion on behalf of vegetarianism 15–16
commensurability issue
    commensurability of values 247
    conception of good man and 241
compensation, rights and duty of 79–81
concerned individual
    and argument from pain and suffering 175–7, 181–8
    and the good man 240–2
    inconsistency 219–21, 227
    insincerity 219–27
    Singer's concession 215–16, 218
conditional vegetarianism *see* vegetarianism, conditional
consequences, and exercise of rights 77
consequentialism 70–2
    and practice 94–5
    rights and 86–90
consistency
    approval and action 228–31
    concerned individual and 219–21, 227
    demands of consistency 232–3
    liberal view of 234
    severe view of 234, 237–40
    strict view of 234–7
consumption *see* meat consumption

Cottingham, John 188n
craniotomy case 139n
    attempts to render control responsibility superfluous 128–33
    avoiding injury 133–5
    bringing aid 133–5
    control responsibility 125–8
    immoral omissions 129–30
critical thinking, and assessment of argument 5

Descartes, René 175, 188n
Diamond, Cora 82
diet
    as grounds for non-moral vegetarianism 9
    and health 10
Diet for a Small Planet (Lappè) 9, 23
Director of Public Prosecutions v. *Smith* 138n
doctrine of double effect (DDE)
    bringing aid and avoiding injury 133–5
    conditions for employment 119–20
    control responsibility 125–8
    direct and oblique intention 120–3
    immoral omissions 129–30
    killing and 118ff.
    order of causation between effects 135–8
    responsibility 123–5
drugs, use for animals 10, 12, 13
duty
    and moral criticism 131–3
    prima facie 53
Dworkin, Ronald 55
    fundamental moral rights 61–5, 67–9, 70, 81n, 84, 155n

economy
    claim of progressive collapse 203–6
    practicalities of vegetarianism 197–203
effect on character of commercial farming 20
effectiveness
    and choice of tactics 39–40
    of becoming vegetarian 206–9, 213
effects, order of causation between 135–8

emotion as grounds for non-moral
vegetarianism 8
employment
and claim of progressive collapse
203–6
meat industry and 187
practicalities of vegetarianism
197–203
environment, opposition to change
193–4
environmental ethic 141ff.
artifacts and nature 150–1
biotic community 149–50
conflicts in values 144–5
feelings and attitudes 145–6
mistakes about inherent value
146–8
moral standing and inherent value
142–4
value theory and ethics 151–5
ethics, value theory and 151–5

farming, factory 216
and animal interests 22–3
and argument from pain and
suffering 37–8, 175–6, 182–3,
203
consistency and action 233
and counter-arguments 33–4
and moral rights 49
positive moral vegetarianism 36–8
reducing suffering 208–9
reforms, 184–5, 207–8
and replaceability 167
and tactic of concerned individual
218
Third World 19
farming methods and grounds for
vegetarianism 33–4, 38
fast food industry
growth of 15, 185, 210
practicalities of vegetarianism 198
feelings and inherent value 145–6
Feinberg, Joel 79
Foot, Philippa 133–5
Fox, Michael W., reverence for life
ethic 104–8, 113–14
freedom, constraints on 77
Fried, Charles, positive and negative
rights 71–2

genetic engineering
and ability to feel pain 180
and life proper to species 186–7
Gewirth, Alan 43
Glover, Jonathan 72, 102n, 161
good man, conception of
concerned individual as 240–2
Griffin, James 241

Hare, R. M. 62, 65n, 68
two-level account of moral thinking
90ff.
Hart, H. L. A. 55, 66n, 121, 138n
health, argument from 10–14
carcinogens 11, 12, 13
cholesterol 11, 14
drugs in animal flesh 10, 12, 13,
16n
moral vegetarians and 27
saccharin 13–14, 16n
Hinduism 8
Hohfeld, W. N. 77, 78, 82n
human welfare
argument from effect on character
20
argument from violence 20–1
increased shortage argument 18–19
moral vegetarianism 17
redistribution argument 17–18
waste argument 19–20

increased shortage argument 18–19
infanticide 161
injury, avoiding, cf. bringing aid
133–5
insincerity
becoming an expression of sincerity
223–4
concerned individual and 219–21,
230, 231
pretended cost 226–7
relation to fuller context 221–3
sincerity and action 224–5
intention, direct and oblique 119,
120–3, 133
interests, animal 22 *see also* rights
Interests and Rights (Frey) 44, 45, 49,
102, 141, 164
intuitionism, *prima facie* rights 52–3,
54, 60, 63

Jainism 8
Jamieson, Dale 247
Johnson, Edward 155n

Keating Thomas, and inherent value
    147–8
Kenny, Anthony 124, 223, 226
killing
    appeal to wrongness of 99ff.
    argument for vegetarianism from 4,
        27, 28–9, 30, 37
    attempts to render control
        responsibility superfluous
        128–33
    bringing aid and avoiding injury
        133–5
    conception of status of
        vegetarianism 31
    control responsibility 125–8
    diminution in pleasure and
        replaceability 161–3
    direct and oblique intention 120–3
    doctrine of double effect 118ff.
    morality of 100–2
    population policy 165–6
    replaceability 159ff.
    responsibility 123–5
    self-consciousness and food animals
        164–5
    side effects 159–60, 161–2
kinship and reverence for life 104–8
knowledge, Singer's claim of 209–13

land ethic 141
Lappè, Frances Moore 9, 23
Leopold, Aldo 35n, 141, 149, 152
life, value of *see also* animal life
    diminution in value 110–11
    kinship and reverence for 104–8
    life principles 103–4
    value of animal and human 108–10
    vivisection 111–16
lobby, agribusiness 193–5
Lyons, David 69

McCloskey, H. J., and intrinsic moral
    rights 56–7, 58, 61–5
MacCormick, Neil 62, 67, 81n
Mackie, J. L., and fundamental
    moral rights 58–9, 60–4

market forces, effect of vegetarianism
    on 211–12
Martin, Michael 180, 187, 189n, 191,
    209, 216n, 227, 242n
Mason, James 175
meat consumption
    Britain 12
    United States 12, 184–5, 210
meat industry
    claim of progressive collapse 203–6
    practicalities of vegetarianism
        195–203
Mill, John Stuart, amenability to
    moral rights 83, 84
Miller, Peter 156n
moral concepts and moral rights 47–8
moral criticism and duty 131–3
moral standing and inherent value
    142–4
moral taint and conception of good
    man 240
Moral Status of Animals, The (Clark) 21,
    49, 245, 247
moral thinking, Hare's two-level
    account of 90ff.
Moral Thinking (Hare) 90
moral vegetarianism *see*
    vegetarianism, moral
morality and serious intent 4
Muslims 8

Nagel, Thomas 118
Narveson, Jan 82n
needless suffering 243–8
Nozick, Robert 68

omissions, immoral 129–30

pain and suffering, argument from 4,
    21–3, 27, 28–9, 30, 102, 174ff.
    and alleged reasons for choice of
        vegetarianism 190ff.
    amelioration argument 159ff.
    argument and concerned
        individual 175–7
    bases of argument 174–5
    claim of progressive collapse 203–6
    and conception of status of
        vegetarianism 30–5
    concerned individual's tactic 181–3

life proper to species 183–7
miserable life and single experience
  views 177–81
cf. moral rights 44, 49
and negative moral vegetarianism
  36–8, 39
valuing suffering but not life 187–8
Palach, Jan 137
pleasure potential
  population policy and 166
  replaceability and 169–71
political-economic power and reasons
  for choice of vegetarianism 193–5
population policy, replaceability
  argument and 165–6
positivism, legal, Dworkin and 61
Practical Ethics (Singer) 21, 49, 159,
  160, 164, 167–8, 177, 178
practicality of becoming vegetarian
  206–9
prices, meat, support of 212–13
principles and superfluity of rights
  49–51
Prior, Arthur 223, 226

Rachels, James 24n, 110
Ralston, Holmes 151
Rawls, John 62
Raz, Joseph 67, 81n
rearing methods *see also* farming,
    factory; veal calves
  argument from pain and suffering
    185
  evolution in 185
redistribution argument, and
    enhancement of human welfare
    17–18
refraining and acting 130–1
Regan, Tom 142–5
  inherent value 146–51, 155n
  needless suffering 243–5
  utilitarianism 196–7
religious conviction as grounds for
    non-moral vegetarianism 8
replaceability
  and animal generations 171–2
  diminution in pleasure and 161–3
  failure to bar 168–71
  killing and 159ff.
  and miserable lives 166–8

of non-persons 162
of persons 162–3
self-consciousness and 164–5
responsibility
  attempts to render control
    responsibility superfluous
    128–33
  control responsibility 135–8
  doctrine of double effect 123–5
Returning to Eden (Fox) 104
rights
  and consequentialism 86–8, 89
  duty to compensate 79–81
  exercising 76–7
  loosening preconceptions about
    74–8
  as mirrors of absolute wrongs 70–2
  negative 71
  non-interference view of 77–8
  positive 71
  strong 67, 69, 70
  as trumps 67–70
  weak 67
rights, absolute
  as mirrors of absolute wrongs 70–2
  and *prima facie* rights 72–3
rights, infringed, and duty to
    compensate 79–81
rights, institutional 84
  and moral rights 47
rights, legal, cf. moral rights 74, 77,
    78, 84
rights, moral 46
  accommodation towards 84
  acquired 63–6
  and act-utilitarianism 83ff.
  animal welfare and 27, 28, 30
  appeal to 43–5
  argument from pain and suffering
    37
  basic 55–62
  basic rights as self-evident 56–8
  and conception of status of
    vegetarianism 30, 31
  conflict of 51–2
  correlative thesis 53–4
  dispensing with diversions rights
    create 62–3
  fundamental rights as
    recommended 58–61

Hare's account of moral thinking
90ff.
hostility towards 84–6, 95n
cf. legal rights 74, 77, 78, 84
and moral concepts 47–8
prima facie 52–3
principles and superfluity of 49–51
repudiating rights 54–5
right to equal concern and respect
61–2
superfluous 85
unacquired 63–6
wrongs, rights and protection 48–9
rights, *prima facie*
absolute rights and 72–3
correlative thesis 53–4
to life 100
repudiating rights 54–5
and strict intuitionism 52–3
Right and Wrong (Fried) 71
Rodman, John 180
Ross, W. D. 50
basic moral rights 57

Sanctity of Life and the Criminal Law, The
(Williams) 121
Schindler, Oskar 221
self-consciousness
and food animals 164–5
Singer's view 163
sexual potency, and vegetarian diet
10
Should Trees Have Standing? (Stone)
142
sincerity and concerned individual
219–27
Singer, Isaac Bashevis 21
Singer, Peter
alleged reasons for choice of
vegetarianism 190–95
appeal to thresholds 213–15
argument from pain and suffering
21–3, 38, 102, 174ff.
claim of knowledge 209–13
claim of practicality/effectiveness
206–9
claim of progressive collapse 203–6
concession to case of concerned
individual 215–16, 218
consistency 227

on killing 101
moral absolutism 31–3
moral rights 44, 49
needless suffering 245, 247, 248
pleasure potential 170
population policy 166
positive and negative moral
vegetarianism 38, 39
practicalities of vegetarianism
196–7, 202
replaceability argument 159–65,
167–8, 171–2
self-consciousness 163–5
sincerity 219ff.
tactical conception of
vegetarianism 33–5
trade-offs in values 241–2
squeamishness as grounds for non-
moral vegetarianism 8
Stone, Christopher 142–4
suffering, argument from pain and 4,
21–3, 27, 28–9, 30, 102, 174ff.
amelioration argument 159ff.
argument and the concerned
individual 175–7
bases of argument 174–5
claim of progressive collapse 203–6
conception of status of
vegetarianism 30–5
concerned individual's tactic 181–3
life proper to species 183–7
market forces and 211–12
miserable life and single experience
views 177–81
cf. moral rights 44
needless 243–8
and negative moral vegetarianism
36–9
and reasons for choice of
vegetarianism 190ff.
Regan's view of needless 243–5
valuing suffering but not life 187–8
symbolic gesture, as reason for choice
of vegetarianism 191–3

Taking Rights Seriously (Dworkin) 55,
61, 67, 68, 84
taste, as ground for non-moral
vegetarianism 7
Taylor, Paul 154

test conditions, drug 14
Third World
    food shortage 18–19
    moral rights and 43
Thomson, Judith Jarvis 79ff.
thresholds, appeal to, Singer and
    213–15
Tooley, Michael 163

unnaturalness as grounds for non-
    moral vegetarianism 8
unusualness as grounds for non-moral
    vegetarianism 9
utilitarianism *see also* act-
    utilitarianism
    act-utilitarianism account of
      strength of rights 73–4
    and basic moral rights 59, 60, 67,
      68–9, 70
    classical 160, 162–3
    Dworkin and 61
    and the good man 240
    Mackie and 59
    practicalities 195–203
    preference 160, 162, 163
    Singer and 33–5, 44, 49, 241–2
utility 49, 74
    degree to override rights 75, 81n

values *see also* value theory
    conflicts in 144–5
    trade-offs in 241–2
value, inherent
    artifacts and nature 150–1
    feelings as guide to 245–6
    Leopoldian picture of 148–50
    mistakes about 146–8
    moral standing and 142–4
    value theory and ethics 151–5
value theory and theory of ethics
    151–5
VanDeVeer, Donald 243
veal calves
    factory farming 22, 24, 34, 207,
      208–9
    life proper to species 184
    moral rights 37
    replaceability argument 170, 173
vegans 7

vegetarianism, alleged reasons for
    choice 190ff.
    claim of political-economic power
      193–5
    claim of practicality/effectiveness
      206–9
    claim of progressive collapse 205–6
    claim of symbolic gesture 191–3
    practicalities of utilitarianism and
      vegetarianism 195–203
vegetarianism, conditional 31–3
vegetarianism, forced 6
vegetarianism, moral 4, 6–7
    argument from effect on character
      20
    argument from health 10–15, 27
    argument from pain and suffering
      21–3, 36–8
    argument from violence 20–1
    increased shortage argument 18–19
    moral grounds best means of
      persuasion 15
    negative 36–40, *see also*
      vegetarianism, negative moral
    positive 36–40, *see also*
      vegetarianism, positive moral
    redistribution argument 17–18
    waste argument 19–20
vegetarianism, negative moral 99,
    191, 218
    argument from pain and suffering
      36–8, 159, 248
    change in requirements for success
      38–40
vegetarianism, non-moral
    aesthetic grounds 7–8
    diet 9
    religious conviction 8
    squeamishness 8–9
    taste of meat 7
    unnatural 8
    unusualness 9–10
    wastefulness 9
vegetarianism, positive moral 99,
    191
    argument from pain and suffering
      36–8, 159
    change in requirement for success
      38–40
vegetarianism, status of

conditional and unconditional
    conceptions 31–3
counter-argument and competing
    tactics 33–5
partial and absolute exclusions
    30–1
vegetarianism, unconditional 31–3
violence, meat-eating and heightened
    aggression 20–1
vivisection 175

and value of life 111–16

waste argument 19–20
    as grounds for non-moral
        vegetarianism 9
Williams, Glanville 82n, 122
Wordsworth, William 20
wrongs, and moral rights 48–9
wrongs, absolute, rights as mirrors of
    70–2